SCREENWRITING

The Sequence Approach

Paul Joseph Gulino

continuum
NEW YORK • LONDON

2009

The Continuum International Publishing Group Inc
80 Maiden Lane, New York, NY 10038

The Continuum International Publishing Group Ltd
The Tower Building, 11 York Road, London SE1 7NX

www.continuumbooks.com

Printed in the United States of America

Library of Congress Cataloging-in-Publication Data

Gulino, Paul Joseph.
   Screenwriting : the sequence approach / Paul Joseph Gulino.
      p.   cm.
   Includes bibliographical references and index.
   ISBN 0-8264-1568-7 (pbk. : alk. paper)
   1. Motion picture authorship.   I. Title.
   PN1996.G84   2004
   808.2'3—dc22

                                                    2004007969

For Peachie and Pootie

Contents

Acknowledgments   ix

Author's Note   xi

Foreword   xiii

1   An Introduction to Sequences   1
    Why Sequences?   1
    The Origin of Sequences   3
    How A Screenplay Works   4
    How Sequences Work   12

2   *Toy Story*: Firing on All Eight   20

3   *The Shop Around the Corner*: Fractured Symmetry   41

4   *Double Indemnity*: Flashback to the Future   64

5   Fellini's *Nights of Cabiria*: Nocturnal Episodes   80

6   *North by Northwest*: 1,700 Miles in Nine Sequences   97

7   *Lawrence of Arabia*: Sixteen Sequences and an Intermission   114

8   *The Graduate*: Passive Main Character   145

9   *One Flew Over the Cuckoo's Nest*: Midpoint Reversal   158

10   *Air Force One*: Eight Sequences Eight Miles Up   172

11   *Being John Malkovich*: The Disappearing Lead Actor   182

12   *The Fellowship of the Ring*: The Shotgun Approach   199

Sources   225

Index   227

Acknowledgments

My sincere thanks to many who have helped on this journey: first and foremost to my beloved wife Charla, who has been my courage and strength, to my beloved daughter Gina who has been my inspiration, Paul Wolansky, who told me to write it, Warren Buckland and Alison McMahan who were kind enough to be my guides throughout its conception and execution, Joyce Bivans who kept me in the fight, Richard Herman, who's been a stalwart, my parents, who've been there from the beginning, and my students over the years who have been learning with me.

Author's Note

This book is a study of the use of "sequences" in movie making. To illustrate the points I am making about the nature and function of sequences and related storytelling tools—historical, critical, theoretical, and practical—I have reproduced a few images from especially significant movies.

Each image is a single frame taken from the full-length motion picture and is used here for educational purposes pursuant to the Fair Use Doctrine.

My book is not endorsed by or affiliated with any of the performers, directors, producers, or screenwriters who created these movies or by the studios that produced and distributed them, and the single-frame images are used here for purposes of criticism and commentary only.

Readers who are interested in seeing these historically significant motion pictures in their entirety are encouraged to buy or rent copies of the movies from authorized sources.

Foreword

It begins with an idea, an idea that gnaws, that haunts, that spills into the quiet moments, and refuses to go away. With nurturing, the idea grows. It finds purchase in a fertile imagination and unfurls itself, opening into its very own world. Characters arrive. Sometimes they step out of the mist of the mind fully formed, other times they're lumps of clay that must be sculpted. You can't wait to give them voice. You can't wait to tell their tale.

Then comes the terror of the blank page. If you're a beginning screenwriter you ask, "How do I fill 120 pages?" If you're a seasoned professional you ask, "How do I contain my story to only 120 pages?" And no matter who you are, you ask, "How do I make it good?" It's enough to send you running to Starbucks for non-fat latte and an afternoon of procrastination.

I arrived at the University of Southern California's Graduate Screenwriting Program in the Fall of 1990 with a head full of stories and no idea how to write a screenplay. I'd read most of the popular screenwriting books and had written a couple of lousy scripts where everything happened in the right place but nothing seemed to matter. Luckily, at USC, I learned the craft of screenwriting from one of the form's master educators, Frank Daniel, who designed the program's curriculum around the sequence method.

On the surface, the sequence method may appear to be just another formulaic, by-the-numbers approach to structuring your script. Nothing could be further from the truth. Instead of providing a dead structure, sequencing helps writers create the dynamic, dramatic engines that drive their stories forward. And unlike other popular approaches to screenwriting, the sequence method focuses on how the audience will experience the story and what the writer can do to make that experience better. Sequencing gives writers the clarity to understand and manipulate dramatic tension to maximum effect, playing off the audience's expectations and controlling its hopes and fears.

The sequence method doesn't just make a screenplay better; it also makes it easier to write. Sequencing helps clarify character motivation and drive, and illuminate which scenes are dramatically necessary and which are irrelevant. It breaks the 120-page monster into manageable sections, and provides an easy to follow dramatic road map that helps writers avoid the typical second-act morass.

What I learned from a master teacher at USC, Paul Gulino has now committed to paper and ink in this remarkably helpful volume. In it, he has managed to provide a thorough yet succinct introduction not only to the notion of sequences, but also to the theory that underlies them and all dramatic storytelling. Further, he has provided concrete illustration of the use of these theories in the insightful, detailed analysis of several significant feature films. In this, he echoes Frank Daniel's notion that, ultimately, the only true teachers are the masters of the form, and that learning how to study them can lead to a lifetime of discovery and enrichment.

I am much indebted to Frank Daniel, my instructors at USC, and the sequence method for making me a better storyteller and a better screenwriter. I hope that this volume will in some measure do for others what they did for me. Over the course of my career, I've discovered that when I employ the sequence method, my screenplays turn out well. When I've strayed . . . well, so have my screenplays.

—Andrew W. Marlowe

An Introduction to Sequences

Why Sequences?

The great challenge in writing a feature-length screenplay is sustaining audience emotional involvement from page one through 120. Most writers can dash off a ten- or fifteen-minute script with little planning; as the length stretches to an hour or more, it becomes difficult both to conceive a script in its entirety and execute the individual scenes at the same time. Most professional writers use various tools to solve this problem—writing a treatment, outline, step outline, beat sheet, or using file cards. The function of all of these is to allow writers an overall view of their work while they toil away at the specific scenes.

The division of a feature film into acts—commonly three acts nowadays, corresponding generally to the setup, development, and resolution—is likewise a way for writers to divide the vastness of 120 pages into digestible pieces that can be attacked individually, without the need to be mindful of the overall work.

Even in using the three-act approach, though, navigation through a screenplay can be difficult. Most commonly, the first act is understood to occupy the first thirty pages, the second act the next sixty, and the third act the final thirty. For most writers, it is the sixty pages of the second act—the true heart of the script—that present the greatest challenges, a bewildering descent into a swamp of seemingly limitless choices, replete with the perils of wrong turns down dead ends and quicksand from which the writer cannot extricate the story.

The use of *sequences* is an important tool that is often overlooked in handling this problem. A typical two-hour film is composed of sequences—eight- to fifteen-minute segments that have their own internal structure—in effect, shorter films built inside the larger film. To a significant extent, each sequence has its own protagonist, tension, rising action, and resolution—just like a film as a whole. The difference between a sequence and a stand-alone fifteen-minute film is that the conflicts and issues raised in a sequence are only partially resolved within the sequence, and when they are resolved, the resolution often opens up new issues, which in turn become the subject of subsequent sequences.

The advantage of understanding that a feature film is composed of a series of shorter films is that it mitigates the problem of a seemingly amorphous second act. In general, a two-hour film will have two fifteen-minute sequences in the first act, four in the second, and two more in the third. Variations on this arrangement can be seen in many films, mostly in the length of the sequences and sometimes in their number, but as a tool for planning and writing a feature film this approach can be very valuable.

In the pages that follow I will explore the notion of sequences in detail—their historical origins, how they are defined and how they function to make a screenplay fulfill its most basic task: engaging a reader/viewer. Since understanding sequences requires understanding of some basic principles of storytelling, I will also examine these, with an eye toward the question of how a screenplay goes about engaging an audience. I will then explore eleven films representing a wide variety of styles and time periods and show how sequences function within each.

Academically, the sequence approach to feature-length screenwriting was taught at Columbia University in the early eighties, and has been taught for the last decade at the University of Southern California and more recently at Chapman University. Its use as a teaching tool grew out of the experiences of Frank Daniel (1924–1996), the inaugural dean of the American Film Institute and later the head of the film programs at Columbia University and USC, who found that teaching the three-act approach to screenwriting resulted in the difficulties discussed above, and so resurrected the notion of sequences to help students write more successful screenplays. One of the films analyzed in this volume, *Air Force One,* was written by Andrew W. Marlowe, who learned of the technique while studying at USC's Graduate Screenwriting Program.

In putting this approach down in book form for the first time, my hope is this simple truth—that big films are made out of little films— can be of help to others in conceiving and writing a feature-length screenplay.

The Origin of Sequences

In the beginning was the sequence.

Or more properly, the one-reeler. With the advent of projection of movies in 1897, the celluloid carrying the images was wound up around spools that could hold about a thousand feet. At 18 frames per second, these lasted between ten and fifteen minutes.

By the early 1910s, for reasons both artistic and economic, films were extended beyond one reel. Because most theaters only had one projector, this required the projectionist to stop the projector, swap reels, and start the show again, during which time the audience waited in the dark or, more typically, was regaled by intervals of live entertainment.

Artistically, filmmakers dealt with this interval by making sure the films had a fade-out at the end of the first reel and a fade-in at the start of the second—often marked with a title noting the "End of Act I" and "Start of Act II,"—which in turn required that the narrative be adapted to conform to the constrictions imposed on it by this interruption. This was particularly necessary when—as happened early in the feature film era (1913–1920), the films were sometimes shown in installments—one or two reels at a time over the course of several weeks (much like a serial or modern-day daytime TV drama series) rather than all during the same evening. Each reel thus had to have its own integrity.

Some screenwriting manuals of the time advised writers to structure their work around this division into reels.[1] By the late 1920s, with the full-length feature film coming to dominate the cinema, most theaters had two projectors, and thus the viewing experience became essentially seamless. In this context, formal and rigorous adherence to writing for each reel became unnecessary, but the structure persisted, evidenced by

---

1. Ben Brewster, "Traffic in Souls: An Experiment in Feature-Length Narrative Construction," *Cinema Journal 31, No. 1, Fall 1991,* p. 39. Brewster cites articles by Epes Winthrop Sargent in *The Movie Picture World* (22 June 1912 and 24 February 1912), and Sargent's manual *Technique of the Photoplay,* 2d ed. (New York: Moving Picture World, 1913), p. 121–24.

the organization of screenplays into *sequences* identified by letter (A, B, C, etc.), a practice that lasted into the 1950s.

If the notion of writing in sequences played a role in feature film writing for the decade and a half after 1913, the craft of screenwriting underwent a dramatic change starting in 1927, which saw the advent of the talking picture. Till then, writers had only to script physical action and title cards. With this new innovation, they had to write dialogue, and Hollywood producers turned to the experts to solve the problem—the thriving community of playwrights working on Broadway, which pulled the craft more firmly into the three-part structure first expounded upon by Aristotle (360–322 BC). The result was an eight-sequence structure married to three acts.

In fact, the underlying structure—eight sequences in a feature film—persists to this day, long after its origins and practice have been forgotten. Rather like Monsieur Jourdan in Moliere's *The Bourgeoise Gentleman* who is shocked to realize he's been speaking prose for forty years without knowing it, feature film screenwriters continue to structure their films in sequences—and can get into trouble when they don't.

The persistence of this arrangement suggests that something deeper is at work than the somewhat accidental arrival of cinema with 1,000-foot reels. The notion of a feature film having eight parts is, like all else in dramatic theory, tied to human physiology. Drama has been a one-and-a-half to three-hour experience for 2,500 years. Apparently, beyond that length, people become restless and uncomfortable, and attention suffers.

The division of two hours into sequences of ten to fifteen minutes each also most likely speaks to the limits of human attention, i.e., without the variation in intensity that sequences provide, an audience may find itself fatigued or numb rather than enthralled by what is on screen.

How A Screenplay Works

This book puts forward and articulates the division of feature films into eight segments. Many discussions of screenwriting begin either with Aristotle's influential work *The Poetics* or Syd Field's more recently influential work *Screenplay* (1979), which articulate different ways of dividing up a dramatic work. Aristotle described tragedy as a "whole action," and, to him, a whole is that which has a "beginning, middle and end." This is the first formulation of drama in three parts, and though he also further broke down tragedy into five parts ("prologue," "episode," "exode," "parados" and "stasimon") the first three roughly corresponded to the beginning, middle, and end, while the latter two were inserted in the middle, marking where the chorus entered and then sang odes.

Syd Field's book described a three-act division of screenplays as "beginning," "confrontation," and "resolution," separated by "turning points," and, though he did not originate the notion of thinking of screenplays in terms of acts, the popularity of his book has helped make the "three act structure" the most common model. Other screenwriting manuals that have been published since 1979 espouse the notion of three acts, and give various insights into what they mean and the function they play in writing the screenplay.

Variations exist, of course. Kristin Thompson, in her thoughtful and informed book *Storytelling in the New Hollywood* (1999), studied over a hundred films from the 1910s to the 1990s and discerned in them what might be considered four acts, not three (which she terms "setup," "complicating action," "development" and "climax"). David Bordwell, in *Narration in the Fiction Film* (1985), described six parts of what he calls the 'canonical' story format: "introduction of setting and characters," "explanation of a state of affairs," "complicating action," "ensuing events," "outcome," "ending."

While much insight is to be gained from these books, aspiring writers may understandably get the mistaken impression that the task of the writer consists primarily in following theorists' notions or recommendations, and, failing to do so, they will fail.

There was, of course, a group of extremely successful playwrights who did not base their work on Aristotle's *Poetics*, or any other known guide or manual of dramatic writing—this group includes Sophocles, Aeschylus, Aristophanes, and Euripides—the playwrights of Greece's Golden Age of drama—whose plays constituted the body of work that Aristotle studied in order to generate his treatise. And of course for most of the history of movie making, writers did not have access to Syd Fields's book, and, indeed, screenwriting manuals were comparatively rare during Hollywood's own "Golden Age" of the 1930s and 1940s.

While the playwrights who flourished before Aristotle, and the screenwriters who did so before Field, worked within the framework of specific conventions and formulae, their basic task can be understood in a way that is more empowering to the writer and more helpful to her in realizing her vision than aiming to conform to a formula and connecting its dots.

In his 1927 study *Aspects of the Novel*, E. M. Forster (1879–1970) described somewhat caustically the root nature of story: "It has only one merit: that of making the audience want to know what happens next. And conversely it can only have one fault: that of making the audience not want to know what happens next."[2]

A decade earlier, in his book *Playmaking* (1912), theater critic and theorist William Archer (1856–1924), wrestling with the issue of what, ultimately, constitutes the essential characteristic of drama, came to the following conclusion: "The only really valid definition of the 'dramatic' is: any representation of imaginary personages which is capable of interesting an average audience assembled in a theater."[3]

As to motion pictures, Kristin Thompson has said the following of the emergence of Hollywood as a world leader in the film industry by 1916: "The techniques of continuity editing, set design, and lighting that were developed during this era were designed not only to provide attractive images but also to guide the audience attention to salient narrative events from moment to moment."[4]

These are three very wide open statements about the nature of the storyteller's task. Their common thread is focus on the audience. All successful plays and films have been successful first, before considering any other positive attributes they might have, in engaging an audience in this way, and if they did not succeed in this task, they either did not survive, or can be found in the discount bin at Blockbuster. And needless to say, if a screenplay does not succeed in the task of keeping a reader or producer wondering what will happen next, it will suffer a fate even worse—remanded to the reject pile, never to see the light of the projection bulb or the video screen.

A writer who understands this as the basic task—keeping the audience attention on what comes next—is free to go about it in any way her imagination and inventiveness allows. If a writer realizes that whatever patterns or rules she encounters in dramatic theory or in screenwriting manuals (including this one) are to be understood as tools to this end, she will be empowered to employ them in more interesting ways than are possible than when seeking to adhere to "rules" or a formula above all else.

2. E. M. Forster, *Aspects of the Novel* (New York: Harvest/HBJ, 1927), p. 27.

3. William Archer, *Play-Making: A Manual of Craftsmanship* (Boston: Small, Maynard & Co., (1912), p. 32.

4. Kristin Thompson, *Storytelling in the New Hollywood* (Cambridge: Harvard University Press, 1999), p. 1.

During the course of the analyses that follow, I will in fact examine films that used various combinations of the tools to achieve this end of audience engagement. Included in their number are some that may seem quite unconventional in their approach, but they all have in common success in engaging an audience.

A successful screenplay, then, is a living thing, in the sense that it "works" to create anticipation in a reader, as opposed to being an inert combination of ink, three-holed paper, and brads. The question is: *how* does it work? This question must be answered before an understanding of sequences can be undertaken, because what applies to features also applies to sequences.

While dramatists and screenwriters have used a variety of techniques over the years, there are, in the main, four basic tools that have been employed successfully to keep the audience attention directed into the future. In order of ascending significance, these Big Four are:

Telegraphing. This is also known as *pointing* or *advertising*. It consists of telling the audience explicitly what would happen in the future of the narrative. A verbal example could be one character saying to another "Meet me at Jerry's Juiceteria at five o'clock" (this is an example of an *appointment*, one form of telegraphing). A visual example of telegraphing would be a character preparing his motorcycle for a ride. Both suggest the direction the story is going. Both help solve one of cinema's challenges—its *selectivity*—what is seen on screen is only a small part of the action. If the audience is told someone is going to meet someone else at a juice bar, we can cut to the juice bar without confusing the audience or providing exposition in the scene explaining to the audience why we're suddenly there.

This tool can also be used as "false" telegraphing—telling the audience where the story is going and then paying it off in the reverse. A character who makes arrangements to see a Broadway show with his mother but instead gets kidnapped is an example of this, yielding a surprise twist. The surprise twist has been a staple of cinema from its first decades, and such twists only work if the audience is made to anticipate something. A character getting kidnapped in the opening shot of a movie can never be a surprise twist, because no expectation has yet been created.

Another type of telegraphing is known as a *deadline* or *ticking clock*. An example of this would be one character telling another: "You have till midnight Friday to bring the Duke back." It not only tells the audience where the story is going, but it can also put a character under time pressure, which intensifies the audience's emotional involvement.

Although telegraphing is used mostly as part of the support system of the narrative flow of a story, it has been used in a more profound way. In *American Beauty* (1999), just after the opening titles, Lester Burnham announces in a voice-over narration, "In a year I'll be dead." This (literal) deadline instantly creates anticipation and gives shape to the story. Much later in the picture, Lester informs the audience, "In a week I'll be dead," and later still, "Today is the last day of my life." I suspect that without these three critical lines of dialogue, audience engagement would be jeopardized, for the film has little else to propel audience attention into the future.

Dangling Cause. This tool carries more emotional freight than telegraphing. In the first decade of the twentieth century, Hollywood films came to be dominated by a narrative model consisting of a series of events linked by cause and effect. A man asks a woman to marry him (cause), and she accepts or rejects him (effect). With the evolution of longer films in the 1910s came the development of the "dangling cause"—a cause that would not have its effect until later—it would, in effect, "dangle" in the audience's mind while other events intruded. For instance, a man *vows* to ask a woman to marry him, but does not do so until the next scene or until several scenes later. In this case, the vow is an example of a dangling cause.

In general, a dangling cause is an expression of intent, a warning, a threat, an expression of hope or fear, or a prediction, which places a question in the audience's mind for which no immediate answer is provided. It thrusts audience attention into the future by arousing curiosity. Early in *One Flew Over the Cuckoo's Nest* (1975; see Chapter 9), McMurphy makes a bet with the other patients about Nurse Ratched, namely that he can "put a bug so far up her ass she won't know whether to shit or wind a wrist watch." This type of dangling cause is known as a *dialogue hook,* for it provides a transition into the following scene, which finds McMurphy slouching in a chair across from Nurse Ratched, presumably ready to make good on his bet. The question arises—can he do what he's said he'll do?

A dangling cause more commonly is not picked up immediately after it is established. In *Lawrence of Arabia* (1962; see Chapter 7), before embarking on an expedition into the desert, Lawrence declares, "It's going to be fun," while his friend Dryden warns him the desert is a "hot, fiery furnace," suitable only for gods and Bedouin—and Lawrence is neither. During the course of the epic, this dangling cause is revisited several times, as Lawrence proves at various junctures to be both god and Bedouin—and ultimately dwells on the question: "Who are you?"

Dramatic Irony. Also known as *omniscient narration*, this is a tool often overlooked by aspiring screenwriters, who tend to believe that the characters in a screenplay need to know everything at the same time that the audience does. Dramatic irony occurs when the audience knows *more* than one or several of the characters onscreen, a condition which pushes audience attention into the future because it creates anticipation about what is going to happen when the truth comes out. That anticipation is known as *ironic tension*, and it is bracketed by a scene of *revelation* (the moment the audience is given information of which a character is unaware) and *recognition* (the moment the character discovers what the audience has already known, which serves to resolve the ironic tension). Dramatic irony comes in two flavors—suspense, which can be used to inspire fear in the audience, and comic, in which a misunderstanding is "milked" to produce laughter.

When the audience learns that two co-workers who dislike each other are unaware that they are writing love letters to each other in *The Shop Around the Corner* (1940; remade as *You've Got Mail* [1998]—see Chapter 3) the question naturally arises—what will the outcome be when the two realize the truth? Dramatic irony has the additional advantage of enriching the scene by giving double meaning to the most mundane lines of dialogue. In *There's Something About Mary* (1998), Ted thinks he's been arrested for picking up a hitchhiker while the audience knows he's being questioned by police about a murder, otherwise innocuous lines he delivers such as "I've done it several times before," and "It's no big deal," generate laughter.

Skillful storytellers employ hierarchies of knowledge in the use of dramatic irony, between not only the audience and the characters but between the characters themselves. In *North by Northwest* (1959; see Chapter 6), Roger Thornhill meets Eve Kendall on the train and she proves to be almost angelic in the way she helps him evade the police. Later the audience learns that she's actually working for the people trying to kill him (first scene of revelation). During the following scenes between Eve and Roger, ironic tension comes into play as we fear the danger he does not see. This ironic tension is so powerful it allowed director Alfred Hitchcock to draw out the subsequent crop-duster scene for more than five minutes with no onscreen activity other than a man waiting for someone near a cornfield. In the scene afterward at the Ambassador East hotel, Roger realizes Eve is working against him, a scene of recognition that resolves the previous ironic tension. But since Roger does not tell her that he knows, a new hierarchy of knowledge is created—now he is aware of something she does not know. This layer of ironic tension is resolved in the following scene, when Roger confronts Eve and Vandamm at the auction house, the final scene of recognition in the relationship between the two.

Dramatic irony is a more powerful tool than telegraphing or dangling causes, and can sometimes sustain a feature-length film all by itself, though almost usually in the comic rather than the suspense variety. *The Graduate* (1967—see Chapter 8), *Top Hat* (1935), *Harvey* (1950), and *Being There* (1979), in addition to *The Shop Around the Corner/You've Got Mail* are comedies that use dramatic irony in large measure to sustain audience engagement.

Dramatic Tension. This tool is the most powerful of the Big Four, in that it can be, and has been, the most common one used to sustain audience emotional involvement in full-length dramatic works for thousands of years, and its use is the primary subject of most books on screenwriting and playwriting. Frank Daniel described it simply yet elegantly: "Somebody wants something badly and is having difficulty getting it."[5] In fact, Daniel articulated two kinds of dramatic stories: chases and escapes, but these are two versions of the same thing: either someone wants something and is having trouble getting it, or is trying to escape something and having trouble doing so.

The notion of dividing screenplays into large segments called "acts" has been discussed previously, and becomes germane when undertaking a study of dramatic tension. This book will explore the notion of eight sequences, but these sequences work within the context of larger segments of a full-length film, and for my purposes three acts are most suitable for articulating and executing dramatic tension. This is because when a character wants something, a question is implied: will the character get it or not? This is known as the *dramatic question*, and a question of necessity has three parts: the posing of the question, the deliberation on it, and the answer to it. A question need not have any

---

5. David Howard and Edward Mabley, *The Tools of Screenwriting* (New York, NY: St. Martin's Press, 1996), p. xii.

more parts to it, and is not complete with any less. So, the first act poses the question: will so-and-so get what he or she wants? The second act sees the playing out of the question, its "deliberation," as the character works against difficulties to get it, and the third act provides the answer. Dramatic tension thus thrusts audience attention into the future with the expectation of the answer to the question.

Understanding dramatic tension in three parts is useful also because it is echoed in the smaller subdivisions of a dramatic work—successfully realized sequences and scenes likewise have dramatic tension, and thus each has a "three act structure": character wanting something, an obstacle, tension resulting from the conflict between the two, and a resolution, leading to a new tension. At the end of the first act in *Double Indemnity* (1944; see Chapter 4), Neff decides to help Phyllis kill her husband for the money and so he can be with her. This poses the dramatic question: will he succeed? The sequence immediately following raises a different dramatic question: can they set up the murder without being discovered? There are a series of obstacles to this end. Within each scene during the setup, there are smaller obstacles, and thus smaller units of dramatic tension: can they get Mr. Dietrichson to sign the contract? Can Walter get off the phone before he arouses Keyes's suspicion? Any time there is dramatic tension, there are three parts: it must be set up (question posed); it must be played out (question deliberated), and it must be resolved (question answered). In film, the "three act structure" is something like a *fractal* in geometry: a nested structure, iterated at three different levels.

Understanding dramatic tension in three basic parts has one last major advantage: it comes to grips with Aristotle's notion of a "whole"—what it is that makes a film *feel* like one film and not, say, eighty separate scenes, or 120 individual minutes of filmic experience. When working with dramatic tension as the primary tool in engaging audience attention, the answer is the *dramatic question* and the tension it creates, known as the *main tension*, to distinguish it from the various smaller tensions arising in scenes and sequences. The main tension is what makes a movie feel like one movie; it's what unifies it; it's what elevates a film above the sum of its parts (providing "organic unity" in Aristotelean terms); it's what we use when we describe what it is *about.* "A man falsely accused of murder and hunted by the police and enemy agents must try to clear his name" describes what *North by Northwest* is about, and it is nothing more than a recitation of the main tension, with the implied question: will he succeed? Likewise with *Saving Private Ryan*

(1998)—"A man is ordered to lead a squad of soldiers behind enemy lines to find an American soldier and bring him back alive," or with *Nights of Cabiria* (1957)—"A lower-class hooker wants love and respectability."

As will be seen in the analyses that follow, the overwhelming pattern in successful feature films is that the first act occupies the first 25% of a film, the second act occupies the middle and runs 50% of the film, and the third act runs the last 25%. It is also worth noting that the main tension is not resolved at the end of the picture; in most cases, it is resolved at the end of the second act; in fact, the resolution of the main tension is what characterizes the end of the second act, and in the third act, a new dramatic tension almost invariably asserts itself. To use the above three examples, in *North by Northwest,* the tension surrounding Roger trying to clear his name is resolved 77% of the way into the movie; the third act revolves around the question of saving Eve. In *Saving Private Ryan,* Captain Miller decides to abandon his mission 70% of the way into the movie; the third-act tension involves defending the bridge from the Germans; in *Nights of Cabiria,* Cabiria gets her love and respectability when the man of her dreams proposes to her 82% of the way into the movie; the third-act tension revolves around her impending marriage and its consequences.

Like dangling causes, dramatic tension plays on an audience's curiosity, but unlike dangling causes, it requires an emotional connection between the audience and a character—the protagonist—in order to achieve its effect. It is the function of the first act, or in Thompson's terms the "setup," or David Bordwell's the "introduction of setting and characters" and "explanation of a state of affairs," to introduce the protagonist—the main character—and create an emotional bond between him or her and the audience. Once this bond is established, the audience will have an emotional stake that goes far beyond mere curiosity and can sustain audience involvement for the length of the feature film.

These, then, are the four basic tools of the storyteller. Other tools exist that can help enrich the experience of a script or movie, and I will discuss these during the analyses. These four are presented here because they are the ones crucial in achieving the most basic task of the screenwriter—keeping the audience wondering what is going to happen next—and thus play the most basic role in how a screenplay "works."

How Sequences Work

Sequences help solve one of the basic problems in all dramatic writing: the fact that a drama is a contrivance, but that it will not work if it *seems* like a contrivance. The action in drama unfolds before the audience's eyes, and the extent to which it seems spontaneous—the extent to which it seems that anything might happen—is the extent to which it will persuade an audience that whatever outcome that eventually transpires is inevitable and therefore satisfying. In this vein, coincidences that hurt a protagonist tend to work in drama, and are viewed suspiciously if they help.

Sequences, by posing a series of dramatic questions within the overall dramatic tension, offer an opportunity to give the audience a glimpse of a great many possible outcomes to the picture before the actual resolution. Screenwriters are sometimes counseled to keep in mind that the characters do not know what the movie is about—in order to create compelling drama, it must seem as though the movie is what happens *despite* what the characters want or expect. Conceiving a story in sequences is a means of achieving this. For example, a writer may invent a story in which, in the setup, a married man becomes obsessed with a woman and decides he's willing to risk everything to have her. Instead of the writer posing the question "how do I make the pursuit of this woman fill up sixty or ninety minutes of screen time?" it is much more fruitful for him or her to ask "what is the quickest and easiest way for this character to get the girl?" Human nature being what it is, chances are the man will do the easiest thing first, and only if that fails will he try a more difficult course of action. The "easiest thing" may only take fifteen minutes of screen time. In developing a story, a writer needs to have the courage to let the second act end after only fifteen pages, if the protagonist is able to achieve his objective in that amount of screen time. It is then easy enough to brainstorm and come up with developments that foil this outcome.

After the first thirty-five minutes of *Being John Malkovich* (1999; see Chapter 11), Craig has figured out how to get Maxine, the woman of his dreams: he's planning to work nights alone with her in the "Malkovich portal" business, and a positive outcome to his quest for her seems readily at hand. Yet fifteen minutes of screen time later his wife has decided she's a transsexual and is in love with Maxine. The next three sequences detail his rejection by Maxine in favor of his wife, his successful abduction of his wife (which then becomes threatened by Malkovich himself), and finally his success in "getting" Maxine by figuring out how to control Malkovich. The means by which he finally achieves her love is hardly something he could have conceived of after first going into business with her, but carefully worked out circumstances have, in the end, forced him to push himself to the limit.

Over the course of a typical two-hour movie, the eight-sequence structure works out as follows. This is, of course, a paradigm—an ideal layout—and variations have been done, very effectively. But it will serve as a starting point.

Sequence A

The first fifteen minutes of a picture answer the questions of who, what, when, where, and under what conditions the picture will take place— the *exposition*. Before such exposition, though, it is crucial to "hook" the audience and get them interested in watching further. The most common technique for achieving this in the first sequence is through the use of curiosity. Most successful movies begin by posing a puzzle to the audience, raising questions in their minds, and promising an answer. *Chinatown* (1974) opens with a puzzling series of photographs showing a couple having sex, accompanied by offscreen groaning. *Sunset Boulevard* (1950) starts with the frantic arrival of police cars, whose officers quickly converge on a man lying face down in a swimming pool.

Once curiosity is used to draw an audience in to the picture, there will be a chance to supply exposition—background material—answering the crucial questions so that the story proper can begin.

Almost always, but not invariably, the audience is introduced to the main character, or *protagonist*, in the first sequence, and is given a glimpse of the flow of life of the protagonist *before* the story itself begins—*in medias res*. An effective first sequence can give us a sense of what the protagonist's life would have been like if the events that lead to story hadn't interfered. In fact, the stronger the sense of flow of life at the beginning of the picture, the bigger the impact of the destabilizing events that intrude to make the story happen. *North by Northwest* is exemplary of this in the extent to which the storytellers cram a full evening and day's worth of appointments for the protagonist, Roger Thornhill, in the opening four minutes; having thus given us a glimpse of the flow of his life, none of these appointments is ever actually realized.

Usually by the end of the first sequence, there arises a moment in the picture called the *point of attack,* or *inciting incident.* This is the first intrusion of instability on the initial flow of life, forcing the protagonist to respond in some way. For Roger Thornhill, it is his abduction; for Jake Gittes in *Chinatown*, it is his realization that he's been duped.

Sequence B

The second fifteen minutes of a film, ending approximately 25% of the way into a typical two-hour picture, tend almost invariably to focus on setting up the main tension, of posing the dramatic question that will shape the rest of the picture. As such, the end of the second sequence tends to mark the end of the first act.

Most commonly, the protagonist introduced in the first sequence spends the second sequence attempting to grapple with the destabilizing element introduced into his or her life during the first fifteen minutes of the picture. The character may have every expectation that the problem will be solved and the story finished, but life itself has other plans. Whatever solutions the protagonist attempts during the second sequence lead only to a bigger problem, or *predicament*, marking the end of the first act and setting up the main tension, which occupies the second. In the *Chinatown* example, Gittes tries to get to the bottom of who hired him and why, and winds up being hired by the *real* Mrs. Mulwray after her husband turns up dead.

Sequence C

The third fifteen-minute sequence of a picture allows the protagonist a first attempt at solving the problem posed at the end of the first act. As mentioned previously, people being what they are, characters tend to choose the easiest solution to the problem, hoping it will be resolved immediately. The character may indeed solve an immediate problem in the third sequence (as in any of the sequences), but the resolution of one problem can lead to much bigger and deeper problems. In *Midnight Run* (1988), Jack Walsh, unable to bring his prisoner from New York to California by plane, opts for a train ride. This is soon thwarted by a rival, and he winds up instead taking a bus, which in turn is attacked by the mob and the FBI, forcing him to borrow a car. The choices of transportation are progressively less desirable, reflecting Jack's increasing difficulty.

Sequence D

The fourth fifteen-minute sequence finds the first attempt at resolution failing, and sees the protagonist try one or more desperate measures to return his or her life to stability.

The end of the fourth sequence very often leads to the *First Culmination* or *Midpoint Culmination* of a film. This may be a revelation or some reversal of fortune that makes the protagonist's task more difficult. Successfully realized scripts at this juncture often give the audience a very clear glimpse of an answer to the dramatic question—the hope that the protagonist will actually succeed at resolving his or her problem—only to see circumstances turn the story the other way. In this sense, the first culmination may be a glimpse at the actual resolution of the picture, or its mirror opposite.

Midway through *Tootsie* (1982), Michael Dorsey reaches a pinnacle of career success, but he is living a lie and doesn't have a romantic relationship with Julie; in the resolution at the end of the picture, his situation is the mirror opposite: he has lost his career but is no longer living a lie, and has a tentative romantic relationship with Julie.

Sequence E

During the next fifteen or so minutes, the protagonist works on whatever new complication arose in at the first culmination. Again, successfully realized scripts can give a glimpse of apparent success or failure, though usually not as profound as at the first culmination. Sometimes this is a place in the story in which new characters are introduced and new opportunities present themselves. This, and Sequence F, are sometimes occupied primarily by subplots, if there are any.

In some pictures, the experience of the first culmination may be so profound as to provide a complete reversal of the protagonist's objective. During the first half of the second act of *Sunset Boulevard*, Gillis works on Norma's script with the aim of escaping her despite her efforts to keep him; after she attempts suicide at the midpoint, he spends the second half of the second act trying to stay with Norma despite Betty's efforts to pull him away.

As with the other sequences, the resolution of the tension in this sequence does not resolve the main tension (i.e., solve the protagonist's problem), it merely creates new complications, usually more difficult with stakes that are higher still.

Sequence F

During this, the last sequence of the second act, the character, having eliminated all the easy potential solutions and finding the going most difficult, works at last toward a resolution of the main tension, and the dramatic question is answered. The end of the sixth sequence thus marks the end of the second act, also known as the *Second Culmination*. As such, it gives the audience yet another glimpse of a possible outcome of the picture.

The Second Culmination, like the first, can be a glimpse of the actual resolution of the picture, or, more typically, its mirror opposite. In *Sunset Boulevard,* Gillis and Betty kiss, marking the high point of their relationship, which is the mirror opposite of the resolution, when he loses everything and winds up face down in the swimming pool. In *Midnight Run,* Jack is under arrest and has lost John Mardukas to his rival, the mirror opposite of the resolution, when he makes it to L.A. in time and winds up a free man with $300,000.

It is a common misconception that the end of the second act needs to be a "low point" in the story. In studying many films, I have not found this to be the case; only three films in this volume—*Toy Story, Lawrence of Arabia,* and *The Graduate*—could be said to follow this pattern. In developing a story, I have found it to be far more useful for the writer to conceive of this moment in the story in relationship to the main tension in some profound way—either by completely resolving it or by reframing it significantly. Seeing it as a "low point" cuts off a writer from a great many story possibilities.

Sequence G

As with the resolutions of tension in sequences A through E, the apparent or actual resolution of the main tension in the sequence F is not the final word. Unexpected consequences of that resolution can come forth, and other story lines and dangling causes previously established bring forth new and even more difficult problems, sometimes forcing the character to work against his or her previous objectives. In effect, the story is sometimes turned upside down and we glimpse it from a very new angle. The seventh sequence is often characterized by still higher stakes and a more frenzied pace, and its resolution is often characterized by a major twist. In *Bullets Over Broadway* (1994), David's play is a success—solving the main tension—and he turns to deal with one of the unexpected consequences—Cheech's obsession with Olive, which results in her murder. In *The Apartment* (1960), Baxter, having achieved success in the corporate world, abandons that ambition and decides to pursue Kubelik, only to have this thwarted by his boss.

Sequence H

The eighth and final sequence almost invariably contains the *resolution* of a picture—the point at last where, for better or for worse, the instability created in the point of attack is settled. Having been given a glimpse of the resolution at the First and Second Culminations and to a lesser extent at the end of each sequence, tension is at last fully and completely resolved. Depending on the picture, the guy winds up with the girl *(Tootsie)* or is doomed never to get her *(Chinatown)*.

Sequence H also almost invariably contains an *epilogue* or *coda*, a brief scene or series of scenes tying up any loose ends, closing off any remaining dangling causes or subplots, and generally giving the audience a chance to catch its breath and come down emotionally from the intensity of their experience.

A note on the analyses

It's easy to tell when a film begins and ends; it's harder to judge when, exactly, an act begins and ends, particularly the end of the second act. A further subdivision into more than three parts can naturally lead to some disagreement as to where, exactly, one subdivision ends and another begins, even with a precise notion of what defines these subdivisions. In some movies, the sequence structure as defined in this volume is readily apparent; these include films that involve journeys (*Lawrence of Arabia* and *Fellowship of the Ring* among those analyzed herein) and those with few if any subplots. Films with subplots (in this volume *The Shop Around the Corner* and *Being John Malkovich*) tend to be more open to interpretation, but the patterns remain. I invite the reader to do their own analyses and compare notes.

A further challenge to this type of analysis is in the variance between classical scripts that were written explicitly by sequence (in this volume, these include *The Shop Around the Corner* and *Double Indemnity*) and my own analysis. Based on my examination of screenplays written from the 1930s through 1950s, it seems that sequences by this time had a variety of definitions, sometimes corresponding to length, sometimes subject matter, and sometimes location. A comparison between how the sequences were divided in the written screenplays of these two films, and my own analysis, is provided in the appropriate chapters. Further, it is important to bear in mind that, with the exception of *The Shop Around the Corner*, *Double Indemnity*, and *Air Force One*, the films analyzed in this volume were not written consciously in sequences. My analyses seek to uncover the sequence structure that exists in these films nonetheless.

In my experience as a writer and teacher, shared with colleagues at Chapman University and the University of Southern California, the sequence approach can be very valuable as a tool for students to develop their screenplays. The charts included in this volume contain exact timings and percentages, which can lend a sense that the technique is more precise than it is. The inclusion of the minute/second timings and percentages is intended as a basis for comparison of patterns across a range of films, and is not intended to give the impression that a writer needs to adhere so precisely to these patterns in the development of his or her screenplays.

With the exception of *Toy Story*, the films are presented in this volume in chronological order. The films were chosen because they represent a variety of storytelling styles, patterns, and subject matter.

Toy Story: **Firing on All Eight**

Arriving in theaters in late 1995, *Toy Story* was acclaimed as a break-through for its use of computer-generated animation, and proved to be a major commercial success. But its success was not due solely to the technology behind it. The simple fact is that the script for *Toy Story* is one of the better ones written during the last century. In fact, if the script hadn't been so good, most likely the computer-generated graphics would not have been noticed.

The film is a good starting point for screenplay analysis for several reasons: one, being an animated piece, there are fewer layers between the conception on the page and the execution on the screen. The art director didn't arrive at the scripted location only to discover that it wasn't right for the scene; the problems of weather didn't intrude, and as parodied during the end titles in *Toy Story 2*, there were no actors throwing tantrums and insisting on making changes in the script. What was written was what wound up on screen, and the film greatly bene-fited from the fact.

The film is also a good starting point because it so profoundly real-izes the three-act, eight-sequence paradigm, even though, like most screenplays written since the 1950s, the sequences are not marked in the script. It also very explicitly utilizes the Big Four tools to achieve its considerable impact, and is strong in the areas of character and theme.

Sequence A: The Unwanted Present

The opening sequence, which runs thirteen and a half minutes, begins with a pre-title sequence that is not part of Sequence A proper, but rather serves more as a prologue that establishes the mundane aspects of the reality of the world in which the story will take place.

Almost all movies open with either an exterior long shot or, more rarely, an interior close-up. The reason for this is the need of the audience to become oriented—an exterior immediately helps give a sense of where the story will take place. An interior close-up answers the same need—the focus begins on one specific object, then works outward until we are oriented. In contrast, use of an interior medium shot as an opening is comparatively rare, and can even lend a sense that the projectionist started with the wrong reel.

Toy Story opens with an interior—but it appears to be an exterior—a blue sky with puffy white clouds, which is soon revealed to be the wallpaper in Andy's room. The use of curiosity now comes into play—we arrive in the middle or end of an imaginary game, utilizing the various toys. Dramatic tension is present within the game—Mr. Potato Head is holding some other toys hostage—but it's not engaging on the dramatic level because we do not know any of the characters involved. The opening *is* engaging because it poses a puzzle where, exactly, are we? Who is playing this game? Why? Many unsuccessful scripts begin by trying to start the story immediately, with expository dialogue and conflict. As discussed in Chapter 1, most successful ones, in contrast, hook the audience initially by tapping into its natural curiosity, then starting the story once curiosity is aroused.

Soon after the puzzle of the opening play-scene, the titles begin along with theme music, and Woody's role as Andy's favorite toy is shown, not only in the game Andy plays but also in the subsequent jaunt they take through the house. This activity solves the puzzle of who was playing the game, and where was it taking place, posed by the opening shots.

When Andy brings Woody downstairs, the first use of telegraphing is seen: a banner reading "Happy Birthday Andy," and dialogue about an impending move, create a deadline. Thus six minutes into the film, and four pages into the shooting script, the audience's attention is shifted from solving a puzzle to anticipation of the future.

The end of the titles—with Woody lying on Andy's bed—marks the beginning of the movie proper. Having been given a glimpse of a mundane, ordinary world, the magic begins, when Woody stirs on the bed and immediately voices concern about the birthday party. Here, again, curiosity comes into play rather than dramatic tension—we quickly learn the birthday party means trouble, though we're not told why. Once the puzzle is posed— why is a birthday a problem?—we get the first real exposition of the movie, during Woody's speech before the "staff meeting," revealing that every year, Christmas and birthdays are a traumatic experience for toys, who fear they will be replaced by some new plaything. Woody's speech also contains telegraphing—he reminds the toys they have one week till the move—and marks the first use of a dangling cause—his assurances that no one will be replaced is an emotion-laden prediction about the future.

The continuing turmoil among the toys, despite Woody's attempts to assuage their fears, leads directly to what can be regarded as the end of the "first act" of the sequence—Woody agreeing to call out the troops if that will calm everyone down. By this time it has become clear Woody is the protagonist of the sequence (he is the one with whom we spend the most time; he is the also the one who recognizes a problem and takes the action of calling a meeting)—and his desire is made clear—he wants to calm down the toys. This thread of dramatic tension, beginning five minutes after the titles, flows through the rest of the sequence and carries with it the implicit dramatic question: will Woody succeed in calming them down?

Exposition

At the dawn of drama in Ancient Greece, *exposition*—the information the audience needs to know about the characters and circumstances in order to become emotionally involved in the play—was handled by a character named ''Prologue'' who would appear onstage and simply deliver this information. Since then, writers have become more adept at smuggling such information in without the audience knowing about it. The two chief means by which screenwriters handle this nowadays are through a scene of conflict—''exposition as ammunition''—and by posing a puzzle to the audience and then having a character solve the puzzle with information. The storytellers here in *Toy Story* employ both: when Woody tells Slink that there's trouble without saying why, it poses a puzzle; when he explains it, it's couched in an argument—he reassures the toys that no one will be replaced, in the process delivering information that this happens every birthday and Christmas.

As long as the dialogue delivering the exposition has a subtext, i.e., an underlying action (for example, *attack, defend, persuade, seduce, reassure*) the audience won't notice that it's getting exposition. The only subtext to avoid is *explain*—it's too neutral and will probably yield a dull scene. And worst of all, the audience probably *will* notice.

This dramatic question is unrelated to the main tension of the film, and does not carry with it high stakes or extremes of action or emotion, but it does provide a crucial thread that binds the first thirteen minutes of the film together. It is the wellspring of conflict during the staff-meeting scene, it justifies the action of calling out the troops, and it provides conflict in the scene after Woody is knocked off the bed. Further, the arguments Woody uses to calm the toys—the assurance that no one will be replaced, and that what is important is what Andy wants, not what the toys want—become central to the main tension of the film and Woody's predicament therein, and likewise provide the framework in which the theme of the picture—love, and attempts to will it—is explored.

When the troops are called out, the dramatic tension shifts slightly, centering on the objective of the troops—to spy on the party down below—and the obstacle—the troops must not be discovered. This obstacle, dramatized well when the soldiers are caught in the open at the entrance to the kitchen and have to freeze—provides crucial exposition into the way the world works—namely, toys have a secret life unknown to adults and only pretend to be inanimate objects. This rule imbues the entire film with a layer of ironic tension—the audience is let in on the secret—and plays a crucial role in the third act of the film when it is broken.

The troops' mission is an apparent success until Mom pulls out a surprise present, which leads to consternation among the toys listening upstairs in the bedroom, where a new obstacle arises from an old one—because of the toys' anxiety, Rex, the most neurotic, knocks the two-way radio off the nightstand, interrupting the flow of information from the troops. This leads to a brief interlude of ironic tension—the audience is shown that Andy and his friends are heading upstairs, but the toys, whom we know by now must pretend to be inanimate when humans are around—are unaware of this.

This ironic tension is resolved when the toys tune in again just in time to find out the boys are on their way upstairs, inspiring a frenzied attempt by everyone to take his place. Andy and his friends enter the room and deposit the mysterious new toy on the bed, then exit quickly, bringing the sequence to an end.

The tension in the sequence—will Woody be able to calm down the toys?—is resolved to the positive when the last toy is announced to be a Battleship game—an evidently innocuous present. The toys are in a relaxed, celebratory mood, and Woody is their triumphant leader.

When Mom springs the surprise present, this mood is reversed and leads abruptly to the end of the sequence. The dramatic question is finally rendered moot when the party is over and a mystery toy takes Woody's place on top of the bed.

The first sequence of *Toy Story* is a tour-de-force of screenwriting, and not just because of its more obvious merits—its clever dialogue and interesting, engaging characters. The reject pile in Hollywood is replete with broken scripts heavy on clever dialogue and interesting characters. What makes *Toy Story* special is the way it so masterfully uses the Big Four tools of screenwriting to engage the audience from its opening moments. Crucial exposition—the nature and rules of the world in which the story will take place, the principal characters and their relationships and routines—is skillfully smuggled into the film while the audience is enthralled by the concerns, aspirations, and reversals of the characters onscreen.

The opening sequence also demonstrates effective use of *preparation*, in one of its variants, *retardation* (see text box).

An example of preparation by contrast in the opening sequence is the celebration that occurs among the toys when the last of the presents

---

Preparation

An important tool that can greatly enrich an audience's experience of a film, a scene of *preparation* is one which is explicitly designed to create an expectation in the audience—usually hope or fear—which is then paid off either directly (we are led to expect something terrible will happen, and it does) or by contrast (we are led to expect something terrible will happen, but something wonderful does, or vice versa—the classic "reversal"). These are scenes that can usually be cut out of a film entirely without affecting the plot, but they greatly enhance the emotional impact of a film. *Retardation,* an example of which is the "dramatic pause" in an actor's speech, is a form of preparation in which some promised event—the arrival of a character, for example, or the revelation of some information—is presented to the audience, which is then made to wait for it, the effect being the buildup of anticipation. Captain Spaulding's entrance in the Marx Brothers film *Animal Crackers* is a good example of retardation—Captain Spaulding's imminent arrival is the subject of excited discussion and two elaborate songs before he shows up. In this case, the preparation is paid off in reverse—as soon as he arrives, he announces he's leaving.

has been opened, and the present-opening ritual has apparently ended with none of the toys threatened with replacement. As soon as our hopes are raised in this way, Andy's Mom brings on the surprise present, and fear takes the place of hope.

The effective use of retardation is demonstrated immediately afterward. More than two minutes elapse between the revelation that Mom has a surprise gift and our first glimpse of Buzz on top of the bed. During this interval there transpires much frantic activity, consternation, and trepidation among Andy's toys, and clever shot selection that thwarts the audience's ability to determine just what this new toy is. This footage could easily be cut out—the audience and toys could be told immediately the fact that the last toy is a Buzz Lightyear, and the plot would have remained intact. In fact, Buzz could have been the first toy opened, saving several more minutes of screen time without affecting the plot at all. But by teasing the audience thus, the effect of Buzz's arrival is greatly magnified.

As mentioned previously, one of the most common misconceptions of novice screenwriters is the belief that the audience and characters must know everything all the time as soon as it is knowable; in fact, a skillful screenwriter knows what information to withhold, when to withhold it, and when to reveal it for maximum impact. Such knowledge comes only with practice, experiment, and experience, and when developing a screenplay, it is worth experimenting with the story in this regard.

The first sequence also features clever use of *motifs* (see text box, page 45). These are props or lines of dialogue or even patterns of behavior that are introduced (*planted*)—usually surreptitiously—by the writer, which are brought up later in a different context (*paid off*). In the opening sequence, motifs that are planted include Woody's habit of playing checkers with Slink, Sketch's skill at drawing, Potato Head's desire for a Mrs. Potato Head, and Rex's desire to develop a frightening roar. All are paid off in various ways in the sequences that follow, and the ease with which they are embroidered into the script is a testimony to the extent to which it was worked and reworked by knowledgeable craftsmen.

Sequence B: Falling With Style

The second sequence is a short one, running six minutes length, and is also unified by dramatic tension—Woody's assertion of his superior position over Buzz, an issue that did not exist before.

After the boys' hurried departure, the toys emerge from hiding, looking up at the bed in awe. Woody peeks out from beneath the bed, and
the toys suggest that Woody has himself been replaced (something
which literally occurred when he was knocked off his place on the bed).
Woody makes his way up to the bed and introduces himself to Buzz.

The arrival of Buzz constitutes the point of attack of the picture. The
stable world of the opening sequence has had a new, potentially destabilizing element introduced to it. It is not yet clear what the movie as a
whole is about, but Buzz's arrival is clearly something with which the
characters must contend before "normality," or stability, can be re-
gained.

Two and a half minutes into the second sequence, Woody tells Buzz
that there has been a mistake—the spot on the bed just occupied by
Buzz is his own spot, a moment which constitutes the end of the "first
act" of the sequence—Woody is again the protagonist of the sequence,
and his objective is to disarm the threat Buzz apparently poses to his
place at the top of the heap of toys. During the rest of the sequence, he
attempts to accomplish this by simple argument, then, when the other
toys become increasingly impressed by Buzz's considerable technologi-
cal attributes, by verbal harangues against the new arrival, culminating
in Woody's derisive claim that Buzz can't fly—followed by Buzz's successful "flight" around the room.

Buzz's flight (which plants a significant motif), and Bo Peep's subsequent statement, "I've found my moving buddy," bring about the resolution of the tension of the second sequence—to the negative. Woody's
attempts to defend his position as the most esteemed toy have failed.
The sequence ends with Woody making a declaration that is a classic
example of a dangling cause known as a dialogue hook: "You'll see. In
a few days, everything will be the same. I'm still Andy's favorite toy."
This declaration marks the end of the first act of the picture, and not
insignificantly is delivered in a close-up of the protagonist, something
not uncommon at the end of the first act.

All the necessary pieces of the dramatic *predicament* are present: we
know whose story it is (Woody); we know what he wants (to regain his
place as Andy's favorite toy), and we know what the obstacle will be
(Buzz). The dramatic question has been posed: "Will Woody regain his
spot as Andy's favorite toy?" and the main tension of the film is thus
initiated. The audience's hopes and fears will be tied up to Woody's
hopes and fears about obtaining his objective.

When discussing the three-act structure in films, it is worth noting
that no curtains mark the ends of the acts, as can be the case in theater.

However, some films *do* have curtains, and *Toy Story* is one of them: the musical montage, which follows (and in fact refutes) Woody's declaration that he is still Andy's favorite toy. This musical montage pays off several motifs planted in the opening sequence: Sketch's drawing ability, Rex's desire to make a more persuasive roar, Woody's checkers games with Slink. All of these payoffs attack Woody's standing among the toys, either directly or indirectly.

Sequence C: Buzz Takes A Hit

Like Sequence B, the third sequence is fairly short, running just under nine minutes, including the musical montage, which serves as part of the "first act" of the sequence—giving the audience information needed to setup the dramatic tension of the sequence, the information in this case being the fact that Woody has in fact been displaced by Buzz in Andy's esteem, and in that of the fellow toys.

The montage ends with the planting of an important motif—Buzz showing Woody the fact that Andy has written his name on the bottom of Buzz's foot ("in *permanent* ink!"), a visual confirmation that Andy has accepted Buzz. This, and Woody's sensitivity to it, triggers Woody's first attempt to regain his position at the top: a verbal confrontation with Buzz. This attempt marks the end of the "first act" of the sequence: Woody is its protagonist, and his desire is to eliminate Buzz as a threat to his hegemony. The obstacle is readily apparent: Buzz's popularity with Andy and the other toys. The dramatic question is posed: can Woody eliminate Buzz as a threat?

In this case, the tension of the sequence and the main tension of the picture are identical, a situation not uncommon in Sequence C, because it transpires immediately after the establishment of the main tension. The protagonist is thus freshly armed with an objective, and he or she attempts to solve it as quickly and easily as possible. Complications that arise from this first attempt form subsequent tensions in later sequences, which of necessity differ from the main tension.

Woody's verbal confrontation threatens to escalate into a physical confrontation, when it is interrupted by the arrival of Sid, the disturbed, violently anti-toy next-door neighbor. Sid's execution of a "Combat Carl," witnessed by all the toys, dramatizes the threat Sid poses to the toys, and also plants the motif of his use of explosives to achieve his ends.

The scene ends with telegraphing: one of the toys expressing grati-
tude that they'll be moving soon. After a dissolve to dinnertime, more
telegraphing occurs when Andy's mom offers to take him to Pizza
Planet for dinner, thus explicitly telling the audience where the story
will be going. Because Andy can only take one toy with him, Woody
becomes anxious, hoping he will be chosen, and afraid he won't—yet
another dangling cause. Woody's first attempt at defeating Buzz,
through direct confrontation, has been a failure, so he makes his second
attempt: deception. His ruse—manipulating Buzz into rescuing a toy
trapped behind the desk—has the unexpected consequence of launch-
ing Buzz out the window. The resolution of the tension in the third
sequence is thus at hand, and it is, again, a negative from Woody's point
of view. True enough, he does eliminate Buzz as a competitor for Andy's
affection, but now he is an outcast in his own society, hated by his fellow
toys as a murderer.

At the end of the sequence, Sketch's drawing ability is again paid off,
this time with a drawing of a hangman's noose, directed at Woody. Sequence C thus ends with a dangling cause—in this case a threat.

Sequence D: Double Prizes at Pizza Planet

The fourth sequence, which runs a little over ten minutes in length, begins with Buzz climbing onto the family car, which then conveys Andy,
his mom, Woody, and Buzz to a big gas station. A short period of ironic
tension occurs, during which the audience knows that Buzz is on the
car, but Woody does not. This irony is quickly resolved when Buzz appears in the sunroof and hops down to Woody.

Here, a little over a minute into the fourth sequence, the end of the
"first act" of Sequence D transpires: Woody, upon seeing Buzz, states
his objective: "Great! Andy will see you, he'll take us back to the room,
and you can explain it was all a mistake." Woody is, again, the protagonist of the sequence. His objective is to get Buzz back home so he can
clear his name. The dramatic question: "Will Woody be able to get Buzz
back home?" Woody's *overall* objective remains the same: to regain his
place of love and admiration among toys and Andy. But his specific
purpose within the sequence is much more limited: just get Buzz back
home. The chief obstacle clearly will be Buzz's anger at Woody for
knocking him out the window in the first place. In making his statement, Woody is also telegraphing the future course of the story, though

in this case it turns out to be "false" telegraphing: his hopes, thus expressed, are thwarted by later circumstances. Still, it serves the purpose of creating anticipation—pushing the audience's attention into the future.

At this juncture, the skill of the storytellers is again on display—they have arranged the story in a way that binds the protagonist and antagonist together; in fact, the protagonist is put into the difficult position of having to try to get the antagonist—the one person on earth he likes least—to cooperate with him. This storytelling arrangement is not an accident, and a script can succeed or fail because of storytelling decisions like this. For example, in *The Shop Around the Corner* (see Chapter 3), the protagonist and antagonist are thrown into close and constant proximity because they work together in the same shop. In the 1998 remake *You've Got Mail*, the storytellers chose to put them in rival companies in separate locations, and the result was a loss of intensity in the drama as well as the comedy, and a remake that was less successful than the original.

Soon after Woody explains his plan to Buzz, the latter balks at cooperating with Woody, and a fistfight rapidly ensues. This leads to yet another deeper problem: Andy's departure, which leaves Woody and Buzz stranded. Woody's objective remains the same: get Buzz back home, but this much more formidable obstacle has arisen. After the arrival of a fuel truck, which nearly crushes Woody, Buzz and Woody resume their

---

Recapitulation Scenes

Films have a relentless forward motion; a viewer is not expected to go back and review material he or she may have missed, even as the widespread use of DVDs and videocassettes makes this possible. Filmmakers have dealt with this problem from the early days of narrative cinema by carefully repeating important information. Occasionally, an entire scene is used primarily to review important information and then set up future action; this is known as a *recapitulation scene.* Typically, such a scene has one or more characters recount briefly where the story has been, often in the context of trying to figure out what to do next; thus it serves both to review and create anticipation. These scenes are not uncommon in mysteries and thrillers, which tend to be plot-heavy and involve twists and turns that might leave the audience confused.

confrontation in what is known as a *recapitulation* scene (see text box p. 29). When Woody tells Buzz it's a perfect time to panic, because "I'm lost, Andy's gone, they're going to be moving in two days. . . ." The important issues driving the picture are restated clearly and forcefully.

A scene of preparation by contrast follows their confrontation, in which they go separate ways, and we are led to believe all is lost. At this juncture, Woody sees the Pizza Planet delivery truck and a reversal occurs: Woody recognizes a way to persuade Buzz to cooperate, and despair turns to hope. In Woody's attempt to persuade Buzz to board the Pizza Planet truck, we see again an example of telegraphing, in which Woody explains what the procedure will be ("The truck will take us back to the refueling station, which can then take us home.") This dialogue is also an example of *indirection* (see text box p. 31).

Just prior to their trip on the Pizza Planet truck, Buzz warns Woody not to ride in the back, as there are no safety restraints. This dangling cause is quickly picked up during Woody's brief but painful ride to Pizza Planet.

Once at their destination, another scene of preparation by contrast plays out, this time raising our hopes and leading to the First Culmination of the picture. Woody and Buzz successfully sneak inside, then make their way through the establishment to within striking distance of Andy. The audience is given a clear glimpse of the end of the picture—a positive resolution in which Woody and Buzz get home safely and Woody's name is cleared. Just when hope is at its highest, though— when Andy's sister's stroller approaches the two—Buzz wanders off to another attraction across the room and we arrive at the negative resolution of the sequence.

Buzz winds up with a game machine full of toy aliens; Woody is compelled to abandon his sure ride home and rescue him; the neighbor Sid—cleverly introduced in the previous sequence—appears at the worst possible time and "wins" both Woody and Buzz.

The dramatic question of the sequence has been answered: Woody failed to get Buzz back home so he can clear his name. And, as in Sequence C, the end of this sequence finds Woody's attempts to solve his initial problem—regaining his place at the top of the heap—leading to even graver difficulties. It's useful to note in this sequence the extent to which the storytellers are concerned with keeping the audience oriented—explicitly telling us where we are in the story, what just happened, what it means, what the future plans of the characters are, and their hopes and fears. Storytellers who fail to consider these issues run

Indirection

This dramatic technique comes in two flavors: visual and verbal. The use of verbal indirection is a means by which a writer can avoid writing dialogue that is "on the nose"—characters expressing exactly what they mean in the most direct possible terms. Aside from being dull, such dialogue tends also not to be particularly lifelike: people tend to be more complex in the way they express themselves.

Indirection is another example of a tool that is easier to use in a rewrite than in a first draft. A useful exercise a writer can perform when he or she encounters a scene with dialogue that is too direct is to try the opposite—can a character who is angry express himself by being ironically playful instead of just plain mad?

Indirection can also be motivated by the needs of the characters within a scene. In *Toy Story,* while stranded at the gas station, Woody describes a plan to get Buzz back to his home planet by getting onto the delivery truck, but the audience recognizes that he is indirectly describing a secret plan to get Buzz home to Andy's house.

The other type of indirection—visual—involves implying events rather than showing them. This can mean using sounds of an event instead of the sight, or showing reactions rather than actions. An effective example in *Toy Story* is Sid's destruction of the Combat Carl in Sequence C. When the firecracker explodes, the image shown is not of the Combat Carl but rather the toys watching from the window. We hear the explosion, the camera shakes, debris flies, and the toys are knocked about, but we never actually see the destruction.

the risk of writing a script that leaves the reader lost, disengaged, and disenchanted.

The sequence ends with Sid uttering a dialogue hook into the Sequence E: "Let's go to my house and . . . *play.*"

Sequence E: Falling Without Style

The fifth sequence begins immediately with a dangling cause—Woody warns Buzz and the alien toy: "You guys don't get it: Once we go into Sid's house, we won't be coming out." It's an outright prediction of the future, and contributes to a scene of preparation—the creation of dread about Sid's house—that begins with ominous music and is further developed when Sid feeds the alien toy to his ravenous dog.

When they arrive in Sid's room, Woody and Buzz watch while Sid does a "double bypass brain transplant" on his sister Hannah's rag doll. The operation is an important motif, paid off in two important ways subsequently.

When Sid leaves the room moments later, we arrive at the end of the setup, or "first act" of Sequence E, three minutes into the $9^{1}/_2$-minute sequence, when Woody tells Buzz: "We are gonna die. I'm out of here." Woody is again the protagonist of the sequence, and his objective is to escape from Sid's house with Buzz. Again, this will serve Woody's overall objective—regaining his place at the top—but is it a different tension, a more specific, smaller task en route to achieving the larger one.

Following this are several attempts by Woody and Buzz to escape, each one thwarted by a new obstacle: the door is locked, the room is populated by frightening, deformed toys (that are, apparently, cannibals), the dog Scud bars their escape. While contending with these obstacles, a cutaway to Andy's room occurs, where the other toys hear of Woody's disappearance and see it as conclusive evidence of his guilt. This cutaway serves to remind us of Woody's overall objective even as the characters concern themselves with the more specific problem of trying to get out of Sid's house.

During their escape from the dog Scud, Woody and Buzz split up, and Buzz finds temporary refuge in a room where the television advertises Buzz Lightyear dolls. This leads to the major culmination—that is, turning point—in Buzz's character arc (see text box p. 33). Suffering from the beginning under the delusion that he is a real superhero and not a simple toy, Buzz blunders through the story until he witnesses the television commercial, whose disillusioning message is reinforced soon afterward by Buzz's failed attempt to fly out the window (the first payoff of his "flight" in Andy's bedroom during the second sequence).

After his failure to fly, Buzz is retrieved by Hannah, bringing on the end of the sequence. Woody's objective—to escape Sid's house with Buzz—has been resolved in the negative. Far from escaping, Woody is now in hiding and Buzz has undergone a crushing disillusionment.

Buzz's experience of disillusionment is noteworthy because it brings about a significant mood and tone shift. Buzz's realization and the actions he takes—accentuated by the music—bring us out of comedy. Just as dramas can suffer if they are relentlessly downbeat, and thus employ moments of "comic relief," so too comedies can be tiring if they are funny all the time, and benefit from moments of "dramatic relief."

Character Arc

This notion contrasts a character's *want* with his or her *need,* and how the relationship between the two plays out in the course of a story. The paradigm works like this: a character begins the second act with a conscious desire (e.g., Woody wants to regain his place at the top of the heap) and an unconscious need (e.g., Woody needs to realize that Andy's love cannot be willed; he must accept his place in the hierarchy, wherever it may be). During the course of pursuing his desire, he suffers sufficiently to become conscious of his need and let go of his want. This process of transformation is the character arc. In *Toy Story*, three characters—Woody, Buzz, and Sid—go through significant transformations, and several of the minor characters go through minor ones.

The danger for a writer of thinking in terms of character arc is the temptation to force characters to change in a way that fits the scheme, resulting in a shallow character and/or a predictable outcome. The best defense against this is to develop a story that is significantly challenging enough for the character as to force such a transformation.

Quite often, the character arc of the protagonist is what defines the theme of the picture, contained in the truth the character doesn't realize until after his or her transformation.

Sequence F: The Big One

The sixth sequence, which runs just over eleven minutes, finds a subtle but significant shift in tension from the previous one. The objective remains the same—Woody wants to escape from Sid's house with Buzz— but Woody has during this sequence one new, significant obstacle: Buzz's loss of interest in trying to escape, owing to his disillusionment. The dramatic question of the sequence becomes: can Woody overcome Buzz's lack of cooperation in order to escape from Sid's house with him? This is a new tension not present in Sequence E.

The sequence begins with Woody falling out of the closet and finding Buzz participating in a tea party with two of Hannah's decapitated dolls (a payoff of Sid's "triple bypass brain transplant" of the previous sequence). Woody uses a ruse to get Hannah out of the room so he can rescue Buzz, and immediately this new problem—Buzz's loss of interest in the fight—asserts itself. The "first act" of Sequence F thus ends after its first two minutes. Woody deals with this new problem by striking Buzz with his own dismembered arm to shock him back to reality, then leads him to Sid's room, where an open window promises an escape route at last. Woody even succeeds in tossing a string of Christmas lights to Andy's toys across the yard, and we are given another glimpse of a possible ending, since escape seems so easily within reach.

Buzz refuses to cooperate, though, and resists Woody's desperate pleas. As a result, Andy's toys rebuff Woody, and audience expectation goes from hope to fear, in a classic example of a *reversal* (see text box, page 168). Soon after Andy's toys abandon Woody, Sid reappears in the room with a new and more dangerous explosive device (the anticipation for which was planted in the previous sequence) and the situation deteriorates rapidly. Woody succeeds in hiding, but Buzz refuses to move and is thus chosen by Sid to be the victim.

A timely thunderstorm—one of the rare coincidences that actually helps the protagonist—delays the planned demolition, and Sid sets the alarm clock and creates a deadline: "Tomorrow's forecast: sunny." The choice of a thunderstorm is noteworthy because its dark, stormy atmosphere enhances the sense of hopelessness the characters—and the audience—will soon feel.

The "sequence third act" begins when Sid is asleep, Buzz is taped to a rocket and Woody is trapped beneath a milk crate. Here, Woody makes one last desperate plea for help to Buzz: "You've got to help me get out of here so we can make a break for it." Buzz again refuses to cooperate, and Woody at long last gives up, and urges Buzz to forget about him and escape on his own, admitting for the first time his own fears and frailties about being accepted by Andy.

Here we arrive at the second, or main, culmination of the picture, the end of the second act, in which the main tension—"Will Woody regain his spot as Andy's favorite toy?"—is resolved, not because Andy has accepted or rejected Woody, but rather, because Woody stops trying to achieve this goal. At Woody's moment of greatest extremity—when all appears lost—he goes through his own crushing disillusionment, realizing that he cannot make Andy love him, and that all his efforts to do so—which has led to the series of calamities that constitute the story—were futile. At this moment, the contradiction between the protagonist's desire—to regain his position as Andy's favorite toy—and his need—to realize that he cannot will Andy's love and the path to wisdom lies in acceptance—is resolved, making clear the theme of the picture, i.e., the basic truth it seeks to explore and express.

In these moments of despair, a hint of hope arrives when Buzz, listening to Woody's words about how much better it is to be a toy than a space ranger, looks at the bottom of his foot, where Andy had inscribed his name. This visual payoff sets up a major shift in tension to follow in the third act.

Sequence G: "The Toys Are Alive!"

The clearing up of the thunderstorm—and the coming of dawn—are the atmospheric elements that enhance the change of mood accompanying the arrival of the third act. Even as Woody continues to despair, Buzz, his spirits revived, begins to affect a rescue, picking up on a dangling cause of the previous sequence—Woody's plea for help. Buzz announces his arrival with another dangling cause: "Come on, Sheriff. There's a kid over in that house who needs us." Even as Buzz begins to push the milk crate in order to free Woody, the moving van pulls up next door, reminding us of the imminent deadline. The sudden alliance between two characters who have spent all of the preceding scenes in bitter conflict adds a special emotional surge to the picture.

A new problem arises as soon as Woody is freed from the milk crate—the noise of the rescue almost awakens Sid. In a quick example of preparation by contrast, Sid falls back to sleep, Buzz and Woody breathe a sigh of relief, then the alarm clock goes off, awakening Sid after all. With Sid's seizure of Buzz for the rocket ride downstairs, Woody appeals to Sid's toys for help, and with another dangling cause—"We're going to have to break a few rules, but . . .", we arrive at the end of the "first act" of sequence G, at which point the tension of the sequence is in play: will Woody be able to rescue Buzz before he's blown up by Sid?

A cutaway to Andy dejectedly leaving his home without his two favorite toys reminds us again of the deadline of the move as a backdrop to the more urgent deadline of Buzz's imminent demise, and reinforces the stakes involved in any failure by Woody to achieve his objective.

The cutaway also allows the storytellers to return to Woody laying out his plan with Sid's toys, without the audience knowing what precisely the plan is. In this case, the storytellers have opted for mystery rather than irony. Another option would have been to reveal to the audience the plan in detail, creating tension during its execution, playing on our hopes and fears as various phases are carried out.

Instead, while the objective is made clear—rescue Buzz—the means are left mysterious, and anticipation is created not only by dramatic tension—will they succeed in rescuing Buzz?—but also through promising an answer to the mystery—what precisely is their plan? In this, the viewer is in a mid-level position as to dramatic irony—we know more than Sid, but less than Woody. The approach chosen has the effect of saving time at a point in the film when speed is crucial. The tempo of the third act tends to accelerate, leading to the resolution as an emotional high point. Laying out a plan in considerable detail runs the risk of dragging out the sequence, which, as written, runs only eight and a half minutes.

The execution of the caper constitutes the bulk of the sequence's second act—Woody and the other toys act to achieve their objective, overcome obstacles, and succeed in saving Buzz's life. In the process, Sid's character undergoes his own transformation—his perception of and attitude toward toys changes.

As soon as Woody and Buzz shake hands, marking the positive resolution to the tension of the sequence, the honk of a horn reminds them (and the audience) of the moving deadline, and the final sequence begins.

Sequence H: A Finale That Soars

The chase in the final sequence of *Toy Story*, which runs just under ten minutes, is among the most successfully realized in cinema history. The tension of the sequence is obvious at the outset and has been carefully set up and nurtured throughout the preceding action—Woody and Buzz have to get on the moving van before it drives away and the two are lost forever. The sequence is executed as a rapid series of alternations between hope and fear, between obstacles encountered, obstacles overcome, and new obstacles. Many of the obstacles, and the solutions to them, arise from elements carefully set up and/or planted previously.

The deadline of the family move was set up in the opening minutes of the film. The first obstacle—the dog Scud's interference—is an unintended consequence of Woody's plan to rescue Buzz. When Buzz jumps onto Scud—showing his willingness to lay down his life for Woody—the complete transformation of their relationship is made vivid. Woody's solution to the Scud problem—employing RC, the remote-controlled car, to rescue Buzz—is a payoff of its use in getting Woody into trouble in Sequence C. The hope that arises from Woody's rescue of Buzz using RC is dashed when the other toys rise up against Woody and interfere with the rescue; this is a payoff of their chronic misunderstanding of Woody's real intentions, and the other toys' ignorance of Woody's now-positive relationship with Buzz.

The new setback that arises when the toys throw Woody out the back of the truck is solved rather inadvertently when Woody winds up on the front of RC, united again with Buzz. When the other toys see the three—RC, Woody, and Buzz—approaching, the moment of recognition occurs—they realize the mistake of their ways—and join at last in the rescue effort.

The hope that arises from this development is an opportunity for another reversal, and here the storytellers deliver once again. RC's battery starts to fade just as rescue seems imminent. When the van goes around a corner, Slink, the "stretchy dog," is stretched to the limit and disaster looms. At last, Slink lets go, and Woody, Buzz, and RC come to a stop in the middle of the road, the moving van fading in the distance. Woody suddenly comes up with a solution—lighting the rocket for propulsion—and even has the match ready, which was planted in Sequence G. This newfound hope is an opportunity for yet another reversal, when a car goes by and its wind blows the match out.

Here we arrive at what is sometimes called the *black moment*, late in the third act, when all seems truly lost. Here, the storytellers rely on another payoff—the magnifying glass Sid had used earlier on Woody—to effect the reversal. When Woody succeeds in lighting the rocket using Buzz's helmet as a magnifying glass, the hopes of the audience soar—literally as well as figuratively—despite Woody's ominous observation that "rockets explode." Just before this deadline is realized, Buzz jettisons the rocket and the resolution of the picture is at hand, in the second payoff of "falling with style."

When Woody and Buzz arrive safely on the seat next to Andy, all the significant lines of dramatic tension, dangling causes, and deadlines have been resolved or closed off. A thread of ironic tension remains in that the humans still don't know about the secret life of toys, but when Woody and Buzz "freeze" in order to pretend they're just toys, even this tension is rendered moot.

The epilogue is very brief, though it is very necessary after such an extraordinarily emotional roller coaster of a sequence. It is set at the following Christmas (a payoff of Woody's first-sequence observation that birthdays and Christmases are always the hardest for the toys), utilizes the technique of payoff skillfully, with the soldiers doing their mission once again, the toys listening in rapt attention to their reports, Bo Peep connecting at last with Woody (picking up at last a dangling cause from the opening sequence—her invitation to "come visit any time—I'm only a couple of blocks away"), and Mr. Potato Head getting his Mrs. Potato Head at last (another payoff from the opening sequence).

TOY STORY
Sequence Breakdown

Seq.	Description	Length	Running Time
ACT I			
A	Opening titles to Buzz's arrival on the bed. *Unifying Aspect*: Dramatic Tension. *Protagonist*: Woody. *Objective*: To reassure the toys that the birthday party poses no threat.	13:40	13:40 (18%)
	Point of attack: Buzz's arrival		
B	Buzz's appearance to Woody's assertion that he's still Andy's favorite toy. *Unifying Aspect*: Dramatic Tension. *Protagonist*: Woody. *Objective*: To disarm the threat that Buzz poses to his position.	6:00	19:40 (25%)
	Predicament: Buzz has usurped Woody's position as Andy's favorite toy; Woody has to try to get his position back.		
ACT II			
(Main tension: Will Woody be able reclaim his place at the top?)			
C	Musical interlude showing Buzz's ascendancy, followed by Woody's attempts to attack Buzz verbally and physically that lead to his bouncing Buzz out of the window by mistake. *Unifying Aspect*: Dramatic Tension. *Protagonist*: Woody. *Objective*: To attack Buzz so as to regain his position.	9:20	29:00 (37%)
D	Buzz and Woody get stranded at gas station, wind up at Pizza Planet, only to be captured by Sid. *Unifying Aspect*: Dramatic Tension. *Protagonist*: Woody. *Objective*: To get Buzz back home.	9:48	38:48 (51%)
	First Culmination: Woody almost gets Buzz into the stroller at Pizza Planet (48%).		
E	Woody and Buzz make several unsuccessful attempts at escape, which leads inadvertently to Buzz's realization that he's not the real Buzz Lightyear. *Unifying Aspect*: Dramatic Tension. *Protagonist*: Woody. *Objective*: To escape from Sid's place with Buzz.	9:45	48:33 (63%)
F	Woody attempts to revive Buzz's spirits, but winds up imprisoned by Sid and doomed. *Unifying Aspect*: Dramatic Tension. *Protagonist*: Woody. *Objective*: To get Buzz to cooperate so they can get out of Sid's place.	10:54	59:27 (78%)
	Second Culmination: Woody is imprisoned with no escape; Buzz is discouraged and awaits the end.		

ACT III

G	The main tension has been resolved as to Woody's aspirations—he no longer desires to suppress Buzz in order to regain his spot as Andy's favorite. Now the tension shifts—will Buzz and Woody together make it back before Andy moves? In this sequence, Woody enlists the other toys in a plan to defeat Sid, and successfully carries it out. *Unifying Aspect*: Dramatic Tension. *Protagonist*: Woody. *Objective*: To carry out his plan.	7:46	1:07:13 (89%)
H	Climactic chase to the moving van. *Unifying Aspect*: Dramatic Tension. *Protagonist*: Woody. *Objective*: To get on van with Buzz.	9:16	1:16:29 (100%)

Resolution: **Woody and Buzz make it to Andy's car.**

Epilogue: **Brief wrap-up scene at new house.**

The Shop Around the Corner:
Fractured Symmetry

The sixth collaboration between screenwriter Samson Raphaelson and director Ernst Lubitsch, this picture, based on a stage play by Hungarian playwright Miklos Laszlo, appeared in 1940. Its basic kernel—about bitter rivals who have unwittingly fallen in love with each other—has proven durable, finding itself remade as *In the Good Old Summertime* (1949) and more recently as *You've Got Mail* (1998).

It is a challenge for study because in so many ways it violates the paradigm laid out in the classic construction of a movie like *Toy Story*. In fact, it breaks one of the most basic of the "rules" of screenwriting: it does not have a protagonist with a strong objective, much at stake, and a relentless drive toward achieving that objective over any obstacles that may come in the way.

Because it is a very successful picture despite these violations, studying it can open the mind to look beyond conventions to the deeper level at which a film can engage its audience. That deeper level, in this case, is the use of Tool #3—dramatic irony—rather than Tool #4—dramatic tension. The use of a different tool can change the landscape of a picture substantially, while allowing it to achieve its most basic objective: keeping the audience wondering what's going to happen next.

The construction of the sequences in *The Shop* is again a contrast to *Toy Story*: the dramatic tension that unifies six of them tends to be less strident, with dramatic irony shoring up audience interest, and two of them are ensemble pieces, unified by time and place rather than a protagonist with an objective. Further, *The Shop Around the Corner* contains a major subplot. As a result, all of the sequences include material from that subplot in addition to the main plot, and two of the sequences are concerned primarily with the subplot.

Aside from being valuable as an object of study for its unconventional approach to engaging audience attention, *The Shop Around the Corner* is a very rich example of several other screenwriting techniques: the use of *indirection* (primarily verbal—see text box, page 31), the extensive use of props and "business" for the actors, and the planting and payoff of motifs.

Sequence A: Getting Acquainted

The first sequence runs eight and a half minutes and is unified by place (the shop) and time (one morning). It has no identifiable protagonist and no thread of dramatic tension.

The picture actually begins with a title that is not in the script: "This is the story of Matuschek and Company—of Mr. Matuschek and the people who work for him. It is just around the corner from Andrassy Street—on Balto Street, in Budapest, Hungary." This amounts to a subtle acknowledgement of the predominant storytelling pattern that audiences were (and still are) used to—character with objective—and a way of signaling to the audience that what follows will be somewhat different. Since the end of the first act of the movie occurs as a surprise twist, without any hint of the direction of the story prior to this, there is a danger the audience attention will drift. The title is, in effect, a subtle reassurance that the storytellers know what they're doing, and that the slow start of the picture from a plot viewpoint is not an accident.

In the 1998 remake *You've Got Mail*, the storytellers dealt with this problem by eliminating the twist—the audience knows from the get-go the leading man and woman are lovers, even before we (and they) find out they are rivals. The price the storytellers paid for that choice is that while the direction of the story is made clear immediately, the audience is now way ahead of the characters, waiting for them to catch up, and this lends the film a sense of slowness and predictability.

As in *Toy Story*, the opening images of *The Shop Around the Corner* present something of a puzzle—a young man riding a delivery bicycle down a busy street and stopping next to another man, who is waiting alone on a sidewalk. The writing on the side of the bicycle, and that of the shop behind them—"Matuschek & Company: Novelties and Leatherware" provides the first information about the two. The exposition technique that follows is *exposition as ammunition* (see text box on page 22), with identifiable subtext in the dialogue, subtext that belies its outward appearance of simple chatter. Pepi's opening line, "Always the first one, eh?" is not a neutral observation—it is a subtle attack, which provokes a defense from Pirovitch: "It doesn't hurt to be early." Pepi's reply is a renewed attack: "Why? Who sees you? Me. Who sees me? You. What does it get us? Can we give each other a raise? No."

By listening to them trade alternate accusations of disobedience and obsequiousness, we learn they work in a shop for a Mr. Matuschek, that one of them, Pirovitch, is always trying to impress the boss while the other, Pepi, is always slaving away for Mr. Matuschek's wife on company time. Soon Flora appears, followed at last by Kralik, who immediately asks Pepi to go to the drugstore to get some bicarbonate of soda—a motif used twice later in the scene. Vadas next appears; his loud clothing and cocky attitude immediately identify him as a fop, and his relationship to everyone is immediately shown as antagonistic. A conversation about Kralik's dinner the previous night with the boss yields more information, this time about Kralik: he's the favorite of the boss (and thus one level above everyone else), and he has an open, active mind.

Pepi returns with the bicarbonate of soda (its first payoff)—which Vadas seizes upon as a way to attack Kralik, as it reflects poorly on Mrs. Matuschek's cooking. During the ensuing argument, Matuschek arrives in a taxi, which provides an opportunity for planting another motif—Pirovitch's attempt to open the door for the boss (he's beaten to it this time by Pepi). Mr. Matuschek asks Pepi to get him some bicarbonate of soda (the second payoff of the motif) and leads them all inside the shop.

In just over four minutes, all of the workers in the shop have been introduced, as have their various relationships. No one character's objective carries the scene; rather, audience engagement is achieved first through curiosity, then by following the playing out of the various conflicts between the characters.

Once inside the shop, Kralik discloses to Pirovitch his anonymous correspondence with a woman on "intellectual subjects." Here, instead of delivering exposition through argumentation, curiosity is used. Kralik rather secretively asks Pirovitch: "Psst. Want to hear something?" Kralik then proceeds to read a few snippets from a letter without revealing what it is he's reading from. After Pirovitch becomes curious (reflecting the audience's curiosity), Kralik only deepens the mystery by beginning a roundabout tale of looking in the newspapers for encyclopedias because he wanted to know how people live in Brazil. Finally, after Pirovitch is completely bewildered, Kralik clarifies the mystery he created: he's corresponding anonymously with a woman, and neither of them knows what the other does for a living—crucial information the audience needs to make sense of what happens shortly afterward. The scene also reinforces the sense that Kralik is intellectually curious and values self-improvement.

The scene is interrupted by Mr. Matuschek, who wants Kralik's opinion about a cigarette box he's thinking of buying from a wholesaler. The cigarette box is an important motif that is revisited many times throughout the picture. Its use here is significant in that it's a prop—i.e., a visual element—which is used to express the relationships between Mr. Matuschek, Kralik, and the others in the store: Mr. Matuschek admires Kralik and respects his opinion, but sometimes resents Kralik for being *too* smart, while the others in the shop lack any real insight, or the courage to stand up to the boss.

This scene is the first in the picture to employ dramatic tension—Matuschek serves as the protagonist of the scene, and his objective is Kralik's approval for his decision to go ahead with the box. The obstacle is Kralik's honest disapproval of the box; Mr. Matuschek counters by trying to get others to agree with him. The resolution is negative—he never wins Kralik over to his point of view. In the coda of the scene, Mr. Matuschek takes a call from the cigarette-box seller and turns him down: Kralik has won the argument. The scene also introduces another motif—Matuschek's line about wanting an "honest opinion," and Pirovitch's craven response to it.

Sequence B: "I want a job"

The arrival of the female lead, Klara, marks the beginning of the second sequence. It is unified by dramatic tension; its protagonist is Klara, and her objective is securing employment. The first scene of the sequence is remarkable in that in the space of four minutes, screenwriter Raphaelson forcefully utilizes all four of the major screenwriting tools: dramatic and ironic tension, dangling causes, and telegraphing.

Klara's dramatic objective (both in the scene and sequence) is made clear within the first two minutes of her entrance, when she asks to

Motifs: Cinematic Poetry

Cinema is a thoroughly "concrete" medium. Unlike poetry and literature, which employ words—which are abstractions—cinema uses photographic images. Still, the use of *motifs* offers the screenwriter an opportunity to be poetic, creating resonances throughout a film that are analogous to rhyme in poetry. They come primarily in two forms: verbal (lines of dialogue or ideas expressed in dialogue) or visual (props or patterns of behavior). They are introduced *(planted)*—usually surreptitiously—by the writer, then brought up later in a different context *(paid off)*. They can be paid off more than once; a motif repeated with variations for comic effect is a *running gag*.

Toy Story and *The Shop Around the Corner* are richly embroidered with such motifs. When writing a script, keeping an eye out for opportunities to plant such motifs is a good practice to maintain, and can result in a more coherent and powerful screenplay. It can be difficult for a writer to anticipate where to plant motifs in the first draft—when at that stage, it's best simply to note places where they might come in handy, and insert them in a rewrite. Often a writer will see places to pay off a motif first, and then figure out where to plant them, hence the notion that a screenplay is written backwards—only when a writer gets to the ending can he or she understand exactly how to set up that ending.

Subsequent rewrites can provide opportunities for further embroidery. The cigarette box in *The Shop Around the Corner* is a motif that is paid off seven times during the course of the film.

speak to the boss, while Kralik, misinterpreting her intentions, tries to sell her on various products (bringing the use of props again into play). As soon as she discloses her real intent to Kralik, exposition resumes in earnest—we discover Klara's extensive background as a salesgirl and Kralik's nine years' experience at Matuschek & Company—all smuggled to the audience during a vigorous argument.

A brief interlude of dramatic irony occurs late in the scene, when Mr. Matuschek overhears Kralik telling Klara that he knows his boss inside out and can predict his reaction. Mr. Matuschek, assuming Klara is there to buy something, sits her down and assures her the word "impossible" is not in his vocabulary. This allows the audience to experience the opening part of the scene—when Klara was trying to get a job and the audience didn't know it—through the prism of irony, because now we do know what's coming and Mr. Matuschek does not.

Figure 1. Sequence B of *The Shop Around the Corner* (1940) is unified by Klara's desire to get a job at Matuschek and Company. The means she uses—demonstrating her salesmanship—utilizes a prop (the cigarette box) that was introduced in the opening sequence. The planting and payoff of such motifs as the cigarette box, the wallet, and the bonuses make it an unusually richly textured film. (Frame enlargement)

When Mr. Matuschek replies to Klara's job request with an "Impossible!" the tension of the scene is resolved in the negative: Klara does not get the job. Afterward, Klara tells Kralik "I *have* to have a job!"—initiating a dangling cause—and he replies that he'll call her during inventory in two weeks—an appointment.

Kralik is called away to Matuschek's office, where Matuschek proceeds to ask him a series of questions about the dinner party of the night before. The exchange is an example of the masterful use of *indirection* (see text box, page 31): on the surface, Mr. Matuschek is asking Kralik how he liked the previous night's party; in the subtext, he is warning Kralik to stay away from his wife, concluding with the line: "Mrs. Matuschek thinks an awful lot of you, and I think an awful lot of Mrs. Matuschek."

This scene is interrupted by Vadas, who announces he has a buyer for the controversial cigarette box (its first payoff). When the "buyer" turns out to be none other than Klara, who is still hanging around the shop, Mr. Matuschek picks up where he left off earlier and tries to get her to agree with him that the box is a good product. She takes advantage of the situation to demonstrate her considerable salesmanship by selling the box to a customer at above the asking price. Klara's success brings the scene and sequence to a positive resolution: Klara gets the job (though this is only implied; we do not get a confirmation of this until the following sequence). The storytellers' choice of the already-planted cigarette box as the means by which Klara gets her job is not an accident: the shop is readily seen to be full of novelties, and any of these could have served the same function. The cigarette box, though, is already imbued with meaning, having been the battleground between Matuschek and Kralik. In using it here, it picks up additional layers of meaning and grows in potency. This kind of embroidery is what distinguishes a truly outstanding screenplay from one that is merely adequate.

The sequence ends with Matuschek asking one more time for Kralik's honest opinion, a request overheard by Pirovitch, who quickly slinks away—the second payoff of that motif.

Sequence C: The Revelation

The third sequence, which runs over sixteen minutes, is unified by dramatic tension: the protagonist is Kralik, and his objective is the night off. It also contains a revelation for the audience that initiates the main tension of the film.

The function of the first part of the sequence is the same as in the opening sequence: exposition. This is because several months have passed since the previous scene, and the audience needs to be caught up. The movie thus revisits the initial location and time of day, with Pirovitch waiting for the shop to open. The shop window displays the cigarette boxes, reduced considerably in price, the second payoff of that motif. This one image tells a story: Klara won the argument about the boxes, but Kralik was ultimately right (see Figure 2).

Kralik arrives, and immediately announces he has a dinner date that evening at 8:30—an appointment that will become the central interest of the next three sequences. Pirovitch assumes it is with the boss; Kralik tells him the boss never invites him any more, to which Pirovitch remarks how difficult it is to get along with him these days—important

Figure 2. The opening scene of Sequence C of *The Shop Around the Corner* (1940) closes off two dangling causes left over from the previous sequence: the issue of Matuschek buying the cigarette boxes, and Kralik's prediction that they are not a wise investment. This image reveals that Matuschek did go ahead with the purchase, but Kralik was proven correct. Shortly afterward, it is revealed that Klara got the job, providing the resolution to the dramatic tension of Sequence B. (Frame enlargement)

information for the "B" plot, which is soon to blossom. Kralik next announces he plans to ask Mr. Matuschek for a raise—another echo of the opening sequence, when the issue of raises was brought up—and a dangling cause that will be picked up repeatedly during the next two sequences.

Klara's arrival at this point provides an opportunity for the storytellers to smuggle in yet more exposition in an argument she has with Kralik over a green blouse with yellow dots on it, planting that visual motif. The thrust of that exposition is that Klara and Kralik have had a very antagonistic relationship.

In a subsequent conversation with Pirovitch, Kralik discloses his plan to ask the girl with whom he's been anonymously corresponding to marry him. Their discussion is pregnant with the future—Kralik lays out his hope—that she's beautiful but not too beautiful (otherwise she may not like him)—and his fear—that he won't find her attractive. He compares her to a bonus check whose envelope he has not yet opened—the possibilities are limitless until you open it. The use of this analogy plants the motif of the bonus, paid off (literally) in the last sequence, and echoes the motif of the raise.

A taxi now arrives, and Pirovitch, in the payoff of yet another motif from the opening scene, rushes to the taxi and opens the door (thinking it's Mr. Matuschek) only to have Vadas step out. Vadas is decked out in even more expensive clothing, shows off a big wad of cash. Like Pirovitch's remarks about how difficult the boss has been lately, Vadas's behavior is part of the setup of the major subplot involving Mrs. Matuschek.

Mr. Matuschek now arrives and once again Pirovitch is beaten to the punch by Pepi, who opens the door for the boss. Matuschek looks at the shop-window display with disapproval, and announces everyone will stay late that night to redecorate—an appointment that threatens Kralik's dinner date. Kralik reacts with alarm, and, unknown to him, so does Klara, who confides to Ilona that she has a date at 8:30 that night, and tells her she *has* to get out of it somehow—a dangling cause picked up a few scenes hence.

With the disclosure that Kralik and Klara have unknowingly been corresponding with each other, we arrive at the end of the first act of the picture. Kralik is the protagonist. What he wants is the girl. The problem is that he doesn't know that the girl he loves is also the girl he hates. This is an example of a predicament that is *invisible* to the protagonist. Unlike a film relying on dramatic tension, in which the first act ends when the character becomes aware of his objective and begins his pursuit of it, in a story that relies on ironic tension, the character is unaware of the problem he faces. The main tension in this case exists solely in the audience and not in any of the characters onscreen. True enough, Kralik does have *problems*, which can create tension for him—for example, he worries about whether he'll find the girl he's been corresponding with attractive, but he is unaware of the predicament that powers the film, the *main* tension, which can be best stated as: Will Kralik wind up with Klara despite the misunderstanding? The overriding question for the audience until the middle of the film is: what will happen when the truth comes out? In this, the audience's hopes (that they'll wind up together) and fears (that they won't) play out independently of the protagonist's hopes and fears, because for most of the picture the protagonist is not aware of the situation.

Figure 3. The blocking helps establish the dramatic irony of this scene in Sequence C of *The Shop Around the Corner* (1940). Kralik has just given Pepi the night off, inspiring Klara to ask for the same. Kralik's back is turned so he can't see Klara's reaction, but the audience can. Note the use of props by the actors: almost all the scenes in the script specify business for the actors—the handling and sorting of luggage and other sales items, along with documents, keys, pencils, and various other objects that help keep the scenes dynamic. (Frame enlargement)

Another consequence of the fact that the tension is purely in the audience is that there is no clearly articulated point of attack in the picture—no hint of the direction of the story until the predicament is established. It's important *not* to give a hint, or the surprise is lost. The opening title, discussed earlier, serves subtly the function of a point of attack, insofar as it lays out in very broad strokes what the story will be about, i.e., people in a shop. Klara's arrival can also be seen as a point of attack, since before she arrived, the story could not have unfolded as it did. But Klara's arrival serves this function only in retrospect; when she enters, she is just another of the many people trying to make a living.

Usually a predicament is established at the *end* of a sequence, reflecting the function of sequences as subunits of a character's overall objective. That this one occurs in the middle of one demonstrates the disjunction between the tensions created in the individual sequences and the overall main tension, at least at this point in the film. In *Toy Story,* the tension of the third sequence is identical to the main tension: Woody wants to regain his top spot against the usurper Buzz. In *The Shop Around the Corner,* the tension of the third sequence revolves around Kralik getting the night off.

From the moment the audience realizes that Kralik and Klara are the two anonymous lovers, every subsequent scene involving them, until the final minute of the film, is imbued with dramatic irony. Even Klara's first line after the revelation occurs—her declaration to Ilona that she plans to wear the polka-dotted blouse to the café that night—is more than simply a payoff of a motif. It has an added meaning, since the man she's trying to impress with the blouse has just, unknown to her, criticized it.

In the remainder of the sequence, while Kralik's and Klara's concerns are paramount, the major subplot of Mr. Matuschek's wife gradually grows in prominence, though it is not completely independent of the main plot—in fact, it asserts itself as an obstacle to Kralik's objective of getting the girl of his dreams.

Once everyone is inside the shop, Mr. Matuschek is shown on the phone talking to his wife, who seems to be running through her money very quickly. He promises to send her more, a dangling cause that is picked up at the end of the sequence. As soon as he hangs up, Kralik enters to ask for a raise, picking up on the dangling cause from the previous scene.* Mr. Matuschek coldly puts him off before he can even ask; afterward Kralik expresses his frustration to Pirovitch, who cautions him not to do anything rash. During their conversation, Vadas, listening in, reacts with alarm to Pirovitch's suggestion that Matuschek is having trouble with his wife. Like Matuschek's phone conversation with his wife, this is part of the setup for the marital affair subplot.

Pirovitch succeeds in calming down Kralik, who heads to the stock room to work with Klara and Pepi. Here, Pepi asks for the night off, claiming he's a child. Kralik assures him he'll work it out with the boss. The ease with which Pepi gets the night off is readily noticed by Klara, but Kralik does not notice *her* reaction. The resulting scene shows masterful use of both dramatic and ironic tension as well as indirection.

---

*It is not completely clear what Kralik is intending to ask Matuschek in this scene; he might plausibly be planning to ask for a raise or for the night off. In the screenplay Kralik only says that what he wants to talk about is "important to him."

Subplots

When a writer has an initial inspiration for a feature-length script and is contemplating how to develop it, he or she is always faced with a basic choice: whether to make it a *long* story or a *broad* one. A "long" story concerns itself primarily with a protagonist experiencing a succession of events, and a "broad" one introduces one or more subplots that run in parallel to the protagonist's story, involving subordinate characters. The choice is independent of the amount of time portrayed in a film. Subplots are often informally referred to alphabetically—the "A" plot is the main story, and the "B" plot one of the subplots, "C" plot if there is another, and so on.

Subplots, like dramatically structured main plots, have a protagonist with an objective, and follow the same three-act shape of setup, development, and resolution, (thus they almost invariably have a minimum of three scenes), and often their resolution involves a culminating moment that changes the subplot character, in a small-scale echo of the protagonist's character arc. Subplots basically have three functions: one, the *plot* function—they intersect with the main plot to help or hinder the protagonist; two, the *thematic* function—they show variations on the main theme of the picture by presenting alternating ways in which characters deal with the situation the protagonist may himself be confronting; and three, the *structural* function—by cutting away from the main plot to a subplot, especially at moments of high suspense, the storyteller can *retard* the action and by thus delaying it intensify the anticipation.

The subplot in *The Shop Around the Corner* serves all of these functions. Matuschek is the protagonist; his objective is to discover who his wife is sleeping with and punish him; the subplot poses a major obstacle to Kralik, it presents a variation on the theme of secret lovers and mistaken identity, and it's used at critical times to cut away from the suspense surrounding Kralik's and Klara's relationship.

Klara is the protagonist of the scene. Her objective is getting the night off and the chief obstacle is that the person who can get her the night off is her antagonist, Kralik. She goes about pursuing her objective using indirection: instead of coming right out and asking him, she acts extremely nice to him, complimenting him as a boss, claiming that she's learned a lot from him, and even thanking him for telling her not to wear the green blouse with the yellow dots—the second payoff of that motif. All the while, she's helping him rearrange luggage—business that the actors are given by the storytellers to enrich and render visual the verbal aspect of their interaction. In addition to the dramatic irony of Klara using subterfuge to manipulate Kralik, the whole scene plays, too, with the subtle line of irony that, unknown to Klara, the person she hopes to meet by getting the night off is none other than the man she's asking to help her get the night off.

When at last she judges the moment is right, she asks him the big question. This is the moment of recognition for Kralik, who, outraged at realizing her game, rejects her request. Both dramatic and ironic tension are simultaneously resolved. In the stormy aftermath, Klara tells him she *does* plan to wear the polka-dot blouse after all (its third payoff), then heads out into the shop and pleads directly with Mr. Matuschek. When Kralik piles on and also asks for the night off, Mr. Matuschek explodes in a tirade, momentarily interrupted by a comic interlude with a customer and an ill-timed personal phone call to Pirovitch. In the end, Mr. Matuschek saves his most bitter words for Kralik, who responds that "perhaps it's time to call it a day"—a dangling cause that is picked up in the following sequence.

The dramatic tension of the sequence—will Kralik get the night off?—has seemingly been resolved with a positive outcome, but the price paid in anguish makes it seem a pyrrhic victory.

At this point, Mrs. Matuschek phones again, reminding Mr. Matuschek to send more money. Matuschek asks Vadas to deliver it, closing off the dangling cause introduced at the start of the sequence.

Sequence D: The Advantage of Being a Boss

The major subplot, or "B" plot—Mr. Matuschek's marital problems—is the primary focus of this sequence, which runs just under fourteen minutes. It is unified by dramatic tension: it has a clear protagonist, Mr. Matuschek, who has an objective—to discover who is sleeping with his wife.

His first order of business is to fire Kralik, the man he's convinced is the guilty party. There is a brief scene of preparation by contrast before he gets fired, in which Kralik straightens out his tie and the other employees give him signals of encouragement as he heads into the boss's office. When Kralik emerges afterward, he delivers the news using indirection—instead of telling them he's been fired, he reads aloud the letter

Aftermath Scene

While the bulk of the tools discussed in this volume deal with creating anticipation and otherwise directing the audience's attention
toward the future, it is worth briefly discussing a type of scene that
deals more with what just happened than with what is about to happen: the *aftermath scene* or *aftermath beat*. Like a scene of preparation, an aftermath scene provides punctuation in the story, allowing
the storyteller to lend emphasis to certain moments deemed important. They invariably follow emotionally charged scenes, and are usually characterized by little or no dialogue or activity, and are heavily
atmospheric, often enhanced with music. Two of the most famous
aftermath scenes are contained in movies in this volume: the last
scenes of *Nights of Cabiria* and *The Graduate*. As with scenes of
preparation, aftermath scenes can usually be cut out without affecting the plot, but they have a profound impact on the emotional impact of a film.

of recommendation Matuschek had given him. He then uses a series of
props to express his inner state—he crushes underfoot the carnation he
was going to use as an identifier in his anticipated meeting with his lover
(first payoff of the carnation motif), then turns in the tools of his
trade—his sales record book, pencils, and key, the latter the planting of
a motif paid off in two sequences hence. Kralik says his good-byes, and
Pirovitch assures him they will see each other again—a dangling cause
picked up later in the sequence.

A brief, silent *aftermath scene* (see text box, above) occurs after the
door slams behind Kralik and all the employees stand silently. The moment is interrupted by a phone call to Mr. Matuschek, who excitedly
invites the caller to come over immediately. This in turn leads Matuschek to let everyone go for the evening. Before he goes, Pirovitch leaves
a message for Kralik, telling him he'll be stopping by that night—
picking up on a dangling cause and setting up an appointment. After
this, Vadas approaches Mr. Matuschek and tries to invite himself to dinner in another example of verbal indirection: he talks about how beautiful the dining room table is, and how wonderful it must look at a dinner
party, but never explicitly says what's on his mind. This motif—
someone attempting to invite himself to dinner—is paid off in the last
sequence of the picture.

After everyone is gone, a private detective arrives and delivers the news to Mr. Matuschek: Vadas is the employee having the affair with Mrs. Matuschek, much to Mr. Matuschek's surprise, who had clearly thought it was Kralik. Mr. Matuschek dismisses the private eye and, emotionally devastated, attempts to kill himself. The effort is thwarted by the timely arrival of Pepi. The suicide scene is done using visual indirection: we hear the gun and see the damage the bullet makes to a chandelier, but never see Mr. Matuschek fire it.

A brief aftermath scene ends the sequence, with Pepi staring at a distraught but evidently unharmed Matuschek.

Sequence E: Fractured Symmetry

The "A" plot resumes in this ten-minute sequence, which is again unified by dramatic tension: Kralik as protagonist, whose objective is to salvage the relationship with his lover. It opens with Kralik and Pirovitch arriving at the café so that Pirovitch can deliver a note to the unknown lover. The moment of recognition—at least for Kralik—is at hand, and audience anticipation of that moment is intensified by *retardation* (see text box on page 24), derived through a running commentary by Pirovitch on the various women in the restaurant, then by his partially obscured view of Klara, and finally by his roundabout way of giving Kralik the news ("if you don't like Miss Novak, I can tell you right now, you won't like this girl").

When the moment of recognition comes at last to Kralik, the main line of ironic tension is only partially resolved: now Kralik knows the truth, but Klara does not. This asymmetrical treatment of the ironic tension is noteworthy. It would have been entirely possible for the storyteller to continue developing the dramatic irony purely symmetrically, with both characters remaining in the dark until the resolution at the end, whereupon both would recognize the mistake. By fracturing the symmetry in this way, the screenwriter is able to explore the premise from a new, fresh angle while in the middle of telling the story, in effect giving the audience two films for the price of one: the first one about two lovers with a mutual misunderstanding, and the second about a man who pursues a woman by using secret information he has about her—i.e., her delusion about who he is. Such changes in the angle of exploring a premise are central to the success of many movies, and lack of such variations can make a film feel "one-note," predictable, or boring.

The scene ends with Kralik putting the note back into his pocket and walking away from the café, intent on leaving Klara to wait in vain.

The film now switches to inside the café, where another scene of preparation occurs between Klara and the waiter, who relates stories about previous blind dates at the café, and how some had gone well, but others hadn't. These stories do more than stoke Klara's anxiety about her anticipated date; they also advise the audience about what to hope for and what to be afraid of—the function of a scene of preparation. The dramatic irony of Kralik's expressed intent to leave her there hangs heavily over the scene.

Kralik enters the café soon after the waiter departs and pretends to run into Klara by accident. Henceforth, the scene takes on a traditional dramatic shape: Kralik is the protagonist, and his objective is reconciliation with Klara. The emotional impact of the scene is of course greatly intensified by the irony caused by Klara's ignorance of the fact that Kralik is the one for whom she's waiting.

Kralik uses indirection in his attempt to break the news to Klara and salvage their relationship. Instead of announcing that he's the "dear friend" of the correspondence, he talks about how little the two really know each other, and how he thought highly of her when she first started working for him. He tells her that people seldom go to the trouble of scratching beneath the surface to find their inner truth—a succinct statement of the theme of the picture. At one point he offers to take the place of her date if he doesn't show up—as close as he gets to disclosing the truth about himself. Unfortunately, she rebuffs him at every turn, at last calling him an "insignificant little clerk," and the scene is resolved in the negative: Kralik fails to woo her. Further, he fails to tell her he's the "dear friend," and so that line of ironic tension is left dangling as the scene ends.

This moment comes 58% of the way into the film, within range of a first culmination. It represents a significant, plausible outcome of the story: Kralik and Klara don't wind up together. It is in fact the mirror opposite of the resolution, which occurs in the last minute of the film. But this moment actually fulfills two functions. In terms of overall structure, it provides an emotional upheaval near the middle, but in terms of the main plot line, it actually serves as more of a second culmination—the end of the second act. The following sequence actually returns to the main subplot, and when the film returns to the main plot

Figure 4. Klara calls Kralik an "insignificant clerk," prompting him to abandon her at the café. This moment, occurring at the end of Sequence E, proves to be the low point in their relationship and provides a reasonable glimpse of a possible outcome of the picture: the two never wind up together, and Klara never finds out the identity of her pen pal/lover. The actual resolution is, of course, the mirror opposite. (Frame enlargement)

line in Sequence G, the dramatic question—Will Kralik wind up with Klara despite the misunderstanding?—has undergone a significant change.

Sequence F: The Keys to the Kingdom

This eleven-minute sequence is a contrast to the "dramatic relief" of the previous two in its return to a more upbeat, comedic tone, and is unified by dramatic tension, but only slightly so: the protagonist is Kralik, and his objective is to take over the reins of the business, but there is little in the way of obstacles.

After Pepi has a brief comic exchange with the doctor, he takes Kralik in to see Mr. Matuschek, who is bedridden but in a good mood. Matuschek rehires Kralik and elevates him to store manager, handing him the store key. The use of this prop not only pays off the motif established earlier when Kralik was saying his good-byes, it is also a visual expression of the change in their relationship. Three dangling causes mark the end of the scene: Kralik's promise that this Christmas will be the best in the history of the store, Pepi's success in eliciting a promotion from Mr. Matuschek, and Mr. Matuschek's instructions to Kralik to fire Vadas quietly.

The last of these is picked up first, when Kralik, happily returning to the shop and receiving congratulations from everyone, quickly assigns Vadas a time-consuming and pointless task. This scene is imbued with dramatic irony—as Kralik toys with Vadas, the latter is unaware of the fact that Kralik knows about his affair, and that he's soon to be terminated.

The next dangling cause is picked up when Pepi emerges from a haberdashery, done up in expensive-looking new clothes and a hat—visual evidence of his transformation in status. He delivers the news about Vadas's affair and Matuschek's attempted suicide through indirection— letting the others listen in on his phone calls.

After this, Kralik finally finds an excuse to fire Vadas (his criticism of Klara). In the ensuing scuffle, Vadas is knocked into the display of cigarette boxes—yet another payoff of that motif.

Sequence G: The Pursuit of Klara Begins

The remaining two sequences return the focus to the main plot, centered on Kralik's pursuit of Klara. This refocusing of attention also marks the transition from second act to third. As noted previously, the main tension was premised on symmetry—neither Kralik nor Klara knew the truth, and the hopes and fears of the audience were bound up in the question of whether the misunderstanding would doom their relationship. Now, with the fracturing of the symmetry yielding light on the situation for Kralik but not Klara, a new question has replaced the old: will Kralik succeed in wooing Klara despite the misunderstanding? The character-with-objective pattern of the third act imbues it with dramatic tension, but dramatic irony remains a significant element of audience involvement right through to the end of the picture.

The sequence begins with Klara reaching forlornly into an empty post office box, then returning to work, only to discover Kralik has become the manager—a development that causes her to faint. Klara winds up in bed, and Kralik visits and begins to woo her—using, appropriately enough, indirection. Rather than reveal immediately and directly who he is—the "dear friend" of their correspondence—he chooses instead to seduce her by writing a letter to her and pretending he is not the one who wrote it, said letter being very complimentary to him (describing him as a "very attractive young man"). The scene has no dramatic conflict and is sustained instead with the dramatic and comic irony (Klara tells him it's "difficult to explain a man like him to a man like you"). Kralik's approach amounts to a distant echo of the sales technique Klara used on him twice before—while trying to get a job during their first meeting, and later when she tried to manipulate him into giving her the night off.

The effect of the letter is intoxicating on Klara—she promises Kralik she'll be back the next day and will sell more goods than ever before—a dangling cause picked up later in this sequence and the next. Motifs come into play in the scene—the word "psychological" is planted here, the cigarette box is paid off yet again—this time with Klara announcing her intention to get her "dear friend" one for Christmas (much to Kralik's dismay), and the motif of the wallet bearing family pictures is planted.

The film now switches to daytime in front of the shop, where Pepi berates Rudy—the new errand boy—about being on time, in the process disclosing to the audience the fact that it's Christmas Day. Inside the shop, Kralik announces that Mr. Matuschek is much better—an update of his condition that serves to disarm confusion that might arise in the final sequence, when Matuschek shows up at the shop.

The twelve-minute sequence ends with a scene that picks up on the dangling cause of Klara's intention to buy the cigarette box for her "dear friend." Pirovitch persuades her to buy a wallet for her friend instead, using—as usual—indirection: he starts by telling her he wants to get a perfectly awful present for a relative he dislikes, and he thought the cigarette box would be perfect. After the scene, Pirovitch informs Kralik that he's succeeded, a surprise twist revealing the two had been in cahoots on the issue.

Sequence H: The Best Christmas Since '28

The final sequence of the film, like the first, is unified by place and time, in this case the shop on Christmas Eve. It begins with Mr. Matuschek arriving outside his store in the bustle of Christmas Eve. Here, in yet another example of verbal indirection, he attempts to sell a suitcase to two women by pretending to be just another window shopper.

After this blows up in his face, Mr. Matuschek enters the shop and congratulates everyone on the best Christmas sales since 1928. The following scenes—involving the handouts of bonuses (a payoff of a motif from Sequence B) and Mr. Matuschek's attempts to get himself a date on Christmas Eve (paying off the motif planted by Vadas)—amount to an epilogue: the script revisits all the various characters, with references to issues developed during the story (Kralik having other plans, Pirovitch staying home with his family, Pepi going off on a date, and finally Rudy, the new errand boy, with no place to go). This unusual placement of the epilogue before the resolution of the story is a bow to the fact that the remaining tension is largely ironic: what will happen when Klara finds out the truth? The resolution of that tension does not deliver the emotional impact of a more dramatically driven piece (such as *Toy Story*), so the need for an epilogue to bring the audience down from that emotional high is not as great. By placing the epilogue before the resolution, the remaining tension imbues an epilogue that otherwise might not have the emotional power to sustain audience interest.

With only Kralik and Klara remaining in the shop, all that remains on the agenda is the moment of recognition for Klara: how will she react when she finds out the truth? Will she still love the "dear friend" when she finds out who it is? Here, the screenwriter exploits the situation for maximum effect, delaying the moment of recognition—milking the comic and dramatic irony of the situation—through a full ten minutes before finally delivering the goods.

First Kralik sees Klara wrapping the wallet for her "dear friend," closing off that dangling cause. Klara tells him she thinks she might have an engagement ring when she returns to the shop, and Kralik replies that he's meeting someone that night, and it's serious; Klara suggests they may both be engaged come Monday—a dangling cause delivered in full comically ironic fashion. During the conversation, Kralik gets some timely exposition about her initial attraction to him, in which the "psychologically mixed up" motif is paid off twice.

After learning this, Kralik uses verbal indirection to finally land her, creating an elaborate story about how he'd already met Klara's lover, a Mr. Popkin, and proceeding to torment her with less-than-flattering details about him. He proves to be the ultimate salesman, drawing such a dreary picture of her anonymous lover so that when he finally reveals the truth of the situation to her, he is a much better catch by comparison.

Once this last thread of ironic tension is resolved, there remains only a brief gag about Kralik's bowleggedness, a payoff of the motif planted at the café, before a loving embrace ends the picture.

Sequences in the original screenplay: a comparison

As was standard practice in 1940, Samson Raphaelson's original screenplay was marked by sequence. There are six in all, labeled A–F, and vary in length of running time from six to twenty-three minutes. Sequence A encompasses both of what I identify as the first two sequences—the ensemble setup and Klara's quest for a job. It's logical to group these together in the sense that, together, they constitute the bulk of the setup for the film as a whole. As detailed above, though, Klara's arrival signals a significant shift in the action; in fact, with the exception of a one-and-a-half minute scene between Kralik and Matuschek, Klara is onscreen continuously from the moment she enters to the moment she succeeds in selling the cigarette box, and her objective—getting a job— touches on all the action, including the brief scene between Kralik and Matuschek. From a writer's point of view, it's more useful to see them as two distinct sequences to be tackled in succession, rather than one large chunk of story.

The screenplay's Sequence B and my own Sequence C (Kralik and Klara trying to get the night off) are in accord; the screenplay's Sequence C combines both of my Sequences D and E. The logic of the screenplay's grouping appears elusive at first; of those twenty-four minutes of screen time, fourteen take place at the shop and involve the "B" plot—Matuschek fires Kralik, finds out Vadas is the guilty party, and attempts suicide. The next nine move to a new location—the café—and return to the "A" plot—Kralik finding out Klara is the "dear friend." Their unity seems to be thematic—both depict a man discovering something about the woman he loves. However, from a writer's viewpoint, tackling these two portions of the story separately makes the job easier.

The screenplay's Sequences D and E are largely similar to my own divisions (Sequences F and G); on the final sequence, my analysis and the screenplay's demarcation are in agreement.

THE SHOP AROUND THE CORNER
Sequence Breakdown

Seq.	Description	Length	Running Time
	ACT I		
	(Script Sequence A)		
A	Opening of film (excluding titles, which run 1:17) to Matuschek telling the Miklos Brothers on the phone that he doesn't want the cigarette boxes. *Unifying Aspect*: Place and time. *Protagonist*: Ensemble.	8:39	8:39 (9%)
	Point of attack: Klara's entrance.		
B	Klara enters and tries to get a job; she finally succeeds by selling the cigarette box to the female customer. *Unifying Aspect*: Dramatic Tension. *Protagonist*: Klara. *Objective*: A job.	8:50	17:29 (18%)
	(Script Sequence B)		
	ACT II **(Main tension: Will Kralik and Klara get together despite the misunderstanding?)**		
C	Kralik and Klara argue about the polka-dotted dress; Kralik reveals to Pirovitch he's going to ask Mr. Matuschek for a raise and then meet his pen pal.	16:19	33:48 (35%)
	Predicament: **Kralik has unwittingly fallen in love with a woman he hates (23:45—25%)**		
	Matuschek talks on phone to his wife, who is asking for yet more money; Kralik is rebuffed by Matuschek—and his offer to make a delivery to Mrs. Matuschek is refused. *Unifying Aspect*: Dramatic Tension. *Protagonist*: Kralik. *Objective*: The night off.		
	(Script Sequence C)		
D	Matuschek fires Kralik, sends everyone else home, discovers true identity of the man his wife is seeing—and attempts suicide. *Unifying Aspect*: Dramatic Tension. *Protagonist*: Matuschek. *Objective*: To find out who is sleeping with his wife.	13:52	47:40 (49%)
E	Pirovitch and Kralik venture to restaurant; Kralik discovers it's Klara; Kralik goes to talk to her. She rebuffs him, calling him an "insignificant clerk." *Unifying Aspect*: Dramatic Tension. *Protagonist*: Kralik. *Objective*: To keep hope for love with Klara alive.	8:51	56:31 (58%)
	First Culmination: **Klara calls Kralik an "insignificant clerk," Kralik exits the café (56:22—58%).**		

(Script Sequence D)

F	Kralik is re-hired by a bedridden Matuschek, fires Vadas. *Unifying Aspect*: Dramatic Tension. *Protagonist*: Kralik. *Objective*: to take the reins at Matuschek & Co.	10:42	1:07:13 (70%)

ACT III

G	The film returns to the main plot, and refocuses onto Kralik's quest for Klara, which initiates the third act tension. Kralik will try to use his newly won power and position to rescue their relationship. In this sequence, Klara reaches into empty mailbox, then faints upon seeing that Kralik is indeed the new boss; Kralik visits her in bed—then, with the help of Pirovitch, gets her to give him a wallet.	11:50	1:19:03 (82%)

(Script Sequence E)

Unifying Aspect: Dramatic Tension. *Protagonist*: Kralik. *Objective*: Klara.

Second Culmination: Kralik visits a bedridden Klara (1:09:30—72%).

(Script Sequence F)

H	Matuschek arrives outside store on Christmas Eve, then goes inside, congratulates everyone, hands out bonuses, gets himself a date. Alone with Klara, Kralik seduces her away from her fictitious lover, then finally reveals the truth about himself and the letters. *Unifying Aspect*: Place. *Protagonist*: Ensemble.	17:47	1:36:50 (100%)

Epilogue: **Matuschek congratulates them on a fine job, gives out bonuses, gets himself a date.**

Resolution: **Klara embraces Kralik.**

Double Indemnity: Flashback to the Future

Released in 1944 as a much-anticipated cinematic adaptation of a James M. Cain novel considered too risqué for the screen, *Double Indemnity* wound up winning several Academy Awards, among them Best Screenplay. It is noteworthy as a collaboration between Billy Wilder (director) and Raymond Chandler (detective novelist who wrote the script) that generated the classic film noir.

Because it uses the principle of flashback, *Double Indemnity* tests the basic theory of dramatic tension—that audience attention is achieved by creating in them hope and fear about the outcome of a question: will a character get his or her objective? In this picture, the protagonist, Walter Neff, tells the audience at the outset the outcome of his quest, yet the movie remains intensely involving. This is because while the audience knows the ultimate outcome, it is unaware of when it occurs and under what circumstances. Thus, as the scenes unfold, the storytellers can still manipulate the audience's hopes and fears, though the question posed to the audience differs slightly from when the audience does *not* know the outcome. That is, whenever Neff runs into an obstacle, the question becomes not so much "will he overcome this obstacle?" as "will *this* be the obstacle that proves his undoing?" The hope remains the same: that he'll overcome the obstacle. And the fear that he won't is, if anything, enhanced by the audience's awareness that Neff is ultimately doomed.

Sequence A: Doing Ninety in the Parlor

The first sequence runs fourteen minutes and is unified by dramatic
tension: Neff is the protagonist and his objective, contained in a single
scene, is to sell insurance to Phyllis. The first six minutes of the sequence
set up Neff's circumstances that render the scene with Phyllis compre-
hensible.

The opening of the picture begins with a puzzle, aimed, as is typical
in a successful picture, at arousing curiosity. The title sequence itself
features a silhouetted figure on crutches moving ominously toward the
audience while grand, intense music announces the dark, dangerous,
suspenseful nature of the subject matter. The riddle of the man on
crutches is not answered, but is instead supplanted by another puzzle: a
car driving recklessly late at night on rain-slicked streets. Who's driving
it? Why? What's wrong? Is someone after him?

Even when the car skids to a stop and the door opens, we are not
allowed a glimpse of the face of the person who emerges, so even that
mystery is milked for a minute or so longer. In the elevator shortly
thereafter, the answers to the puzzle come at last: the man's name is
Neff, he works in the insurance business, and he's not much interested
in small talk at that time.

More substantial answers to the mystery do not come until Neff be
gins dictating a memo to his friend Keyes, almost five minutes into the
film. Even here, though, the answers are given as pieces of a tantalizing
puzzle, with important parts left out. Neff mentions the Dietrichson
case, the fact that it was murder, and confesses his guilt in it. In this
confession, he describes himself using the terminology of the insurance
business: age, height, occupation, health, even though he is addressing
a friend who would know these things. This use of irony in the dialogue—Neff pretending that his friend doesn't already know these
facts—serves both the function of adding extra richness to a painful
confession, while simultaneously giving exposition to the audience—
facts about the protagonist are thus smuggled in without the audience
realizing it. After confessing his guilt, Neff begins to relate the tale, sending the narrative into the past, where the story proper begins—six minutes into the sequence.

Neff's introductory monologue runs just over two minutes, and even
though it amounts to a monologue, it still has within it a subtext: an
action verb, something Neff is trying to do aside from relating information. The memo is presented as a polemic—an argument with Keyes, in

which Neff will show how Keyes has an over-inflated opinion of himself, thinking himself "such a wolf on a phony claim." When Neff begins relating the story, "It began last May . . ." he is doing more than regaling an old friend with an interesting tale; he's setting out to show how Keyes was wrong. This dangling cause is finally closed off in the last minutes of the film, when Keyes acknowledges, "You can't figure them all, Walter."

In the flashback, Neff arrives at Phyllis's house to sell her husband on insurance. The scene plays out in simple dramatic fashion, with Neff playing the protagonist whose objective is to sell Phyllis a policy, and the chief obstacle is his sexual interest in Phyllis. When Phyllis responds to Neff's flirtation with an accusation that he is exceeding the speed limit, there follows a famous example of verbal indirection: a discussion about a traffic stop on the surface conceals sexual sparring just beneath it. In this scene, the anklet is planted, as well as the notion of accident insurance; in fact, Phyllis's query about accident insurance, and Neff's subsequent ruminations about it, constitute the point of attack of the picture. Neff's initial confession also serves the role of the point of attack, focusing the audience attention on the future and giving us a very strong sense of what the story will be about. The scene ends with an appointment: Neff will return Thursday night at 8:00 p.m. to talk to her husband about the auto-insurance renewal.

Neff returns to his office, where he witnesses Keyes interrogating a truck driver named Garlopis who has submitted a false claim. Here, Keyes's great talent for smoking out phony claims is dramatized, the dialogue motif of the "little man" inside of him is planted, as is the visual motif of the cigarette-lighting routine.

The sequence ends when Neff arrives in his own office and finds a message from Phyllis, rescheduling the appointment. In voice-over, Neff indicates his intention to go, a dialogue hook that binds the first sequence to the second.

Sequence B: The Red-hot Poker

The next sixteen minutes of the film introduce and develop a line of tension quite distinct from that of the first fourteen minutes, which is why what is marked as Sequence A in the screenplay can be split into two at this juncture. Whereas the first fourteen minutes hooked the audience with curiosity and found Neff trying to sell insurance, the next sixteen follow Neff's resistance to temptation to cooperate with Phyllis in a murderous plot, resistance that ultimately proves futile.

The sequence begins with Neff keeping an appointment established in the previous scene. Though ostensibly there to sell auto insurance, it becomes quickly apparent to him that Phyllis has something else on her mind, which he readily misinterprets as sexual interest in him. His objective in the scene is a sexual liaison with her, and the chief obstacles to that objective are her persistent questions about insurance. In the end, when Neff realizes what precisely she is asking for—an accident policy on her husband which would enable her to murder him and collect a large sum of money—he abandons his sexual objective and retreats.

The dramatic tension of the sequence is thus set up four minutes into it: Neff must resist Phyllis and her devious plan. He does this at first by food, drink, and bowling, then, when Phyllis arrives at his apartment, by stridently pointing out all the things that could go wrong with such a scheme. As Neff describes how Keyes would react if she were to file a claim after murdering her husband, he is doing more than fighting off temptation and trying to talk Phyllis out of it; he is also smuggling exposition to the audience (explaining all the obstacles that await them) and setting up a *reversal* (see text box on reversals, page 168).

The reversal is crucial because of the implausibility of the premise. What would drive a relatively normal, law-abiding citizen who has never done anything more ethically questionable than sell vacuum cleaners to agree to kill a perfect stranger for the sake of money he doesn't need and a woman he's just met? The storytellers had several options at their disposal; they could've made Neff desperate for money for some reason, or given him a history of criminal activity, or given him some personally acrimonious relationship with Mr. Dietrichson. Instead, they left the character and situation essentially as presented in the Cain novel, and opted for a reversal, in which the protagonist resists the temptation full-bore, giving the audience a glimpse of an alternate outcome (he successfully resists), then succumbs. (Note: while present in the Cain novel, the reversal is less developed). A cutaway to the present day, with Neff continuing his memo to Keyes, provides the audience with additional justification: Neff had long been tempted to try to "crook the house," because he knew the industry from the inside.

When Neff finally tells Phyllis he'll help her do the murder, the dramatic tension in the sequence is resolved in the negative. In the three-minute epilogue of the sequence, Neff launches into a series of dangling causes, hooking the sequence with those that follow: they're going to get away with it because he knows how to do it right; everything will be perfect—nothing overlooked, nothing weak—he and Phyllis must never be seen together, they must watch every move carefully, "it's straight down the line."

When Neff watches Phyllis's car drive off in the rain—a classic example of both visual indirection (we hear the car but see only Neff's face as he watches it) and *aftermath* (the scene is light on dialogue and heavy on atmosphere; see text box, page 54), both the sequence and first act draw to a close. As in *Toy Story*, there is something of a curtain between the acts—in this case, a cutaway to Neff in the present, speaking into the Dictaphone and explaining the next phase of their scheme.

Sequence C: Setting Up the Murder

At the outset of the second act, the main tension is clear: will Neff get the girl and the money? This sounds like two objectives but since they're entwined, they function as one. The answer to this question was of course given explicitly by Neff in the opening Dictaphone scene. What drew the audience into the story at that time was curiosity—not whether he'll obtain his objective, but rather, how did he fail? By this point in the movie, dramatic and ironic tension are both used to engage the audience's emotional involvement—irony created by our fore-knowledge of the outcome, which creates a sense of anticipation—and dramatic tension as well, since, as discussed previously, the audience doesn't know *which* obstacle Neff encounters will be the one that dooms him, so the issues of hope and fear central to dramatic tension remain in play.

The fourteen minutes of Sequence C are concerned with Neff and Phyllis setting up the murder, and involve two reversals, the second of which spins into Sequence D and the murder itself. The opening scene is set up in the voice-over narration—Neff has to get Dietrichson's signature without Dietrichson's knowing about it, and with some witness present. The rest of the scene proceeds with dramatic irony as the primary means of audience engagement: there is little conflict in the scene, just Neff trying to sell Dietrichson on an accident policy, Dietrichson refusing, and Neff getting him to sign twice. The emotional power in the scene comes from the audience's superior knowledge—and fear that Dietrichson will find out what it is he's really signing. One bit of infor-

Figure 5. Walter Neff watches Phyllis drive away in a brief aftermath scene in *Double Indemnity* (1944), a medium shot that ends Sequence B (and first act) of the picture. Like *Toy Story* and *The Graduate,* this film features a "curtain" after the first act—in this case, a cutaway to Neff narrating into a Dictaphone at his office, where he sets up the dramatic tension of Sequence C. In both *Toy Story* and *The Graduate,* a musical interlude serves as a curtain. (Frame enlargement)

mation revealed by Dietrichson becomes important immediately afterward: his anticipated trip to Palo Alto. After succeeding in getting Dietrichson's signature, Neff explains to Phyllis the "double indemnity" clause, and tells her that Dietrichson must take the train—a forceful dangling cause.

When Neff leaves the house, he encounters the first potential obstacle: Dietrichson's daughter Lola is in his car, in need of a ride. Neff maintains his cool, and in the process the Lola–Nino subplot is established. The dramatic irony of the scene—audience knowledge that Neff is actually planning to kill Lola's father—infuses it with emotion, so that the expository function (giving the audience information about Lola's circumstances and romantic aspirations with Nino) is concealed.

The first reversal of the sequence comes in the following scene at the Los Feliz market, where Neff explains to Phyllis how everything is falling into place, only to have her deliver the unfortunate news that Dietrichson has broken his leg, and the trip to Palo Alto has been cancelled. Phyllis wants to go ahead with the plan in some form, but Neff warns her against it, a dangling cause closed off at the end of the sequence.

The following scene, featuring Keyes trying to talk Neff into taking a desk job, utilizes preparation by contrast in order to set up another reversal. In Neff's voice-over narration, he speaks of the fates watching over him to prevent him from doing something he shouldn't do, and in the scene with Keyes he is generally upbeat. This moment is really the first glimpse of a potential outcome of the film—Neff doesn't go through with it. When Phyllis calls with the news that Dietrichson is going to Palo Alto after all—and on the train, as they'd planned—the reversal is effected. The scene, which had previously been driven by dramatic tension—Keyes trying to persuade Neff to take a desk job—now switches to ironic tension, with Keyes hovering in the background while Neff and Phyllis speak surreptitiously on the phone. When Neff lights Keyes's cigar at the end of the scene, the sequence also comes to an end, with the plan having overcome its one significant obstacle.

Sequence D: Dietrichson Makes a Wrong Turn

This thirteen-minute sequence is in essence a short film about two people committing a murder, and it ends when the murder is complete. Its engine is overwhelmingly dramatic—will Neff and Phyllis pull off their murder? Still, two layers of irony suffuse it—the overriding layer of the audience's foreknowledge that the two will ultimately fail, and the intermittent layer that occurs whenever the two are in contact with other characters, who don't know about their conspiracy.

Neff's voice-over narration at the outset provides the sequence's "first act" setup, and also a good deal of preparation. He recounts how he set up his alibi and arranged the doorbell and phone so that he'd know if he had visitors or callers. These steps help enhance the anticipation of the actual murder, which has been planned for some time.

When Neff gets into the back of Dietrichson's car three minutes into the sequence, the setup is complete and the sequence's "second act" begins. After some ironic dialogue between Dietrichson and Phyllis, in which he assures her he'll be back in a few days, Neff kills him. When they arrive at the train station, Neff and Phyllis exchange words in a recapitulation scene, in which Neff lays out a series of dangling causes to be picked up as the conspiracy unfolds. Once on the train, Neff hobbles to the observation car at the rear (paying off the motif of the silhouetted man on crutches from the title sequence) and is about to leap onto the tracks when the character Jackson interferes. Dramatic irony infuses this scene, forcing Neff to be discreet as he attempts to get Jackson off the platform. When he succeeds, Neff leaps from the train and he and Phyllis complete their "impersonation." A last-minute problem with their car's engine threatens to be their undoing until Neff is able to start it.

The sequence concludes when Neff drops off Phyllis, then heads home, and we revisit the preparations he made for the night of the murder. Neff's voice-over narration ends with a chilling dangling cause: he expresses fear that everything will go wrong, that he is walking the walk of a dead man.

Sequence E: Apparent Triumph

The fifth sequence, which runs just under fourteen minutes, is unified by Neff's desire to weather the stormy aftermath of the murder without giving himself away, and is comprised of two important reversals set up by preparation by contrast, both of which are notably absent from the James M. Cain book. How these moments of the story are handled is a good example of the virtuosity of the Wilder–Chandler collaboration.

During the first five minutes of the sequence, much attention is given to creating a sense of impending doom, picking up on the dangling cause of the previous sequence. This is accomplished by withholding important information from the audience as long as possible, then delivering it for maximum effect.

The sequence commences with Neff narrating in his office and describing his fears of exposure. The scene flashes back to his office building, where Neff runs immediately into Keyes, who says something is wrong with the Dietrichson case, and who leads Neff to a meeting with their boss, Norton. The scene is infused with dramatic irony—audience fear that the secret will come out and Neff will be exposed.

In the meeting with their boss, Norton announces he is not satisfied with the conclusion of accidental death in the Dietrichson case—but he does not say why. The meeting is interrupted by the arrival of a visitor—a new development that delays Norton's delivery of his objections to the case. This is a classic example of *retardation* (see text box, page 24)—the audience is made to fear Norton's conclusion, but is also made

Figure 6. Neff's best friend, Barton Keyes, makes an unexpected and un-welcome appearance at Neff's door while Phyllis is en route in Sequence E of *Double Indemnity* (1944). The scene is driven by dramatic irony, and delivers a devastating blow to Neff's hopes for his scheme's success. Careful use of preparation—complete with Neff declaring that he feels the money is as good as in the bank—is paid off by contrast when Keyes arrives and expresses his suspicions. Neff's upbeat mood before this scene provides the first culmination of the picture—a reasonable glimpse of a possible outcome, namely that he and Phyllis succeed. (Frame enlargement)

to wait before hearing what it is. The suspense is thus milked for maximum effect.

Just before Phyllis enters, Norton urges Neff and Keyes to "watch me handle this"—a dangling cause enhancing our anticipation. When Phyllis arrives, Norton makes introductions and then begins to make his case against her. At last, Norton announces his conclusion that it was a suicide—an innocuous conclusion as far as the hopes and fears of Neff and Phyllis (and the audience) are concerned. This moment of relief is punctuated by some business involving the glass of drinking water that Neff hands to Phyllis, which allows the two to make surreptitious eye contact. Norton's identification of suicide as the problem with the Dietrichson case is a reversal, set up in the previous four minutes by suggestions of impending doom—classic preparation by contrast.

Soon after this, Phyllis launches into a diatribe, denouncing Norton and storming out of the office, earning Norton a rebuke from Keyes: "You sure handled that one"—closing off the dangling cause from just before Phyllis's arrival. Keyes completes the demolition of Norton's case in a memorable lecture about suicide.

The scene with Norton is worth study because it shows two forces simultaneously at work—dramatic and ironic tension. The scene's emotional center is ironic—fear that Neff's secret will be revealed. But the scene is shaped by dramatic tension—Norton's desire to prove he's "no idiot." The "first act" or setup for that tension occurs when Norton tells Keyes and Neff to watch him "handle this," an explicit attempt to show that just because a man has a large office he's "no idiot." When Phyllis exits, the tension is resolved to the negative (i.e., he fails). Keyes's subsequent destruction of Norton's case proves to be the "third act" of the scene, with the business with the glass of water and Keyes's line about wearing a tuxedo providing the exclamation point at the end of it.

After leaving Norton's office, preparation by contrast begins again in earnest—this time in the reverse of the previous eight minutes. Neff's voice-over narration, the lighting, and the music all suggest a positive outcome to the murder conspiracy. When Neff arrives home, Phyllis calls him and the two exchange congratulations, and Neff invites her over; the money, says Neff, is as good as in the bank. These moments amount to the first culmination of the film—the midpoint moment when the movie could reasonably end, with Neff and Phyllis living happily ever after with $100,000 and no one the wiser about their murder conspiracy—the mirror opposite of its actual resolution.

Soon after Neff invites Phyllis over, this glimpse of a positive outcome vanishes in the wake of another reversal: Keyes arrives with suspicions about the Dietrichson case, and, unknown to him (but quite known to the audience) Phyllis on the way. The scene proceeds with the two tools of dramatic and ironic tension, dramatic in that Neff attempts to get Keyes out of the apartment before Phyllis arrives, and ironic in its primary emotional aspect: fear that Phyllis will arrive with Keyes still there, and the conspiracy will be exposed. Neff's casual appointment with Phyllis has turned into the classic deadline.

Phyllis arrives before Keyes leaves, but happens to overhear him before she's discovered. Keyes's dialogue continues ironically in earnest, expressing suspicion about Phyllis while Phyllis secretly listens to him. Keyes enters the elevator after delivering an ominous dangling cause about arresting her "so fast it will make her head spin."

The sequence concludes with Neff recounting the new danger— Keyes will never give up on the case; he'll have her investigated and followed, so they can't see each other for a while. Phyllis objects to the idea that they must be apart, and he reassures her with an embrace and a kiss. This slightly positive note provides a striking contrast to the shot that opens the following sequence: Lola waiting for Neff outside his office.

Sequence F: The Conspiracy Crumbles

The fourteen minutes of Sequence F proceeds as a series of increasingly threatening revelations and crises, and its protagonist, Neff, has as his objective the need to diffuse and disarm them. Along the way, attempts are made by the storytellers to use the momentary elevation of hope to set off further calamity by contrast.

At his office, Neff hears Lola deliver some disturbing news about Phyllis's past: it seems that her murder conspiracy with Neff may not have been her first. The scene is infused with irony: our knowledge, unknown to Lola, that she is confessing her suspicions of foul play in her father's death to the man who engaged in that foul play.

Neff disarms this potential disaster by treating Lola to dinner and taking her to the beach. The mood again becomes upbeat—Neff noting that by the second day Lola was able to laugh—just in time for the next bit of disturbing news: Neff seeing Jackson, the last man who saw him on the train platform, sitting outside Keyes's office.

Ironic tension is milked to maximal effect in the scenes with Keyes and Jackson. First, Keyes announces he is a great man, having unraveled the Dietrichson murder conspiracy. He articulates the conspiracy with devastating accuracy—to the man who was involved in that conspiracy. Neff makes a feeble attempt to undermine Keyes's theory, then Jackson is brought in, and here suspense is created out of the fear that the witness will recognize Neff as the man on the platform.

Neff manages to diffuse the situation by trying to avoid direct eye contact with Jackson, whose examination of Dietrichson's photograph confirms Keyes's theory about the murder. After Jackson leaves, Keyes works on the audience's expectation with several dangling causes: murder conspiracies always fall apart sooner or later; when two people are involved it's usually sooner; Phyllis' lover and co-conspirator will show himself eventually; if Phyllis tries to sue over a denied claim, he'll be waiting. He also plants the dialogue motif about the trolley car.

Afterward, Neff contacts Phyllis urgently for a meeting at the market. Here, he tells her they can't go ahead with their plan to collect the insurance money, and she rejects his assertion. As Phyllis goes away vowing to make the claim (a dangling cause picked up in the following sequence), Neff remarks in his voice-over narration that it was the first time he'd pictured her dead. The moment marks the second culmination—the end of the second act—the resolution of the main tension. The answer to the dramatic question: "will Neff get the girl and the money?" is answered to the negative. The third act turns on a very different question: "Will Neff extricate himself from the conspiracy?"

Sequence G: The Case Busts Wide Open

The thirteen and a half minutes of the seventh sequence concern Neff's realization that murdering Phyllis will allow him to extricate himself from his troubles, and his carrying out the murder.

The plan is germinated in a scene with Lola at the Hollywood Bowl, where Neff learns that Lola believes Phyllis and Nino Sachetti are the two who murdered her father. The involvement of Sachetti is confirmed in the following scene when Keyes reveals to Neff that the "somebody else"—the person who helped Phyllis kill Dietrichson—has revealed himself. This leads Neff to sneak into Keyes's office to find out what Keyes is talking about, and here he discovers that Keyes suspects that Sachetti is Phyllis' co-conspirator.

Neff calls Phyllis and makes an appointment with her: eleven o'clock that night, with the front door unlocked and the lights out. In voice-over, Neff reveals his intention to kill Phyllis in order to gets himself out of the mess he is in, a moment that marks the end of the "sequence first act."

Soon thereafter, Phyllis is revealed to be hiding a gun under her chair prior to Neff's arrival, setting up two lines of ironic tension: each intends to kill the other; neither is aware of the other's intention. In the scene, Neff toys with Phyllis for a few moments, explaining the rationale for his actions. The secret, murderous intentions of both characters infuse the scene with emotion. Neff prepares to kill Phyllis, only to be shot first. The two embrace, and Phyllis confesses a change in her rotten heart to him, which serves as a brief preparation by contrast to Neff's killing her a moment later.

The sequence ends with Neff greeting Sachetti outside the house and urging him to call Lola to make up to her, effectively closing off the Lola–Sachetti subplot.

Sequence H: "Somebody moved the elevators a couple miles away."

The death of Phyllis marks the resolution of the picture, and the final sequence is essentially an epilogue, tying up the relationship between Neff and Keyes. As in the opening scenes, the final sequence takes place entirely in the "present," with Neff completing his narration into the microphone and Keyes arriving on the scene. The sequence has a simple dramatic thrust—Neff's objective, revealed two minutes into the sequence, is to make it across the border. Keyes responds to this intention with a dangling cause: "you'll never even make the elevator," a prediction that comes true a minute or so later.

The sequence and film end with a punctuation mark: the payoffs of two motifs—Neff telling Keyes "I love you, too," and Keyes lighting Neff's cigarette.

Sequences in the original screenplay: a comparison

This screenplay, like that of *The Shop Around the Corner*, is explicitly marked by sequences, this time four in all,* three of them with running times of about thirty minutes and one running about half that. Closer examination again shows that within all the sequences except one (Sequence C) there are significant subdivisions in the development and release of dramatic tension.

Sequence A in the screenplay, like that of *The Shop Around the Corner,* encompasses the entire first act. As detailed above and in the accompanying chart, it clearly has a significant shift midway through. Until Phyllis calls Neff back to her place and discusses accident insur-

---

*There was also a Sequence E—a portrayal of Neff's execution—which was filmed but not included in the final cut.

ance with him, she's just another customer (albeit one he lusts after) and he just another salesman in the middle of an ordinary day. After that point, his focus centers obsessively on Phyllis and her proposal.

Sequence B in the screenplay corresponds to Sequences C and D in my own analysis. These twenty-nine minutes of screen time encompass both the planning of the murder and the murder itself, two very distinct segments of the story, separated by that glimpse of an alternative outcome—the "fates" that Neff thought might be watching over him when the initial plan is shelved by Dietrichson's broken leg.

Sequence C in the script corresponds precisely with my own demarcation of Sequence E, while Sequence D stretches across what I consider three distinct shifts in the story: Neff's effort to control the collapsing conspiracy, his murder of Phyllis, and his attempt at the end to escape to Mexico. These are all united by Neff's attempts to undo what he has done (committed the murder), but they are more easily tackled as separate beats by a writer.

DOUBLE INDEMNITY
Sequence Breakdown

Seq.	Description	Length	Running Time
	ACT I		
	(Script Sequence A)		
A	Opening confession to Phyllis leaving a message for Neff (excluding opening titles). *Unifying Aspect*: Dramatic Tension. *Protagonist*: Neff. *Objective*: To sell Phyllis on a car insurance policy.	14:22	14:22 (14%)
B	Neff visits Phyllis's place a second time—she suggests taking out an accident policy. He resists and tries to escape the entanglement; at the end of the sequence, he is drawn in. *Unifying Aspect*: Dramatic Tension. *Protagonist*: Neff. *Objective*: Resist the temptation posed by Phyllis.	15:40	30:02 (29%)
	Point of attack: Phyllis suggests accident insurance without her husband knowing. Also, Neff's confession in the opening monologue serves this function.		
	Predicament: Neff decides to help Phyllis murder her husband and get the insurance money.		
	(Script Sequence B)		
	ACT II **(Main tension: Will Neff get the girl and the money?)**		
C	Neff and Phyllis set up the murder, only to find it thwarted by Mr. Dietrichson's broken leg. *Unifying Aspect*: Dramatic Tension. *Protagonist*: Neff. *Objective*: To set up the murder.	14:17	45:20 (43%)
D	Neff and Phyllis carry out the murder. *Unifying Aspect*: Dramatic Tension. *Protagonist*: Neff. *Objective*: To murder Dietrichson.	12:41	58:01 (55%)
	(Script Sequence C)		
E	Neff tries to survive the murder's aftermath; his hopes are first raised when Keyes inadvertently comes to his aid—concluding it *was* an accident, not suicide, then dashed, when Keyes becomes suspicious after all. *Unifying Aspect*: Dramatic Tension. *Protagonist*: Neff. *Objective*: To ride out the stormy aftermath without giving himself away.	13:45	1:11:46 (68%)
	First Culmination: Neff thinks he got away with it, invites Phyllis over (1:06:34—63%).		

| F | Neff finds out about Phyllis's past role in a murder (through Lola); Keyes reveals to him that he's figured out how the murderers did it; Neff then survives a close call with Jackson from Medford, Oregon, and at last tells Phyllis it's over. She refuses. Main Tension is resolved in the negative: Neff has failed to help Phyllis pull off the perfect murder—now she has become the enemy. Third-act tension: dealing with Phyllis. *Unifying Aspect*: Dramatic Tension. *Protagonist*: Neff. *Objective*: to weather a succession of crises. | 13:44 | 1:24:54 (81%) |

Second Culmination: **Neff realizes he's not going to get the girl and he's not going to get the money.**

(Script Sequence D)

ACT III

| G | Neff endures revelations about Phyllis and Nino Sachetti, concludes that his only hope is to eliminate her. He goes to her place and kills her. *Unifying Aspect*: Dramatic Tension. *Protagonist*: Neff. *Objective*: To solve his problems by killing Phyllis. | 13:36 | 1:38:30 (93%) |

Resolution: **Neff kills Phyllis.**

| H | Neff sends Sachetti back to Lola, then confronts Keyes in person, tries to make his final getaway, fails. *Unifying Aspect*: Dramatic Tension. *Protagonist*: Neff. *Objective*: To complete his dictation and escape. | 6:54 | 1:45:26 (100%) |

Epilogue: **Sequence H.**

Fellini's *Nights of Cabiria:*
Nocturnal Episodes

This picture, which won the Oscar for Best Foreign Film in 1957, provides a contrast in structure to the others analyzed herein. While by no means as "experimental" as the films Federico Fellini made a few years later, it is still a departure from the American style of cinematic storytelling. Whereas American films are particularly interested in involving the audience in a chronological, cause-and-effect story from moment to moment, *Nights of Cabiria* is primarily interested in the exploration of the title character and her circumstances. The course chosen for this exploration is episodic—the discovery of the character and a series of tales about her. Still, the film must manage audience attention, and how it does so, and how it has come to move audiences for many years, is a subject worth studying, and pays dividends for the screenwriter who wants to avail himself or herself of all the tools in the arsenal of cinema.

Nights of Cabiria has eight sequences, but unlike the other movies analyzed herein, half are connected logically and thematically, rather than causally. As a result, tools such as dangling causes and telegraphing are used less. Anticipation is created within the sequences using the tools of dramatic and ironic tension. Still, an overall main tension is present, and as a result so too is the dramatic three-act structure. Within the first quarter of the movie, we discover Cabiria's desire: she wants love and respectability. Three quarters of the way through the movie, she gets it in the marriage to Donofrio, resolving this main tension. The third act, of course, reveals the falsity of Donofrio's love, resulting in a devastating finale.

Unlike typical American films, though, there is no true resolution. The story is open-ended; Cabiria's problems exist before the movie begins, and they continue after the movie is finished. As in *The Shop Around the Corner,* the transition from Act I to Act II is invisible to the characters: it occurs because the audience becomes aware of Cabiria's situation, not because some specific event happens to her and forces her to act. When Donofrio reveals his true stripes in the end, Cabiria is in essentially the same situation as she was in at the beginning of the picture—still yearning for love and respectability—only she's worse off emotionally and financially.

Even though the character's situation is thus presented as a cycle and the storytelling approach is episodic, the sequences depicted in the film are not interchangeable; the three main episodes—Cabiria's experiences with Lazzari, the pilgrimage to La Madonna del Divino Amore, and the courtship with Donofilo—escalate in emotional intensity, owing primarily to an escalation in the stakes for the main character.

The sequences in *Cabiria* run from seven to seventeen minutes, though as originally screened, it had one 23-minute sequence, which is worth discussing relative to the role that the sequence structure plays in the maintaining of audience attention. Before the picture was screened at Cannes, it had an additional seven-minute segment in the fourth sequence, after the subject of the pilgrimage to La Madonna del Divino Amore is discussed by Cabiria and her friends, and before they set out on the pilgrimage. During this segment, Cabiria encounters an enigmatic man with a sack, and follows him around as he distributes food and blankets to poor people living in caves outside of Rome. A spirited disagreement about the segment erupted between Fellini, who thought it belonged in the final film, and the producer, Dino De Laurentiis, who felt it slowed the pace to a point that was fatal. In the end, the picture screened at Cannes without the segment, which was only restored in the DVD version more than forty years later.

The segment itself is an odd one for several reasons. Cabiria is completely passive in it—she participates only as an observer who asks questions. Further, the only conflict in the segment—two people refusing to answer questions that Cabiria puts to them—seems forced. These alone may not have been fatal to the segment, but what is noteworthy—from a sequence structure viewpoint—is what its presence does to the length of the fourth sequence. Sequences that run more than fifteen minutes run the risk of becoming tedious, because it's difficult to sustain one line of dramatic or ironic tension for longer than that. With the "man with the sack" segment, the fourth sequence runs 23 minutes. Further, the segment is only vaguely related to the subject of the rest of the sequence—the pilgrimage, and the chance for a miraculous transformation. Confronted with an overlong sequence, a screenwriter ought to strongly consider ways to set it up and develop it more economically. The man with the sack sequence is too long for what it accomplishes, and ultimately the film is probably better without it.

Sequence A: Giorgio

The picture opens with the first example of a device used skillfully throughout the film—*preparation* by contrast (see text box, page 24). An exterior long shot reveals a man and woman in a loving relationship, enjoying a tryst in a romantic setting by a river. The use of a puzzle— arousing the audience's curiosity—is in play in the opening minute— who are these two? What are the circumstances? The puzzle quickly gives way to dramatic tension, though, when the seemingly idyllic situation is shattered by the man, who steals the woman's purse, pushes her into the river, and flees.

For the next three minutes, audience attention revolves around the question of her survival. Here, in another example of preparation by contrast, the dialogue among the rescuers suggests that she has died; a late-arriving man pronounces her dead just before she comes back to life. As soon as she does so, she inquires after Giorgio—the man who'd pushed her into the water. The rescuers express perplexity, and Cabiria angrily sets herself to the task of finding him.

On display in the first six minutes of the picture are the two chief concerns of Cabiria—love and respectability. The indignity she's suffered at Giorgio's hands has obviously struck a sensitive spot in her, as evidenced by her less than thankful attitude toward her rescuers. Just how important her dignity is, and her love of love, becomes clearer when she arrives at her shack. In her conversation with her friend Wanda, she betrays herself as a woman deeply in denial—unwilling to admit what the audience has seen and what Wanda suspects—that Giorgio was not a lover at all but a user who seduced her, took advantage of her, and nearly killed her for a meager amount of money in her purse.

The chief dramatic tension of the sequence devolves around Cabiria coming to terms—and to the truth—about Giorgio. The challenge for the filmmaker is that this struggle is an internal one, and the great problem of drama is that it gains its power by having the audience witness an unfolding of life being acted out—as seen from the outside—and the inner struggles of the characters can only be conveyed indirectly. How, then, to make an internal struggle external and seeable?

After Wanda spells out the truth to Cabiria—that Giorgio pushed him in the river for her money—Fellini relies primarily on props and the Cabiria's facial expressions to convey her struggle and transformation. Cabiria, left alone by Wanda, storms angrily into her house, only to be confronted by the photos of Giorgio on her dresser. Upon seeing his image, she smiles and her anger subsides. She heads back out of the house and paces, deep in thought. She picks up a chicken, strokes it, talks to herself, realizing she might have died. With this realization setting in, she throws the chicken into the air —a concrete visual clue to an abrupt change in her inner state—and disposes of Giorgio's photos and all the other physical evidence of him by tossing them into a fire, all the while verbally denouncing him. The scene dramatizes Cabiria casting Giorgio out of her life, without Giorgio even appearing in the scene.

After she destroys his effects, a scene of *aftermath* follows (see text box, page 54), with Cabiria walking slowly into a darkening sky, hurling a bottle in a last expression of anger.

Sequence B: Ladies' Night Out

The second sequence has no causal connection to the first; the audience is transported to a park where Cabiria and her fellow prostitutes ply their trade. This sequence has as its unifying element Cabiria's desire to seek a customer, which she finds in the movie star Lazzari.

More so than the films analyzed hitherto, the exposition in the opening sequence of *Nights of Cabiria* is indirect, and information accumulates gradually. This gradual filling in of pieces of the puzzle of her life continues in the second sequence. First, the "Grande Dame" who strolls on the far side of the street greets Cabiria with the statement "Here comes that psycho again!"—implying a routine and a past relationship, and displaying an attitude. Cabiria immediately notices the new Fiat that one of the hookers has purchased, and uses it as a springboard to express her values—when you ride in a car, life is better; people think you're well-off—a secretary or a daddy's girl. Here, again, a concrete, visual object is used to help express an inner state—aspiration.

A radio provides mambo music, inspiring Cabiria to dance (planting both motifs), while she trades insults with the *grande dame* across the street. Cabiria seems to be enjoying herself until her adversary brings up the issue of Giorgio, which causes Cabiria to rush across the street to assault her. Here, again, a physical response is used to express Cabiria's inner state—her sensitivity to issues that bear on her love life and dignity.

Cabiria is dragged from the brawl and into the Fiat, which speeds off. In the ensuing conversation, Cabiria declares her self-sufficiency—she doesn't need a man to take care of her—and insists on being let off in the high-class district, where Amleto warns her she doesn't belong.

Eventually, Cabiria finds herself outside a fancy club, where she insists on staying put despite the doorman's request that she get lost. Here, she encounters the movie star Lazzari and his girlfriend Jessie in the middle of a quarrel. In this scene Lazzari warns Jessie that that if she walks away, it's over between them—the first dangling cause of the picture.

Lazzari, left alone, invites Cabiria into his car, the car serving as a big, elegant contrast to the tiny Fiat Cabiria had arrived in. With Cabiria's success in getting a customer at last, the resolution of the sequence is at hand, but it plays out in a surprising way: instead of going to some remote location, Lazzari takes her to another club. Here, the issue of class is played out, Cabiria being the lower-class "fish out of water," a free spirit in a more formal world (this expressed with a payoff of the mambo/dance motif), till at last Lazzari decides it's time to go. The sequence ends with an appointment—Lazzari tells her they're heading to his house for dinner—and a payoff—Cabiria insults the two high-class prostitutes she'd first encountered after being dropped off in the high-class district: she's hit it big.

Sequence C: A House As Beautiful As Lazzari

The third sequence runs fourteen and a half minutes and is centered on the relationship of Cabiria and Lazzari. It plays out as an elaborate preparation by contrast, in a distant echo of the opening sequence. For the first nine minutes, the action brings Cabiria and Lazzari gradually closer, both physically and emotionally, till it appears they will have an intimate encounter. The evening is interrupted at the last moment by the return of Jessie, and Cabiria loses out again.

Though Lazzari could be described as the protagonist of the sequence—his objective being an evening of amusement with his new plaything—a street prostitute—the dramatic thrust of the scene is muted. Lazzari is preoccupied with his problems with Jessie, while Cabiria's awkwardness in the large, richly appointed mansion provides only a minimal amount of conflict.

The sequence begins as Lazzari drives up to his mansion. Here, he scolds his servant and warns him to tell Jessie he is asleep if she should call, a dangling cause closed off later in the sequence.

Upstairs, Cabiria finds herself fascinated by Lazzari's material wealth, playing again on the issue of class and respectability. The two begin far apart physically, with Cabiria standing awkwardly on the far side of the bedroom while Lazzari lounges on his bed with his shoes still on. He plays solemn music as a reflection of his somber inner state, and tosses the photo of Jessie aside in an echo of Cabiria's rejection of Giorgio in the opening sequence. The two gradually get acquainted, with Lazzari asking her about her background. In describing her life, Cabiria emphasizes her dignity, bragging about how she owns her own house and is friends only with Wanda— she does not hang out with the other riffraff, and rarely, if ever, sleeps under the arches.

Lazzari urges her to eat—an action that brings the two closer physically to match their increasing personal familiarity. Cabiria confesses she recognizes him as a movie star, then sits down with him and begins to touch him, carrying out her job, but he tells her it's not necessary, and instead answers her request for an autographed photo. She then begins to serve the food, and the scene is set for a romantic evening: the two are acquainted and clearly enjoying each other's company.

At this point, Jessie arrives at the house, closing off the dangling causes established earlier, and Cabiria's expectations are shattered. Lazzari shepherds her quickly into the bathroom and locks the door, promising he'll get rid of Jessie in a minute.

When Jessie enters, dramatic tension and irony intensify the scene, with Lazzari's objective quite simple: to get Jessie out of his bedroom before Cabiria is discovered. While Cabiria watches through the keyhole, Lazzari's efforts sputter and he and Jessie wind up kissing on the bed. In a powerful scene of aftermath, Cabiria slides backward from the view in the keyhole, abandoned again.

Cabiria awakens the next morning and is escorted out of the bedroom; she only reluctantly accepts Lazzari's money for the evening, again expressing her strong sense of dignity.

Sequence D: The Pilgrimage to La Madonna del Divino Amore

The episode with Lazzari is over; a visual clue is the only direct connection between this sequence and the one before—Cabiria's umbrella, which she'd carried resolutely through Sequence C. This, and a sarcastic remark to Cabiria from one of the hookers about Alberto Lazzari, complete the references to that episode.

In the opening of the sixteen-minute fourth sequence—which is centered on the pilgrimage to La Madonna del Divino Amore—Cabiria and Wanda become reacquainted with Limpy, whose presence is explained by Amleto, his nephew: they hope the Madonna will grant him a miracle—a dangling cause creating anticipation for the rest of the sequence. The appointment for the pilgrimage is revealed, and Cabiria is noncommittal about going. In debating the merits of making the pilgrimage, she demonstrates denial, claiming she needs no miracle because she needs nothing, an utterance at odds with her behavior to this point. Soon, a group of pilgrims walks by barefooted, on their way to the church, and the atmosphere is transformed from nonchalant to deeply religious.

The scene now switches from the somber of night to bright daylight and the festive atmosphere at the church.* In the next nine minutes, preparation by contrast is again in use, culminating in the failure of the Madonna to bestow her miracle. From Cabiria's initially flippant attitude, reinforced by the swirl of non-religious activities around her such as the sale of prickly pears and souvenir photos, the mood gradually becomes more somber and religious. Cabiria becomes gradually more humble and fearful as the singing of hymns grows louder and the cries for mercy from the pilgrims more intense. Her transformation is paralleled by Limpy's progress toward the shrine, aided by Amleto, who tells him he feels the Madonna will show him mercy.

At last, Cabiria goes on her knees and tearfully pleads with the Madonna for help in changing her life (a request at odds with her self-

---

*In the first released version; for the DVD version, see the introduction to the chapter.

satisfied opinion early in the sequence), and Amleto lets go of Limpy so he can receive a healing miracle and walk without crutches. Limpy promptly falls down, and the scene switches to a picnic on the grounds afterward. Limpy's failure to receive a miracle closes off the dangling cause from the opening scene of the sequence.

While a scene of aftermath might typically be expected here—marked by wordless performances, thick atmosphere, and somber music appropriate for the profound disappointment Cabiria has just suffered—the storytellers instead revive the carnival atmosphere of the opening through accordion music and the mundane activities of food and games. Cabiria, though, does not join in the fun, and promptly pronounces the pilgrimage a failure: no one has changed. Since the kind of change Cabiria is seeking—a profound, spiritual, inner change—does not lend itself to cinema, Limpy is employed as a reference point. The wounds they all suffer are internal, but Limpy's is external; Cabiria's realization that no miracle has been bestowed on them has been dramatized by Limpy's fall.

In the argument that follows, Cabiria launches into a tirade providing the dangling causes which propel the story through the remaining three sequences: she vows to sell her house and move away from them, saying she is not like them. After Wanda tries to calm her, she storms away and slumps against a bus, looking longingly at the nuns passing in the distance, and the music changes from carnival to religious; the aftermath scene is delivered at last.

Sequence E: The Magic Show

A contrast in light—night replaces day—marks the transition from the fourth to fifth sequence. There is no causal connection except some references to a ride home in the previous sequence; the only visual connection is Cabiria's costume: her raincoat and scarf. The eleven-minute sequence is unified by place (the theater) and action (the magic show, and Cabiria's reluctant participation in it).

Preparation by contrast begins almost immediately when Cabiria inquires with the ticket clerk about the show's quality and he only obliquely recommends it. When she arrives inside, a patron is shown sleeping in his seat, and on stage we catch the tail end of an unconvincing magic trick, greeted by an unenthusiastic reaction from Cabiria.

The magician next announces a demonstration of hypnosis, and quickly asks for volunteers. After several men come up to the stage, he requests a woman, and chooses Cabiria, who happens to be just finding her seat. Getting Cabiria onstage is a storytelling challenge, because the idea that the magician just happens to choose her among all the women in the theater runs the risk of seeming contrived, but if he does not pick her, the sequence won't work. The solution is to make her resist vigorously the magician's entreaties until he finally has to come off the stage and take her by the hand. Cabiria's resistance gives the audience a glimpse of a reasonable alternative outcome (she refuses) before delivering the actual outcome (she accepts), so the sense of spontaneity—as opposed to contrivance—survives.

Just before she mounts the stage, Cabiria makes one more contribution to the lowering of expectations for the magic show—dismissing it as nothing but tricks. This preparation is paid off by contrast at last when the magician "zaps" one of the participants in a dramatic demonstration of mind control, then wows the audience—Cabiria included—during the "boat ride."

As the men file off the stage, Cabiria attempts to join them—giving the audience another glimpse of a possible outcome (she doesn't participate) before the magician stops her and persuades her to stay. What follows is yet another approach to studying the inner life of a character in all her contradictions—making visible and actable what lies inside—this time through the device of hypnosis.

The contrast between what Cabiria says about herself and the truth is immediately demonstrated when the magician asks her where she lives, and she gives two answers, one a lie, the other, under hypnosis, the truth. The magician sizes her up and assumes she would like a husband; she declares forcefully that she is happy the way she is (a demonstration of denial, given the pilgrimage she'd just been on), then, under hypnosis again, acts out a scene of tenderness and longing that is in direct contradiction to her consciously stated attitude toward marriage.

The climax of the hypnosis scene comes when Cabiria lays bare another issue for her—one of trust, of fear of betrayal by her lover—and the magician abruptly ends the show. The hypnosis scene plants three important motifs—the picking of flowers, the hat (of flowers), and the name "Oscar."

When Cabiria comes out of the spell and finds herself the object of derisive laughter, her sensitivity to dignity is assaulted, setting up a situation that connects this sequence more causally to the one that follows.

Sequence F: Donofrio

This sequence, which runs almost seventeen minutes, is centered on dramatic tension: Donofrio's pursuit of Cabiria. The arrival of Donofrio, a self-styled accountant, marks the beginning of the fourth of the four major episodes in the picture, and the one that is the most completely developed. This episode, even more than the three before it, ends in catastrophe, and like the others before, involves a considerable investment in preparation by contrast. In this, Fellini was careful not only in the storytelling but in the casting as well, choosing to place Francois Perier—a French actor known to European audiences as a romantic leading man—in the role of Donofrio, the scoundrel.

Donofrio approaches Cabiria as soon as she leaves the theater, and overcomes her initial objections to his overtures, persuading her to join him for a drink. In their conversation, Donofrio presents himself as a man unique in the movie—he is kind, sensitive, and focused on her. The tension in the scene is centered on Cabiria's skepticism. By the end of the scene he makes an appointment with her for the following Sunday afternoon. His hand gesture—indicating seven o'clock—provides a nonverbal dialogue hook into the following scene, where, at a busy train station, the clock reads 7:00.

Cabiria arrives on time, and appears to have second thoughts before Donofrio catches up to her and presents her with flowers—a brief reversal that allows a glimpse of an alternative ending (Cabiria never connecting with him). Later, Cabiria confides with her friends about the date—how positive the experience was, and how he paid for everything. The other women are skeptical, especially Wanda, who asks her what he's after—a dangling cause closed off in the final sequence. Cabiria, too, is somewhat skeptical—skepticism that helps to disarm any skepticism the audience may have toward Donofrio, who truly seems a dream come true. Cabiria reveals another appointment for the following night, just before the police arrive, scattering everyone. The timing of the police raid—the first in the picture—is critical, because at this point Cabiria seems at last to have something valuable (the budding relationship with Donofrio) that she risks losing. This inner concern is made visible both in Cabiria's loss of the candy Donofrio had given her shortly after the police arrive, and the fearful expression she has while hiding in the bushes.

The dark light of the night raid gives way to the bright sunshine of Cabiria's next date with Donofrio, during which they get further acquainted, though Donofrio always seems to keep his background somewhat vague.

The scenes that follow work on the problem of making visible what amounts to an inner transformation, from Cabiria's despair after the pilgrimage to hope that Donofrio might just be the answer to her prayer. Cabiria is shown listening somewhat contemplatively to music, then taking a stroll outside her house, where she runs into Brother Giovanni and they discuss God's grace. Giovanni urges her to get married, and as he leaves, invites her to get in touch if she needs him—two dangling causes closed off during the final two sequences.

Bright day gives way to rainy night in the following scene, where Cabiria is shown waiting for customers while apparently deep in thought. When a customer shows up, she is too preoccupied to respond to him.

Bright sunshine marks the transition to the next date Cabiria has with Donofrio. Here, Cabiria creates conflict immediately by telling him she wants to break it off; he responds by proposing marriage. She greets this with passionate skepticism—again functioning to disarm the skepticism of the audience of the likelihood of such a rapid courtship—and in the end she begs him not to say he needs her if it isn't true—a payoff of the line she'd spoken under hypnosis.

The resolution of the scene—and the sequence—comes in the following scene, when Cabiria ecstatically announces to Wanda that she is getting married. This marks the second culmination of the picture, the resolution of the main tension—will Cabiria find love and respectability? The answer is an emphatic yes.

Cabiria tells Wanda her plans—a wedding in two weeks (an appointment that is, of course, never kept), and her decision to sell the house and everything she owns (a dangling cause that provides the central focus of the following sequence).

Sequence G: Good-byes

The seventh sequence—the shortest in the film at just under seven minutes—contains only three scenes and is centered on Cabiria's task of selling her house and all her belongings to begin a new life. Aside from her ambivalence at saying good-bye to her friend Wanda, and momentary doubts about the big change she's making, there is little in the way of tension in the sequence.

Figure 7. Cabiria delivers the news of her impending wedding in *Nights of Cabiria* (1957). The scene marks the second culmination of the film, resolving the main tension: will Cabiria find love and respectability? The scene also closes off a cause left dangling in the previous scene—Donofrio's marriage proposal. (Frame enlargement)

In its first scene, Cabiria seeks out Brother Giovanni to confess to him, closing off the dangling cause of the priest's invitation to stay in touch. It also resolves the religious motif in the film, giving the impression that the grace Cabiria had sought from the Madonna at the pilgrimage has been given to her at last, and she in turn is now free from sin.

In the following scene, Wanda helps Cabiria pack the last of her belongings. Here, there is little tension beyond Wanda's doubting Cabiria's decision to sell most of her belongings in addition to the house, a subtle dangling cause picked up in the final sequence.

The final scene of the sequence finds Cabiria saying her last goodbye to Wanda at the bus stop. Here, she predicts Wanda will get married, too—that she, too, will get her miracle. As Wanda fades in the distance, the sequence draws to a close, with a reasonable glimpse of the resolution of the picture—a happy ending.

Sequence H: Donofrio's Betrayal

The final sequence, running just under thirteen minutes, provides the *actual* ending, and it is a payoff in reverse of the "happy" fairy-tale preparation to this point. The sequence is imbued with both dramatic tension—will Donofrio succeed in stealing her money?—and ironic tension—how will Cabiria react when this emotional freight train hits her?

Figure 8. Cabiria and Donofrio share a romantic moment in the final sequence of *Nights of Cabiria* (1957). Note the similarities between this image and the frame shown in Figure 9: Donofrio's sunglasses (which he wears for the first time in this scene), and the composition of the frame—his position and that of the river in the background—are an echo of the shot of Giorgio just before he pushes Cabiria into the river (see Figure 9). These similarities are the first clues the audience is given about the impending disaster, and as the sequence progresses, the clues become more obvious and the resulting dramatic irony more intense. Director Fellini's use of preparation by contrast—portraying Donofrio as a loving, kindhearted answer to Cabiria's prayers only to have him later revealed to be a scoundrel—involved not only the writing but also casting. Francois Perier, chosen to play Donofrio, was known for his roles as a sympathetic romantic lead. (Frame enlargement)

Figure 9. Giorgio glimpses his surroundings just before snatching Cabiria's purse and shoving her into the river in the opening sequence of *Nights of Cabiria* (1957). (Frame enlargment)

The shift from happy to tragic ending comes gradually, and with the shift comes the ironic tension. The first clue is the opening shot of the sequence—the river, running upper left to lower right in the frame—the same composition as the river in the opening sequence. The next clue is on Donofrio's face—the sunglasses that echo those of Giorgio.

Next comes Cabiria's thick wad of money; she holds it, shows it to him, tells him how much it is, and places it in a black purse, in yet another echo of the opening sequence. Cabiria now verbally reinforces the parallel, talking to Donofrio about how some men are only after a woman's money. With these clues in place, Cabiria speaks about how much she suffered to get the money, and her joy at escaping the life she's led, effectively raising the stakes, or at least reinforcing in the audience how high the stakes are for her.

The two set out for a walk at Donofrio's urging, and wind up in the woods. The dramatic tension in the journey is provided by Donofrio's urging her to come onward deeper into the woods, as against her own preoccupation with the romance of the moment. She stops to pick up flowers—a payoff of what she had done under hypnosis—and wears a white hat that echoes the garland of flowers the magician had given her to wear on her head.

The two arrive at the river's edge, where Cabiria laughingly recalls the incident with Giorgio just before the moment when she recognizes that Donofrio plans to do the same thing. With this, the payoff for the half hour of preparation by contrast is at hand. Donofrio flees with the money while Cabiria rolls on the ground in anguish, wishing for the deliverance of death.

From these moments of despair the audience is delivered one of the great aftermath scenes in cinema history. After a time lapse, Cabiria at last gets to her feet and walks slowly out of the woods, where she wordlessly encounters a group of cheerful young people coming home from a party, dancing and singing, surrounding her with music and goodwill as she walks. Their joy proves infectious, and she is able to smile again.

Figure 10. A classic aftermath scene in the last sequence of *Nights of Cabiria* (1957). After Donofrio betrays her, Cabiria lies on the ground in the gathering darkness. The characteristics of a typical aftermath scene are little or no dialogue, an intensity of atmosphere, and music. Aftermath scenes allow the audience a chance to digest a particularly intense emotional moment. Soon after this frame, Cabiria gets up and begins to walk through the woods, and music arises from a group of young revelers. (Frame enlargement)

NIGHTS OF CABIRIA
Sequence Breakdown

Seq.	Description	Length	Running Time
	ACT I		
A	Cabiria is pushed into the river, rescued, seeks Giorgio, finally burns his personal effects (excludes opening titles). *Unifying Aspect*: Dramatic Tension. *Protagonist*: Cabiria. *Objective*: To find Giorgio.	15:05	15:05 (11%)
	Point of attack: Giorgio steals the purse.		
B	Cabiria gets into a fight at the park, goes off in the Fiat, connects with Lazzari and travels to a nightclub. *Unifying Aspect*: Dramatic Tension. *Protagonist*: Cabiria. *Objective*: To get work.	17:07	32:12 (27%)
	Predicament: Cabiria is a low-class hooker who wants to be respectable and to be loved.		
	ACT II **(Main tension: Will Cabiria find love and respectability?)**		
C	Cabiria connects with Lazzari in his bedroom, then spends the night in the bathroom. *Unifying Aspect*: Dramatic Tension. *Protagonist*: Lazzari. *Objective*: A quiet evening with Cabiria.	14:25	46:37 (40%)
D	Cabiria back in the park; Limpy introduced, the pilgrims go by; Cabiria and her friends go to the pilgrimage, are disappointed. *Unifying Aspect*: Dramatic Tension. *Protagonist*: Cabiria. *Objective*: Help from the Madonna.	16:00	1:02:37 (57%)
E	Cabiria goes to the playhouse and reveals herself under hypnosis. *Unifying Aspect*: Dramatic Tension. *Protagonist*: Cabiria. *Objective*: To enjoy a show.	11:14	1:13:51 (67%)
F	In this sequence, Cabiria is wooed by Donofrio, who finally proposes to her. *Unifying Aspect*: Dramatic Tension. *Protagonist*: Donofrio. *Objective*: Cabiria.	16:49	1:30:40 (82%)
	Second Culmination: Cabiria breaks the news to Wanda: He loves me!		
	ACT III		
G	The main tension is resolved—Cabiria has apparently found love and respectability. The new third-act tension involves pursuing this new relationship of love and marriage. In this sequence, Cabiria packs, sells most of her belongings, and says her good-byes. *Unifying Aspect*: Dramatic Tension. *Protagonist*: Cabiria. *Objective*: To leave her old life behind.	6:55	1:37:35 (89%)

H   Cabiria enjoys dinner with Donofrio; they take a walk   12:41   1:50:16
       in the woods; she is crushed by disillusionment when he   (100%)
       steals her money. *Unifying Aspect*: Dramatic Tension.
       Protagonist: Cabiria. *Objective*: A happy marriage.

       Resolution: **Open-ended.**

North by Northwest: 1,700 Miles in Nine Sequences

All writers should be aware of the profound distinction between a story (*narrative*) and the telling of a story (*narration*). A single story can be told any number of different ways, primarily by manipulating what the audience knows and when it knows it. The impact of the story of *Double Indemnity* (Chapter 4) would have been very different if it had been told in simple chronological order. Likewise the experience of *The Shop Around the Corner* (Chapter 3) would be different if the audience didn't find out until the end of the movie that Klara was Kralik's "dear friend." In either case, the *story* may be identical but the *telling* of determines how movies play to the audience.

North by Northwest, made in 1959 at the height of director Alfred Hitchcock's mastery of the form, is what one might call an example of "pure storytelling": the storytelling is so virtuosic that it conceals the fact that the underlying story is nonsensical. This is storytelling sleight of hand: by skillfully directing audience attention toward the future, the viewer is constantly distracted from considering the gaps and implausibilities in the story.

In its development, *North by Northwest* began with the humble inspiration of the main character being a man that doesn't exist, and the vague notion that the story should involve travel in a northwest direction. From this, writer Ernest Lehman and director Alfred Hitchcock crafted a film that has withstood the test of time. It was not written explicitly in sequences (in fact, Lehman was surprised by one interviewer who asserted that the story had ten parts to it). On close analysis, though, the internal structure of nine sequences becomes readily apparent—nine shorter films, ranging in length from nine to eighteen minutes—nested inside the one larger film. Each follows a very direct dramatic impulse; the protagonist of each sequence is the protagonist of the picture, and he has very specific objectives in each. Along the way, the action is constantly enhanced by the play of various layers of dramatic irony.

Sequence A: Assault with a gun, a bourbon and a sports car

The movie begins emphatically *in medias res*, that is, with life unfolding and fully in bloom when the audience arrives to view it. Unlike the other films analyzed in this volume, the use of a puzzle is less apparent in hooking the audience in the opening moments. The title sequence employs a musical overture that suggests action/adventure, and the titles work themselves out as something of a puzzle, gradually transforming abstract lines into the lines of the modernist United Nations building, but when the dialogue begins, we discover the protagonist, Roger O. Thornhill, swept up in the middle of an ordinary, busy day, dictating instructions to his secretary.

In the dialogue, several appointments are made with business associates, and some exposition occurs as well—notably Roger's relationship with his girlfriend and his mother, and his history of drinking to excess, at least in the opinion of his mother. In this dialogue, the appointments made in the future are the most crucial aspect, because the more persuasive our sense of the future plans of the protagonist, the more effective is his sudden abduction, which disrupts those plans.

The telegraphing of Roger's itinerary continues in the Oak Room bar, where he arranges to get a telegram in order to alert his mother of their theater arrangements that night. This action leads inadvertently to his being mistaken for Kaplan, and abducted by two henchmen.

In all, the opening four minutes of the picture are a *tour de force* in establishing the normal routine of a character at the outset of a film. They are minutes rich with content about a character's life—his manner and style, his relationships, his past and plans—issues that are important in the opening minutes of any film, but in this case made more crucial by the fact that this character's very identity is soon to be questioned. Without firmly establishing who he is quickly, there may be some doubt in the viewer's mind as to whether or not he is telling the truth when he denies he is Kaplan. While such a situation can be useful in some movies, in this one it would serve only as a distraction.

When Roger is abducted, the henchmen telegraph the agenda somewhat obliquely: a car is waiting outside, Roger is to say nothing or risk losing his life. The mysterious abduction provides, in effect, the curiosity-arousing puzzle missing in the opening moments of the picture.

Roger's abduction marks the end of the "first act" of the 16-minute sequence; the rest is driven by simple dramatic tension: Roger trying to escape his abductors. In the car, his attempts escalate, from negotiation to a physical attempt to get out of the car. Once at the Townsend mansion, he again tries to reason with his adversary, this time Vandamm (who he mistakes as "Townsend"), and when this fails, tries to escape by physical means, only to be stopped by Vandamm's men.

In his confrontation with Vandamm, several examples of telegraphing come into play. Roger repeats his appointment at the Winter Garden Theater that evening. While trying to rebut Roger's claim that he is not Kaplan, Vandamm reads from an itinerary featuring past and future engagements for this Mr. Kaplan. There are also references to dinner guests who are waiting for him—a deadline that adds intensity to the scene through time pressure, and also signals how long it will last. Vandamm closes the scene with two ominous dangling causes: a warning in which he tells Roger he wants to give him an opportunity of surviving the evening, and a wish of "pleasant journey," after he tells his henchman to give Roger a drink.

When Roger is placed, drunk, in the Mercedes, the "third act" of the sequence begins: what had been a question about whether or not Roger will escape is narrowed to a question of whether or not he'll survive the car ride.

The four-minute chase sequence ends with Roger involved in a traffic accident with a police car, and the henchmen skulking away. This provides the resolution to the dramatic tension of the sequence: Roger succeeds in escaping. It also closes off the dangling causes established earlier by Vandamm involving the threats to his survival. Roger's safe arrival into the hands of the police does *not* resolve the mystery of his abduction, though, and raises new questions about how he will fare in police custody. These are the questions that bind the first sequence to the second.

Sequence B: Proving His Innocence

Roger is taken to the police station, where his next objective soon becomes apparent: convincing the police of the truth of his story about
being abducted. The stakes rise quickly when the police disclose the car
he was driving was stolen. Roger calls his mother for help and an appointment is made for Roger's lawyer to appear the following morning.

The "first act" of the nine-minute sequence ends with Roger's attorney making the case for Roger's innocence in the courtroom. Here, an
appointment is made for the trial to begin the following evening, and
the judge has the county detectives called in to investigate. The courtroom scene ends with a dialogue hook, with the judge telling Roger of
his intention to find out if Roger had made up the story.

The film immediately switches to the Townsend residence, where
that intention is set in action, with the arrival of Roger, his mother, his
attorney, and the detectives. The scene at the mansion is driven by simple dramatic tension—Roger wants to prove his story is true, and the
obstacles he encounters are the lack of physical evidence (absence of
stains on the couch, absence of liquor in the cabinet), and a phony eye-
witness ("Mrs. Townsend") who undermines his story with lies.

The scene culminates with the claim by the woman that her husband
is addressing the General Assembly of the United Nations—a bit of information that demolishes Roger's allegations in the eyes of the detectives.

The sequence ends with the detectives expressing their intent to call
off the investigation, closing off the judge's dangling cause about ascer-
taining the truth of Roger's story, and leaving Roger to prove his innocence on his own. The last shot of the sequence shows one of the
henchmen disguised as a gardener watching as the police car drives
away—this visual clue confirms Roger's story in the audience's mind
even as the police have come to the opposite conclusion. It also provides
something of a visual dangling cause—suggesting that even as Roger
must deal with the police, his problems with the abductors are not yet
over.

Sequence C: Pursuing Kaplan to the UN

First act of the picture could be said to take place here: it is by now clear
who the protagonist is (Roger) and what his objective is: to clear his
name. The story unfolds henceforth with this objective driving the ac-

tion. Yet at this point Roger still seems to have choices that can easily take him out of the story: as his mother suggests, he could plead guilty and pay a fine and be done with it. It isn't until the end of the 11-minute third sequence that Roger finds himself falsely accused of murder, with both the police and Vandamm's men after him, and no choice but to pursue the mystery and clear his name. The main tension is thus initiated after three sequences, not two.

Sequence C is unified by Roger's desire to get to the bottom of the mystery himself, after the fiasco with the county detectives. It begins with Roger and his mother arriving at the Plaza Hotel and discovering that a Mr. Kaplan is in fact staying there, but that he is out and has not answered his phone in two days. Roger reveals the means by which he plans to overcome this obstacle by bribing his mother into getting him the key—another example of a visual dangling cause, which hooks directly into the following scene.

The "first act" of the sequence ends with Roger and his mother approaching Kaplan's hotel room and beginning their investigation. While the scene in the hotel room features some conflict between Roger and his mother, it is driven chiefly by ironic tension—the audience's knowledge that the two are there under false pretenses, leading to fear that they will be discovered by the maid, the valet, and possibly the mysterious Kaplan himself.

The search of the room is interrupted by a phone call from one of Vandamm's men, who makes an implied threat; the pursuit for the solution to the mystery is immediately transformed into an escape attempt, with Roger successfully evading the two killers at the hotel, then setting off for the United Nations to resume his quest to solve the mystery.

The scenes at the UN, when he inquires after Townsend and eventually catches up to him, are driven by ironic rather than dramatic tension, with the audience forewarned about the pursuit and approach of the killers, while Roger remains unaware until a knife winds up in the back of Townsend.

This incident provides the resolution to the dramatic tension of the sequence: Roger's pursuit of a solution to the mystery has failed, and his attempts to solve it have led to his being wanted for murder.

Transition: The Intelligence Agency

A brief transition scene serves as a curtain between Sequence C and D, and Act I and II. The film moves to Washington DC, where intelligence agents discuss the murder at the UN in a *recapitulation* scene (see text box, page 29) that provides, after almost forty minutes of mystery, some exposition that explains that mystery—but to the audience only. In so doing, the storytellers initiate the first sustained layer of ironic tension—the audience is made aware that George Kaplan, the man Vandamm thought he was kidnapping when his men abducted Roger, is a fiction created by American intelligence operatives to divert suspicion from their own, unnamed agent. Roger, naturally, is unaware of this.

By the end of this transition scene, it is emphatically clear who the protagonist is, what he wants (to clear his name of the murder and get to the bottom of the mystery), and what the obstacles are (he is wanted both by the police and the enemy agents, and is unaware of the conspiracy that surrounds his predicament). The main tension is thus established: Will Roger succeed in evading the police and enemy agents long enough to solve the mystery and clear his name? The scene ends with an ominous dialogue hook: after voicing doubt about Roger's chances of survival, the female agent says, "Good-bye, Mr. Thornhill, wherever you are."

Sequence D: The 20th Century Limited

The fourth sequence, the longest one at eighteen and a half minutes, is unified by location—the train ride on The 20th Century Limited—and by a line of dramatic tension created by Roger's objective of evading the police long enough to make it to Chicago, where he hopes to meet up with the mysterious George Kaplan and resolve the mystery. In this, the dramatic tension of the sequence is essentially the same as that of the picture as a whole. Further, much of the time in the sequence is dedicated to the relationship between Roger and Eve; in this sequence it is justified in the context of the plot (Roger takes refuge with her to avoid the police), but at the same time the romance developed here plays a crucial role in all of the later sequences.

The sequence begins with a brief recapitulation scene in a phone booth at Grand Central Station, where Roger talks to his mother and recounts his predicament (he can't go to the police, and Kaplan is the only one who can solve the mystery) and telegraphs his plans (heading by train to the Ambassador East Hotel in Chicago, where he has learned that Kaplan is staying).

Roger's first task is to get onto the train, in which he overcomes the obstacles of a suspicious ticket man and some police. He is unexpectedly aided by Eve, who diverts the police while he hides in the bathroom. The use of Eve in this manner—and their chance meeting—is a risky storytelling strategy since it is an example of a coincidence that helps the main character. The sense of contrivance is diminished considerably later when it is revealed that Eve has ulterior motives, and is mitigated somewhat by the star power of the cast—the sense that the attractiveness of Cary Grant might be enough for a young female stranger to do him a favor (the positive reaction of the bedridden female in the hospital in Sequence H certainly speaks to this).

The idea of a sexual attraction is reinforced shortly afterward, when Roger is seated at Eve's table in the dining car, and she confesses she tipped the waiter to seat him there. The scene itself is characterized by sexual tension, with Eve leading the way to the seduction and Roger the willing target. The ironic tension of Roger's secret helps give the scene an intensity that it would otherwise lack due to the absence of any real conflict.

Shortly after the moment of recognition—Eve reveals she knows his identity and that he's wanted for murder—the arrival of the police reintroduces the dramatic tension of Roger's need to evade capture.

Eve proceeds to help Roger again, lying to the police about him while he hides in the bunk. Here, again to help dispel the sense of contrivance (a female stranger who just happens to want to help him), Roger asks Eve straight out why she is so good to him—and she replies again with sexual innuendo. Having a character raise a troublesome story issue like this is a useful way for writers to disarm the skepticism such issues might arouse in an audience.

In a rather slow-paced scene after the police leave, the sexual tension is released between the two, interrupted only by the porter, who arrives to prepare the bed. The arrival of the porter, and the cutaway that results to Roger hiding in the bathroom, serves the dual function of interrupting the lovemaking so as to intensify the anticipation of its resumption (a form of retardation), and the plot function of allowing Eve a chance to give the porter the message that reveals to the audience the true reason why she's been so good to Roger—she's working for Vandamm.

Roger and Eve continue their lovemaking after the porter leaves, the scene ending with a dangling cause (Eve telling Roger he'll have to sleep on the floor that night) and a furtive look of apprehension on her face, which Roger can't see. This look provides a visual hook into the next scene, in which the porter delivers the note to Leonard and Vandamm. This is the second major scene of revelation—Roger is not only unaware of the nature of Kaplan (he doesn't exist) and the machinations of the Professor and his men, but also unaware that the woman he is falling in love with is working for his enemies.

The sequence ends with an unspoken dialogue hook: the note itself, which reads "What do I do with him in the morning? –Eve."

Sequence E: An Appointment With a Crop Duster

This sequence runs about sixteen minutes and is unified by Roger's attempt to meet Mr. Kaplan. Because of the revelation in the preceding sequence, all scenes between Roger and Eve are now infused with ironic tension, with the audience's knowledge of Eve's secret—that she is lying to him and is conspiring to kill him, not help him.

The sequence begins with Roger, now dressed as a porter, accompanying Eve out of the train in Chicago. Both dramatic irony and tension inform the scene, with Roger trying to conceal his identity from the police while Eve fends them off once more. Once the immediate danger has passed, when Eve offers to help set up the appointment with Kaplan, the full force of her deceit is felt. The blocking of the scene also allows the audience to see another side of her as well—she turns away from him somewhat wistfully after he mentions that she's the smartest girl he's ever spent a night with on a train, concealing from him her heartfelt concern for his fate.

The police discovery of the porter who'd had his uniform stolen leads to a sudden complication—the police start checking out all the porters. By this time, though, Roger has changed back into civilian clothes.

While Roger shaves in the men's room, Eve makes furtive arrangements on the phone with Vandamm's assistant, Leonard. When she reconnects with Roger, she fills him in on the details of this appointment. The scene ends with more elements of the future—Roger thanking her and expressing his desire to stay in touch with her, the moments made more poignant again by the dramatic irony—her conspiracy to kill him.

With the appointment to meet Kaplan arranged, the tension of the sequence is set up, and its "second act" begins, with Roger's arrival at Prairie Stop for his memorable encounter with the crop duster. The seven minutes that elapse between Roger's arrival at Prairie Stop, and the attack of the crop duster, are a powerful example of *retardation* (see text box, page 24). Clearly, in plot terms, Roger could have been attacked immediately after he gets off the bus, but the intensity of the experience would have been muted considerably.

The means by which the anticipation is created for this scene involved careful choices by the storytellers in the hierarchy of knowledge they disclose to the audience. The viewer knows that Eve is conspiring to do Roger harm, but the means by which this harm is to come to him is withheld from the audience. Thus, for that seven minutes while Roger is waiting, the audience is secretly aware that danger can lurk from any number of directions, and each car, truck, bus, or person who arrives is potentially a dealer in death. The suspense is thus milked to maximum effect, something impossible if the audience were told, for example in the phone booth scene at the train station, that a crop duster would be used.

Once the crop duster attacks, the "third act" of the sequence is at hand: Roger is no longer seeking Kaplan, he is merely trying to survive. He makes several attempts to evade the crop duster, settling at last on stopping the tanker truck and stealing the pickup truck after the ensuing explosion.

The crop duster scene is perhaps the best example in the film of "pure storytelling," since upon closer scrutiny, it is revealed as illogical nonsense. Aside from the more obvious logical problem concerning the clumsy choice of weapon—a crop duster, armed with a machine gun no less (a crop duster killing someone may seem like an accident, but a crop duster that puts bullet holes in a victim is sure to arouse suspicion somewhere along the line), there is the deeper logical problem of just who Vandamm and his men think Roger is planning to meet. The story is premised on the notion that Vandamm believes Roger *is* Kaplan; if so, how could they expect to lure him to some remote location to *meet* Kaplan?

That these glaring "plot holes" are not glaring at all, and in fact are difficult to notice, is a tribute to the storytelling skill of Hitchcock and Lehman. They have crafted the scene so carefully to exploit the audience's hopes and fears about Roger, and given it such an exciting texture, that the experience simply overpowers any interest a viewer might have in analyzing the logic of the situation. *North by Northwest* demonstrates that in order to succeed, a film doesn't need a story, only the impression that there's a story.

Sequence F: Appointment at the Ambassador East

In this sequence, which runs almost eighteen minutes, Roger's focus shifts from trying to meet Kaplan to trying to discover the truth about Eve, and it is this thrust that provides the primary line of tension in the sequence and its unifying aspect.

It begins with a visual link to the previous sequence—the pickup truck Roger had stolen in the previous scene is shown being examined by police, abandoned on a street in Chicago, the telltale refrigerator in the back making the identification certain.

Next Roger is shown approaching the Ambassador East Hotel, a location telegraphed both in the opening sequence and early in the second act. Roger inquires here about Kaplan, and discovers the man had checked out before Eve claimed she spoke to him that morning—leading Roger to the recognition that she had been part of the conspiracy to kill him. This realization creates a new hierarchy of knowledge, because although Roger is now aware Eve is working against him, he doesn't reveal that he knows this to Eve. Instead of being equal to her in knowledge, he moves one level ahead.

By chance, Roger spots Eve going into the elevator, and manages to locate her room. In the scene that follows, Eve betrays obvious relief that he'd survived, and obvious affection for him, which he spurns. He proceeds to question her, not letting on that he knows what she'd tried to do. Although there is conflict in the scene—Roger is pursuing the truth about her while she's trying to deflect it—the primary tool used is dramatic irony—the fact that we know that he knows but she doesn't. This allows us to enjoy the way Roger toys with her with his questions and observations.

In their exchange, Roger initiates several dangling causes—revealing his plans to keep her in his sight at all times—"togetherness"—from now on. This encourages her to make her first attempt to get away from him—asking him to leave. He manages to persuade her to let them have one last meal; she manipulates the situation to escape while he's in the shower, and he in turn uses a clue she left behind—the address of her destination—to continue his pursuit.

He arrives at an art auction and discovers Eve together with Leonard and Vandamm, a moment of recognition that completely resolves the line of dramatic irony initiated with the note from Eve to Vandamm on the train at the end of Sequence D.

After an exchange of words with Vandamm, in which he pieces together most of the puzzle and Eve's involvement in it, the "third act" of the sequence begins: Roger declares his intention to go to the police, and his pursuit of Eve soon turns into an attempt to escape the auction house alive. The sequence ends with Roger's success in getting the police to the auction house; as he's led away, another visual dangling cause is initiated: the Professor is seen in a phone booth making an urgent call.

Sequence G: A Harebrained Scheme

This twelve-minute sequence is unified by dramatic tension centering on whether Roger will succeed in getting Eve out of danger. While traveling to the police station, Roger discloses his identity to the police, who then, unexpectedly, deliver Roger into the custody of the Professor at the Chicago Airport. Here, the Professor reveals to Roger the fact that Kaplan does not exist—a scene of recognition closing off a line of dramatic irony sustained since Sequence D—recapitulates some of the story (part of this obscured by the sound of an aircraft engine so as to avoid repetition), and telegraphs a future appointment in Rapid City, South Dakota. The dialogue-heavy scene is sustained by dramatic tension—the Professor's desire to get Roger to cooperate with him, both in moving faster so they don't miss the plane, and in pretending to be Kaplan for another 24 hours. Just as it seems he is going to fail to get Roger's cooperation, the Professor discloses Eve's role as an American agent. The Professor's dangling cause—"Much more than her life is at stake"—is reinforced by Roger's anguished reaction, and both provide a hook into the next scene, which begins with a shot of Mount Rushmore.

When Roger learns that there is no Kaplan, and that the authorities know he's innocent, the main tension ("Will Roger succeed in evading the police and enemy agents long enough to solve the mystery and clear his name?") is resolved, and thus the second culmination—end of the second act—is at hand. In the very scene that it's resolved, a new and urgent tension takes over which unifies the action of the third act: will Roger be able to rescue Eve?

Roger's arrival at Mount Rushmore closes off the dangling cause in the previous scene initiated by the professor—his request that Roger go on being Kaplan for the next 24 hours. The scene between Roger and the Professor at the foot of Mount Rushmore unfolds as a scene of recapitulation—the Professor recounts how Roger managed to get Eve in

Figure 11. Recapitulation scene: Thornhill and the Professor review what got them to this point, and what hopes and fears they have for their up-coming encounter with Vandamm in Sequence G of *North by Northwest* (1959). The scene completes the setup for the sequence, which is unified by dramatic tension surrounding the rescue of Eve. Recapitulation scenes are common in films that have complicated plots, such as mysteries and thrillers. They function to keep the audience oriented so they can focus on wondering what is going to happen next, rather than wondering what the film is about. (Frame enlargement)

trouble—and of preparation—the scene is rife with dangling causes: the Professor supposing that the face of Teddy Roosevelt on the monument is warning Roger to "speak softly and carry a big stick," and Roger countering that the message is that he shouldn't go through with the "harebrained scheme." The scene also contains some exposition—namely, a meeting has been set up (presumably involving Roger, Vandamm, and Eve). Revealing the information here obviates the need to show scenes of the meeting being set up with phone calls and other information exchanged between Roger and Vandamm. The scene ends with the Professor establishing an appointment—Vandamm is scheduled to leave that night—and a dangling cause—his assurance that after that night, Roger and Eve will be free to pursue their relationship.

With this setup complete, Vandamm, Eve, and Leonard arrive, and the scheme—the precise nature of which has been withheld from the audience—is set in motion. The withholding of this information enables the storytellers to work with both dramatic irony and surprise in the scene—dramatic irony because we now know that Roger is pretending to be an American agent and Vandamm doesn't know it, and surprise because the storytellers can give the impression that Eve's behavior—storming away from Vandamm and Roger, then shooting the latter—are not part of the plan but rather a sign that the plan has gone terribly wrong.

The sequence ends with an apparently negative resolution: Roger has failed to rescue Eve, and in fact winds up shot and conveyed from the scene in a vehicle.

Sequence H: Roger Tries to Spring Eve

The station wagon stops in a wooded area, and here a surprise twist reveals that Roger is in fact unhurt, and that the "scheme" Roger obliquely referred to just prior to Vandamm's arrival at the café involved a fake shooting. Eve is already waiting for Roger there, and the two reintroduce themselves, for the first time without any secret role-playing on Eve's part. There is no tension in the scene—dramatic or ironic. It plays instead like an epilogue, and could reasonably suffice for the end of the movie—Roger has cleared his name, and now he has the girl—except for the new surprise twist at the end of it—Eve is going to put herself in danger that night once again, this time on board Vandamm's plane. This revelation brings on the only conflict in the scene, when Roger raises his objections, but he is quickly subdued and Eve departs in a hurry to make her appointment.

The scene switches to Roger's hospital room, where he moves about like a caged animal, trying the door, then feigning cooperation with the Professor when the latter enters. Roger claims he's already lost interest in Eve, and the Professor replies with a deadline: Eve will be gone within an hour. Roger sends the Professor on an errand to get some bourbon (an oblique payoff to the bourbon that Vandamm's henchman had poured into him in the opening sequence), then makes his intentions clear: he plans to escape from the hospital room, then rescue Eve. As soon as the Professor leaves, the "first act" of the eleven-minute sequence ends and its unifying dramatic tension—will Roger rescue Eve?—is initiated.

Roger makes his escape from the hospital room, then takes a cab to Vandamm's place. Here, he surreptitiously surveys the layout of the house, then finds a location from which to secretly observe the goings-on inside. He nearly succeeds in attracting Eve's attention with a stone, then finds his efforts thwarted by Leonard's intrusion.

This failure leads unexpectedly to Roger's witnessing a conversation between Vandamm and Leonard in which the latter reveals both the "secret" the spies have been keeping—government secrets smuggled out of the country on microfilm hidden in the artwork—and the fact that Eve used blanks in shooting Roger, exposing her as a double agent.

This scene of revelation opens a new layer of irony—Roger is now aware of imminent danger (a new dangling cause expressed by Vandamm: "This matter is best handled from a great height, over water") and Eve is not. The realization makes his quest to rescue her even more urgent by raising the stakes—she has gone from going on a dangerous mission to going on a doomed one.

Roger now turns his attention to contacting Eve, who has gone back to her bedroom. He narrowly misses her, then uses a note written on one of his matchbooks—with a distinctive "R.O.T." logo planted earlier—to get her attention. When she joins him in her room, the irony is resolved as Roger spells out the situation and the danger. As Eve returns to the others, Roger utters a desperate warning—a dangling cause— "Whatever you do, don't get on that plane!"

Figure 12. Roger succeeds in rescuing Eve from Vandamm, resolving the dramatic tension of Sequence H in *North by Northwest* (1959). The moment she enters the car, though, the chase is on, introducing a new tension that unifies the final sequence: can Roger and Eve escape from Vandamm and his men? (Frame enlargement)

This cause dangles for the next several minutes as Eve is led steadily toward the plane and Roger is unexpectedly detained at gunpoint by Vandamm's servant. Just before Eve steps onto the plane, gunshots mark Roger's escape, and in the confusion Eve grabs the statue with the microfilm from Vandamm and runs to Roger, who has hopped into a car. With Eve and Roger safely in the car, the tension of the sequence is resolved: Roger has succeeded in rescuing Eve from Vandamm. Now a new question arises in the last sequence: can Roger and Eve escape alive?

Sequence I: Chase on Mount Rushmore

The final sequence runs just under ten minutes. At this point, all the many layers of dramatic irony that embroider the film have been re solved, and the sequence is unified purely by the dramatic tension surrounding the chase. Roger and Eve are unable to drive the car through the locked gate, so they set off on foot and wind up atop Mount Rushmore. Here, they fight off one assailant, then, with both Eve and Roger dangling on the sheer rock face, beg Leonard for help. He chooses instead to kill them, and before he can do so, he is himself killed by the sheriff, who has arrived in a timely manner with the Professor at his side and Vandamm already in custody.

The epilogue —Roger and Eve's honeymoon night—lasts just a minute.

NORTH BY NORTHWEST
Sequence Breakdown

Seq.	Description	Length	Running Time
	ACT I		
A	Roger, introduced in middle of his busy corporate life, is mistaken for George Kaplan and abducted, and escapes in a wild ride in a Mercedes (excludes opening titles). *Unifying Aspect*: Dramatic Tension. *Protagonist*: Roger. *Objective*: To escape his abductors.	15:41	15:41 (12%)
	Point of attack: Roger's abduction.		
B	Roger attempts to get the police to believe his story. After revisiting the Townsend residence, the police disbelieve him. *Unifying Aspect*: Dramatic Tension. *Protagonist*: Roger. *Objective*: To persuade the police.	8:52	24:33 (18%)
C	Roger enlists his mother's help in finding Kaplan; winds up framed for Townsend's murder. *Unifying Aspect*: Dramatic Tension. *Protagonist*: Roger. *Objective*: To find Kaplan.	11:04	36:16 (27%)
	Predicament: Roger, framed for murder and wanted by spies, must try to clear his name to survive.		
	TRANSITION SCENE: Intelligence bureau revelation/ exposition	2:55	39:11
	ACT II (Main tension: Will Roger succeed in clearing his name?)		
D	Roger finds refuge on The 20th Century Limited, encounters Eve; ends with the revelation that Eve is working for Vandamm. *Unifying Aspect*: Dramatic Tension. *Protagonist*: Roger. *Objective*: To get to Chicago without being discovered.	18:32	57:43 (43%)
E	Roger goes to meet Kaplan and instead meets crop duster. *Unifying Aspect*: Dramatic Tension. *Protagonist*: Roger. *Objective*: To meet Kaplan.	15:55	1:13:38 (55%)
	First Culmination: After crop duster scene, Roger realizes that Eve has betrayed him (1:15:00—56%).		
F	Roger discovers that Eve has betrayed him—follows her to the auction, from which he makes a novel escape. *Unifying Aspect*: Dramatic Tension. *Protagonist*: Roger. *Objective*: To get to the truth about Eve.	17:48	1:31:26 (68%)
	ACT III		
G	Roger is taken to airport—the Professor reveals the truth to him. The main tension—will Roger clear his name?—has now been resolved and a new 3rd-act	11:51	1:43:17 (77%)

tension arises—can Roger rescue Eve? The Professor
persuades Roger to save Eve with ruse at Mount
Rushmore. Roger goes through with it. Whose
sequence? *Unifying Aspect*: Dramatic Tension.
Protagonist: Roger. *Objective*: To help Eve through ruse.

**Second Culmination: At airport, Roger has the
mystery explained to him—then is informed Eve's life
is in danger (1:38:16—74%).**

H	After their moment alone together in the woods, Eve is taken away. Roger escapes from his hospital confines to go after her. He succeeds in sneaking into Vandamm's house and speaking to her, but she is called away to the airplane nonetheless. *Unifying Aspect*: Dramatic Tension. *Protagonist*: Roger. *Objective*: To rescue Eve.	10:45	2:04:02 (93%)
I	Final climactic chase to Mount Rushmore, and the ensuing battle thereon. *Unifying Aspect*: Dramatic Tension. *Protagonist*: Roger. *Objective*: To escape from Vandamm with Eve.	9:51	2:13:53 (100%)

Resolution: The battle on Mount Rushmore.

Epilogue: **Roger and Eve on the train.**

Lawrence of Arabia: Sixteen Sequences and an Intermission

Because of its length, *Lawrence of Arabia* stretches the limits of the dramatic form. As first noted by Aristotle and reinforced by others, one aspect that distinguishes drama from the novel and other long narrative forms is that it is intended to be experienced in one sitting. This gives the viewer a unified effect, a glimpse of the overall shape of the piece that is harder to discern when a narrative is experienced in several installments over the course of a longer time. At three hours and forty minutes, the picture stretches the limits of human endurance, and in a nod to the comfort of the audience, an intermission is offered after two hours.

Still, the picture retains a very rigorous three-act structure. Lawrence is on a quest to free the Arabs of Turkish rule. This is made clear a quarter of the way into the picture, and reaches an apparent resolution three-quarters of the way through, before arriving at its true, tragic resolution. The proportions of the acts remain the same: the first ends approximately 25% of the way through the picture, and the third begins about 80% of the way through. The first culmination—the attack on Aqaba—comes at the 48% mark.

To help convey the audience through a picture of this length, the use of sequences is in evidence: sixteen in all, running in length from eight to seventeen minutes. It's worth noting that even though the film and its acts are atypically long, the constituent sequences are not themselves any longer than those found in shorter films. This speaks to the function of sequences as opposed to acts; typical sequences are themselves short three-act dramas that build upon one another in support of the overall film, which usually has its larger three-act structure. As discussed in Chapter 1, if sequences are too long, i.e., if a filmmaker attempts to use one line of dramatic tension to sustain audience attention for more than twenty or so minutes, the effectiveness of the sequence is undermined.

The overall layout of the story of *Lawrence of Arabia*—a series of journeys—lends itself readily to being broken up into sequences. Nine of the sixteen sequences involve travel from one point to another; most of the rest contain adventures at one particular location or another. Only twice to do successive sequences occur in the same location.

Lawrence of Arabia is, from a storytelling viewpoint, a film obsessed with the future. Perhaps, again, in a bow to its length, the storytellers focus tremendous amounts of energy and screen time on the task of making sure the audience is aware of where they are in the story, what lies ahead, what they should be afraid of, what they should hope for. It is also exemplary in the attention given to making the entrances of characters memorable, and its use of contrasts—light and dark, sound and silence, close-ups and long shots—to help punctuate the action.

Sequence A: Creating Curiosity, Launching the Journey

The opening sequence begins with the opening titles, where a man in military uniform is shown from a high angle tinkering with a motorcycle. The odd angle creates a visual puzzle, and his actions provide telegraphing: it can reasonably be deduced that he plans to ride the motorcycle.

The man begins his journey as soon as the titles end, and the puzzle of who he is remains, because the goggles obscure his face. He passes a construction site with a sign that reads "Warning" and "Danger," a subtle foreshadowing, something of a visual dangling cause.

The man swerves to avoid some pedestrians and winds up in an accident, where his death is implied indirectly—through the wreckage of the motorcycle and the goggles hanging from a bush.

The film immediately switches to a statue of the man that identifies him as T. E. Lawrence—again, the audience is given a glimpse of him, but not a clear one, because he is represented only by the statue. The music and costumes suggest a memorial service, and in the conversation of those in attendance, several contradictory descriptions of the man are shared: "extraordinary," "poet," "scholar," "mighty warrior," "shameless exhibitionist," "very great man."

The memorial service scene ends with a dialogue hook—one man remembering that Lawrence "had a minor function on his staff in Cairo." The film immediately switches to the close-up of a hand holding a paintbrush that belongs, it turns out, to Lawrence, whose location is soon confirmed as Cairo. Shortly after this, after more than five minutes of film, the audience is given its first unimpeded look at Lawrence. These five minutes, then, provide the puzzle whose function is it to hook the audience. The storytellers do not assume the audience knows anything about the title character, or that they have any particular curiosity about him. Instead, they go about creating curiosity about him and retarding his true entrance until the anticipation is sufficiently built up.

In the scene that follows, Lawrence expresses unhappiness with his current position, displays knowledge of Arabic and awareness and concern for the Arab cause against the Turks, and finally exhibits certain eccentricities—his indifference to pain (he showcases his habit of putting out matches with his bare fingers) and his overly formal, condescending manner of speaking. During the scene, Lawrence gets a message and announces to those present he has an appointment with the general. After Lawrence leaves for this appointment, the two remaining soldiers exchange still two more opinions about him: he's balmy, and he's "all right."

While en route to the general's office, Lawrence walks through the officers' mess, where he again displays a condescending attitude, in this case toward a superior officer, and receives a rebuke in which the officer proffers yet another description of him: a clown. Lawrence knocks over a table and awkwardly apologizes.

The film now switches to General Murray's office, where Dryden, a friend of Lawrence's, is attempting to secure Lawrence an assignment in Arabia. The scene makes masterful use of the "exposition as ammunition" approach, but goes a step further: it features as many elements of the future (dangling causes) as there are elements of the past (exposition). The general describes Lawrence as an overweening, insubordinate junior officer; gives his opinion that the campaign in the Middle East is a sideshow to the war in Europe; and reveals that a Colonel Brighton has already been sent out to Arabia. But most of the scene is pregnant with the future: Dryden telling the general that Lawrence may be of use to the Arab Bureau, that Lawrence would not be giving military advice; that, as far as the Arab army is concerned, big things have small beginnings. General Murray in turn opines that time spent on the Bedouin is time wasted, but concedes that an expedition to Arabia might make a man out of Lawrence. In the end, Dryden manages to secure an expedition for Lawrence of three months' duration—a deadline that immediately provides a time frame for the action.

The importance of artillery—paid off later in various ways—is also planted in the scene. Further, within the scene, the business about Lawrence's salute is planted and paid off.

Afterward, Lawrence and Dryden confer, and here again the future figures prominently in the scene. Lawrence claims he's the man for the job; Dryden describes the job to him: find Prince Feisal and determine his intentions, a dangling cause that is picked up in the following sequence. Lawrence replies with another dangling cause, in this case a prediction: "It's going to be fun." Dryden replies that only two creatures think the desert is fun: Bedouins and gods, and that Lawrence is neither. This is a motif that is paid off—revisited—in many ways throughout the film. Lawrence's final retort is to insist that it is going to be fun, a dangling cause that hooks the sequence into the next one.

Sequence B: The Journey to the Masturah Well

An abrupt contrast—from a well-lit, interior close-up to an exterior wide shot of the pre-dawn desert—marks the transition from the first to the second sequence. The sequence begins slowly—two long shots occupy over a minute of screen time—but the extensive setup in the first sequence is sufficient to create enough anticipation to allow for the leisurely pace. The sequence runs seventeen minutes, unified by Lawrence's objective of finding Feisal. The obstacles involve the natural and man-made challenges of the desert. An important aspect of the sequence is Lawrence's evolving relationship with Tafas, his guide, and the beginning of Lawrence's transformation into a Bedouin that this relationship marks. Along the way, the inner transformation of Lawrence is expressed through external means—the water, the camel-riding lesson, Lawrence's gun, Tafas's shared meal.

In the first scene between Tafas and Lawrence, Tafas gives Lawrence a chance to drink, which Lawrence declines when Tafas reveals he himself is not drinking. This arouses Tafas's curiosity about Lawrence, and is a payoff of Lawrence's ability to endure pain, dramatized in the first sequence.

The next dialogue scene occurs at night over a campfire, when Tafas queries Lawrence about his background, attempting to satisfy his curiosity about the man. At the end of the conversation, yet another opinion about Lawrence is expressed, this time his own appraisal: he's "different."

Contrast is again used in the transition between scenes—a dark night sky to the bright morning close-up of Lawrence's gun. Lawrence offers the gun to Tafas as a gift (initiating its use as a motif); Tafas makes a counteroffer—he'll accept it after he takes Lawrence to Lord Feisal. This provides a reminder of the objective of the sequence. Lawrence insists, and Tafas in return offers Lawrence some Bedouin food; the exchange of props thus expresses a change in the relationship.

When the journey resumes, Tafas has the two stop at the edge of a ridge and points out a Bedouin camp far in the distance—planting the motif of Tafas's very sharp vision, and a setup of danger ahead: he tells Lawrence that henceforth they will be in Harith country, and that he is not Harith. Lawrence here displays his knowledge of Arabian ways when he identifies Tafas's tribe simply by looking at the color of his headdress, a knowledge that impresses Tafas and provides a further basis for a closer relationship.

Afterward, Tafas gives Lawrence an impromptu camel-riding lesson, leading to a pratfall, then tells Lawrence the rest of the day will be difficult, but that tomorrow there will be good riding—another dangling cause. In the following scene Tafas declares that the Masturah Wells are a day's ride, and Lord Feisal's camp is one day beyond that—telegraphing the plan for the next two days, and thus orienting the audience as to where they are in the journey. Lawrence replies by urging his camel onward, displaying how much he's learned about camel riding during the journey—thus paying off the lesson planted the scene before.

The two arrive at the Masturah Wells, where they take a drink and rest, and where Tafas notes that the water does not taste good because the Harith are a "dirty people." A brief scene of preparation by contrast follows, where Lawrence lies down near a bush and whistles a tune while examining his compass (planting the prop that will become important later), which lends the impression that the stay at the well will be restful.

Lawrence's relaxation is interrupted by Tafas, who noisily drops the waterskin into the well, his eyes transfixed by someone approaching in the far distance—a payoff of his keen eyesight established before. Lawrence notes Tafas's alarm, and asks whether or not he sees Turks. Both Turks and the Harith have already been established as dangers, so the suspense in the scene—drawn out by a long scene of preparation (in this case retardation)—is already in play and need not be explained.

After a long pause, Tafas identifies the intruder as a Bedouin, and after a bit longer, goes for the gun Lawrence had given him—the first payoff of the prop. Tafas is killed by the intruder, dramatizing the antagonisms between the various tribes of Arabia first hinted at by Tafas.

The intruder examines Tafas's body, then takes the gun—its second payoff—and introduces himself as Sherif Ali. He explains why he killed Tafas (he was from a tribe prohibited from using the well). As Sherif Ali starts to go away, Lawrence attacks him verbally, in the process initiating a dangling cause that will be picked up and developed extensively throughout the picture: he tells them that as long as the Arabs fight against each other, they will remain a little people— greedy, barbarous, and cruel. In addition to creating anticipation, and laying out the task Lawrence will face as he pursues his ultimate objective, this line of dialogue is a motif that is paid off two sequences later in Lawrence's meeting with Feisal.

Sherif Ali warns Lawrence that he will die before finding Feisal's camp, and threatens to take away his compass, then ends the scene and sequence with a dialogue hook: "God be with you, English."

Sequence C: The First Battle

The apparently negative resolution to the previous sequence—Lawrence does not get to Feisal—is reversed in the opening of Sequence C, when we soon learn that Lawrence, now alone, has arrived at Feisal's camp after all. The third sequence, which runs just under nine minutes, is unified by an event—the introduction of Lord Feisal—as opposed to a single line of dramatic tension. The first part of the sequence contains Lawrence's arrival at Feisal's camp, the middle features the battle and Lawrence's encounter with Feisal, and the third portrays the retreat of the Arabs as a consequence of the battle.

It's arguable that Sequence B doesn't end till Lawrence actually meets Feisal, because that is truly a resolution to the dramatic question of the sequence. But several changes occur after the first Lawrence–Ali scene at the Masturah Wells that I think justify such a demarcation. The tran-

sition between the Masturah Wells and Lawrence's arrival at Wadi Safra
is marked by three major changes: in cast (Lawrence loses Tafas, a com-
panion from the outset of sequence B, and gains new ones—Colonel
Brighton, Feisal, and Feisal's men), in location (open desert to the rug-
ged terrain of Wadi Safra), and action (the lonely sojourn ends, and a
battle against the Turks ensues). These changes, and the unhurried pace
of Lawrence's approach to Wadi Safra, signal a new segment of the
movie has begun.

Sequence C begins with a brief scene of preparation by contrast, with
Lawrence singing as he approaches Wadi Safra (the same song he'd been
whistling before encountering Sherif Ali), which gives impression of a
leisurely journey ahead—an expectation abruptly reversed with the appearance of Colonel Brighton, whose presence with Feisal has already
been established several times in the dialogue of the first two sequences.

Brighton confronts Lawrence, finds out about his mission ("appreci-
ate the situation"), and then orders him to keep his mouth shut, and to
make his appreciation and leave—two dangling causes picked up and
developed in Sequence D.

Their conversation is interrupted by the arrival of two Turkish aircraft that launch a raid and initiate the first of three battle scenes fea-
tured in the picture. The attack leads to the memorable introduction of
one of the major characters, Prince Feisal, who tries to charge the aircraft on horseback, then encounters Lawrence in a billow of smoke. This
encounter closes off the dangling cause uttered by Dryden in the first
sequence, namely his instructions to Lawrence to find Feisal.

At this encounter, Colonel Brighton urges Feisal to retreat south, and
Feisal agrees—a dangling cause that knits the scene to the next, which
portrays the nighttime retreat of the Arabs. At the end of the scene, Feisal makes reference to the guns—artillery—of the Turks, the first payoff
of this issue, planted in the scene with General Murray.

The retreat provides an opportunity for the memorable introduction
of two more characters, Daud and Farraj, who ask Lawrence for cigarettes, then later offering to be his servants; Lawrence declines, but the
request is a motif paid off two sequences later, when Lawrence does indeed hire the two.

Sequence D: Feisal's Tent

The fourth sequence runs fourteen minutes and is unified by dramatic
tension: Lawrence's desire to solve the military difficulty the Arabs are

having. The "first act" of the sequence finds Lawrence and Col. Brighton in Feisal's tent, where passages from the Koran are being recited. Dramatically, Brighton is the protagonist of the scene—it is shaped by his desire to persuade Feisal to retreat further south and accept British training and command. Lawrence is the unexpected obstacle to Brighton, disagreeing on tactics (thus picking up a dangling cause from the first and third sequences: Dryden's assurance that Lawrence will not give any military advice, echoing Brighton's similar admonition).

Feisal suggests his men could be supplied through the port of Aqaba—planting a very important motif that is paid off during the following two sequences. There follows "exposition through ammunition," during which it is revealed that Aqaba cannot be taken from the sea because it has twelve-inch guns. The verbal motif of artillery is paid off again, as Feisal requests it and Brighton refuses.

The scene ends with an apparent victory for Brighton, though Feisal indicates he will not give his final decision till the morning—a dangling cause. He then gestures for Lawrence to remain behind. Here, Feisal lays out his own dilemma—the need for help from the British, and his fear of British domination. He questions Lawrence's loyalties—furthering the motif of Lawrence's ambivalent identity. Feisal then recounts the former glories of the Arabs, provoking a dangling cause from Lawrence: "Time to be great again." The scene ends with a dangling cause that initiates a verbal motif of considerable significance during the following two sequences: "We need a miracle."

Thus ends the "sequence first act," and, further, the setup for the rest of the movie: the goal is laid out—a return to greatness for the Arabs—as are the obstacles—the Turks, British, and lack of artillery. Lawrence exits the tent into a rising wind that had already become audible in the scene with Feisal.

After a brief aftermath scene with Feisal alone in the tent, which serves to signal the importance of both what has just happened and what is about to happen, Lawrence sets out for the surrounding desert where he becomes lost in thought. Here, the challenge of dramatizing physically an inner state—deep meditation—is met by intensifying the atmosphere (desert winds, darkness, then eventually light again), by the use of music (a gradually ascending scale, increasing volume, and instrumentation), and through the reaction of Faraj and Daud, who watch him intently throughout the night.

The culmination of the sequence occurs when Lawrence declares: "Aqaba. From the land." The rest of the sequence involves Lawrence trying to persuade Sherif Ali to go along with his plan to seize Aqaba. More exposition is handled through their argument: going to Aqaba will require crossing the Nefud desert, which is impossible; Lawrence wants just fifty men; the Howeitat tribe, who are good fighters, are on the opposite side of the Nefud. During the conversation, Lawrence makes a prediction: if fifty men come out of the Nefud, they may be joined by others, and his last line in the scene is a forceful dialogue hook that binds it to the next sequence: "Aqaba is over there. It is only a matter of going."

Sequence E: Crossing The Nefud

The resolution of the previous scene actually occurs in the opening of this sequence; the question is whether or not Lawrence can persuade Sherif Ali to go along with him to Aqaba, and as Sequence E begins, with Lawrence and others making preparations for departure, the outcome is revealed: Lawrence has succeeded.

With the commencement of the journey to Aqaba, the second act of the movie as a whole begins. It is by now amply clear who the protagonist is, what he wants (to help make the Arabs great again—free of the yoke of both the Turks and British), and what the obstacles are (Turkish forces and British intentions). The seizure of Aqaba will be the first stepping-stone in achieving that goal.

Before Lawrence mounts up, Feisal confronts him and asks where he is going with fifty of his men; Lawrence replies "To work your miracle": a payoff of Feisal's line the night before, and a dangling cause that will inform the next three sequences. Feisal replies with a warning: "Blasphemy is a bad beginning for such a journey"—another line pregnant with the future. Lawrence's promise to deliver a miracle—which Feisal had described as something no man can deliver—and Feisal's rebuke— picks up on a motif initiated by Dryden's remark in the opening sequence, that Lawrence is neither god nor Bedouin. This motif—Lawrence as god—plays a major role in the next three sequences, extending through the conquest of Aqaba and his journey through Sinai.

As the journey begins, the storytellers employ a tool used seldom in the picture—dramatic irony. The two boys, Farraj and Daud, follow Lawrence and his men into the desert and spy on them at the oasis before the moment of recognition: they are caught by Gasim. They are brought to Sherif Ali and Lawrence, where they claim their camels strayed and led them to the camp in order to serve Lawrence—evidence, they say, of the will of Allah. This, and Sherif Ali's description of the two as worshippers (while they lie prostrate at Lawrence's feet), and Gasim's reference to Allah afterward, all help embroider the scene with the "god" motif. The scene also has two dangling causes—Sherif Ali's warning that the two boys are not suitable for the journey, and Gasim's prediction that the two will bring luck to Lawrence. Another motif is also planted—Gasim's statement to Lawrence that the two boys are parentless and therefore outcasts, paid off two sequences later when Lawrence reveals himself to be of illegitimate birth.

The end of the "first act" of this sixteen-minute sequence occurs five minutes into it, when Lawrence and his men arrive on a ridge overlooking the Nefud Desert. The scene is fraught with gloomy elements of the future uttered by Sherif Ali: if the camels die, the men will die, and after twenty days the camels will start to die. The rest of the journey through the Nefud is punctuated by pauses in which new elements of the future are introduced, keeping the audience constantly apprised about the progress they are making and what lies ahead.

The party is shown proceeding through the desert vastness, from a distance that emphasizes how few and small the group is—a subtle visual motif paid off later when these men join up with Auda's men on the far side. During this first part of the desert journey, Lawrence spots two dust columns in the distance, vaguely reminiscent of the pillar of fire that led Moses through the desert: a subtle reference to the "god" motif. In viewing them, Lawrence "drifts," a plant paid off later when a rider falls off his camel, and later still when Gasim disappears for the same reason. After Sherif Ali rebukes Lawrence for drifting, Lawrence replies with a dangling cause: an assurance that it won't happen again. This rebuke and rebuttal carries on another aspect of this sequence and those surrounding it: the antagonism between Sherif Ali and Lawrence.

The bitterness of their antagonism is reinforced during the next scene, when Lawrence is shaving at a campsite and Ali accuses him of wasting water. Ali telegraphs the next phase of the journey: it will take place at night, and they will leave in three hours; Lawrence replies that he'll be the one to awaken Ali.

This exchange sets up the following two scenes, the first of their night journey, and the next of a daytime campsite, where the camels and men are eerily still in the bright sun. After this, Lawrence and Ali pause in a rock-strewn stretch of desert, where Lawrence takes a drink of water and is clearly showing strain. He asks Ali if they rest where they are; Ali tells him there is no rest until they cross the next part of the desert—the "Sun's Anvil," which must be done before the sun comes up the next day—an urgent deadline that informs the rest of the sequence.

In the next nighttime phase of the journey, Daud falls off his camel and quickly regains it. Soon afterward, the far side of the Anvil is reached, and a positive resolution of the sequence is at hand. Lawrence declares, "We've done it!" and thanks God for it; the others remind him how much he has tempted God—another embroidery of the god motif. Lawrence asks Ali how far it is to the wells; Ali tells him by noon, thus giving the time frame for the next phase of the journey.

Sequence F: The Rescue of Gasim

As soon as the reality of their triumph sinks in, Daud notices that Gasim is missing from his camel. That he has fallen off need not be explained, since it had been dramatized previously by Daud's fall and Lawrence's drifting in the saddle. The momentary elation at crossing the Nefud thus serves as a scene of preparation by contrast, with the good spirits quickly reversed by the new revelation.

Very rapidly the dramatic tension of the sixth sequence is established, and the relationship between Lawrence and Ali reaches its low point. Lawrence asks Ali why he doesn't stop; Ali makes a prediction: Gasim will be dead by midday. Lawrence announces he will go back alone; Ali tells him he will kill himself—a dangling cause that is played out through most of the rest of the sequence.

One of the men tells Lawrence that Gasim's time had come, saying "it is written"—planting a phrase that continues the "god" motif. The scene marks the end of the "sequence first act," leaving the audience with competing dangling causes: Ali's claim that Lawrence will never make it to Aqaba, and Lawrence's reply that he will.

The handling of the "second act" of the sequence—the actual rescue of Gasim—is noteworthy not only for what is shown but also for what is withheld from view. Gasim stumbles alone through the desert, Daud watches from his camel, Lawrence makes his way alone, Gasim collapses, all this while the rest of the party refreshes itself at the watering-hole and Farraj watches for a sign of Lawrence. What's missing is the scene in which Lawrence actually finds Gasim and hoists him on the camel.

The omission of this scene seems to serve two purposes. First, it allows for the milking of a certain amount of suspense—if we see Lawrence effect the rescue, we cannot experience the doubt that Daud feels as he keeps an eye out. Second, it allows the sequence to have one climactic moment rather than two. Given the importance of the relationship between Lawrence and Ali, the storytellers have put the emphasis on Lawrence's triumphal return and his reconciliation with Ali, rather than his rescue of Gasim, a minor character.

Lawrence's initial encounter with Daud does provide some moments of exhilaration, but it's sufficiently close enough to the reconciliation with Ali as to be part of the buildup to that moment. In fact, having both of the boys watching for Lawrence, in different locations, allows for the exploitation of dramatic irony. Daud's encounter with Lawrence provides a scene of revelation whose spawned irony enriches the emotional impact of Farraj's anxious waiting and Ali's evident discouragement.

Lawrence's return on camelback, feted by the men, each of whom offers him a place to stay, is reminiscent of Jesus' entry into Jerusalem—another subtle payoff of the "god" motif. Lawrence greets Ali by accepting a drink from his waterskin, and tells him "nothing is written"—yet another payoff of the line. He then accepts Ali's bed after telling Farraj to wash his clothes. Lawrence's subsequent collapse provides the moment of aftermath.

In the epilogue of the sequence, later that night, Ali and Lawrence have a conversation that dramatizes the transformation of Ali's relationship with him, from bitter rival and antagonist to true admirer. After Lawrence speaks of his background, he falls asleep again, and Ali takes advantage of the occasion to burn Lawrence's clothes that are hanging to dry.

Sequence G: Recruiting Auda Abu Tayi

The sharp contrast of night and day marks the transition between the sixth and seventh sequences of the picture. Ali presents Lawrence with the white robes of an Arab sherif, and the external evidence of Lawrence's internal transformation from British officer to Arab is delivered forcefully. Any awkwardness in his manner (conveyed both by Peter O'Toole's acting choices and by the costume designer who intentionally provided him with an ill-fitting uniform) vanishes in his flowing, natural movements in the new garb.

Lawrence rides a camel around a hill away from the encampment in order to try out his new outfit, and here he encounters another major character—Auda Abu Tayi—chief of the Howeitat tribe. This encounter marks the end of the "first act" of this fifteen-minute sequence, which is unified by Lawrence's efforts to secure Auda's help in attacking Aqaba. As such, it picks up a dangling cause from the end of Sequence E—Lawrence's prediction that if they can succeed in getting through the Nefud, they may be joined by others.

In order to secure Auda's cooperation, Lawrence utilizes indirection. Auda complains about the thugs drinking from his well; as soon as Lawrence realizes who he is talking to, he compares Auda to another man of that name who would not begrudge water to men who had come out of the Nefud Desert. During most of the rest of the scene, Lawrence uses such indirect means, primarily flattery, to persuade Auda to cooperate.

Auda summons his son and the two proceed to the well to confront the rest of Lawrence's party. Ali and Auda exchange insults before Lawrence stops them and, again, uses indirection: "What are you teaching [your son] today—Howeitat hospitality?" Auda backs off, and the scene ends with his line: "It is my pleasure that you dine with me at Wadi Rumm." This dialogue plants a verbal motif (Auda's phrase "It is my pleasure") and serves as a dialogue hook into the next image, which is of Wadi Rumm, portrayed in a long shot that shows the great size of Auda's tribe.

The scope of Auda's power is reinforced by the scene that follows, where Lawrence's party is dwarfed by the number of men who come out to greet them in a swirl of dust, pounding hooves, shouting, and gunfire.

Contrast is employed in the transition to the next scene—from brightness, noise, and action to a quiet interior close-up of a girl's face. The scene finds Lawrence, Ali, and Auda finishing a meal in Auda's tent. The thrust of the scene is dramatic—Lawrence wants to persuade Auda to join them against Aqaba. Lawrence manipulates him by appealing to his ego—calling him a servant—and to his greed—his desire for money. In the end, he wins Auda over by persuading him that much money can be had in Aqaba, yet closes the deal by again using flattery, telling Auda he will join them because it is Auda's pleasure—the second payoff of the line.

Sequence H: The Attack on Aqaba

This dangling cause knits Sequence G to Sequence H, which opens with Lawrence's and Auda's men setting off for Aqaba. The previous sequence is thus shown to have a positive resolution—Lawrence has persuaded Auda to join them. Sequence H, which runs just under sixteen minutes, is centered on the seizure of Aqaba: the approach marks the first act of the sequence, the battle itself is the second, and the aftermath is the third.

The mighty procession that proceeds from Wadi Rumm stands in remarkable visual contrast to the small band that was shown setting out across the Nefud. They arrive at an encampment overlooking the port of Aqaba. Here, Lawrence and Ali exchange words in a scene of preparation by contrast that also reinforces dangling causes already in force. Ali predicts they will take Aqaba tomorrow—*if* Lawrence is right about the guns. The upbeat mood is interrupted by a gunshot, which in turn leads to a crisis.

Lawrence and Ali investigate and discover that one of Ali's men killed one of Auda's. With the mission in danger of falling apart over a blood feud, Lawrence offers to be the executioner. He takes hold of Ali's gun—which is actually his own gun, planted several sequences before—and aims the gun at the murderer, who proves to be none other than Gasim, the man he'd rescued from the desert. Lawrence carries out the execution, and in a bitter aftermath, Auda remarks that it was written—the last payoff of the line.

Lawrence, distraught over his action, throws away the gun in a brief aftermath scene before the scene switches to Aqaba, where the attack begins. This is the second of the battle scenes, and is larger, longer, and more elaborate than the previous one, and ends with the image of two large guns facing out to sea, paying off the motif planted in Sequence D. It's worth noting that the battle for Aqaba occurs one hour and forty minutes into the film—the place where one might normally find a climactic scene in a film of more typical length. In this, the storytellers manage to accommodate the audience's conditioned expectations while stretching their attention beyond its normal limit.

An aftermath scene follows the attack—Lawrence at the ocean looking quietly out at the crashing waves. Soon Ali arrives to present him with a victor's laurels and congratulate him. The moment marks the first culmination of the picture: Lawrence is triumphant and his relationship with Ali is very close—the mirror opposite of the second culmination of the film. Ali tells him: "tribute for the prince, flowers for the man"—two more opinions about Lawrence.

Their conversation is interrupted by gunfire in Aqaba, where Auda is furious that he has not found the gold he'd been promised. Lawrence arrives after the telegraph has been smashed, and during the rest of the sequence, he is preoccupied with getting word back to Cairo about the victory, and quelling Auda's rage. He first instructs Ali to have Feisal bring the Arab army to Aqaba—a dangling cause picked up after the intermission—and tells Ali he plans to go to Cairo himself across Sinai—an appointment realized in the following sequence. Ali objects, predicting that Lawrence will take off his "funny" Arab clothes and put on trousers when he gets to Cairo so that he'll be taken seriously, another dangling cause.

Auda interrupts with the accusation that Lawrence lied about gold in Aqaba. Lawrence solves the problem by making a promise—he will bring back gold and guns—and sets a deadline for this—ten days. Auda voices skepticism about Lawrence being able to cross Sinai with Farraj and Daud, and Lawrence retorts: "Moses did." This introduces a variation on the "god" motif—this time Lawrence as prophet.

Sequence I: Across Sinai

This sequence, at eleven and a half minutes, is unified by the journey across Sinai and ends with Lawrence's announcement of his seizure of Aqaba in Cairo. Lawrence's intent, and his plan, are all explained in the previous sequence, so the action begins immediately with Lawrence and the two boys en route. Farraj, obviously exhausted, asks if they can stop and rest; Lawrence replies with a line that reinforces the purpose of the sequence: "There will be no rest till they know I have Aqaba." He then promises that by "tomorrow night" they will sleep in the finest beds in the finest hotel in Cairo—a dangling cause that also sets a deadline for the journey. Daud's reply: "Then it shall be so, Lord," is yet another reinforcement of the "god" motif.

In the next scene, Lawrence points out a dust storm in the distance and calls it a "pillar of fire," carrying this motif one instance more. The party is soon overtaken by a dust storm that claims Lawrence's compass—the last payoff for the object. Lawrence announces they need only head due west, into the setting sun—and will eventually strike the canal. This amounts to an updated agenda that maintains the audience's sense of geography—both time and space—in the sequence. As they ride west, they encounter yet another dust storm. This time, Daud falls into a quicksand and dies, despite Lawrence's efforts to save him. The disaster ends with a lingering aftermath scene that actually carries over into the following scene, which finds Farraj riding a camel, following Lawrence, who walks on foot.

In this scene and a few more that follow, the costume department again got to work in a way that enhances the script, because now Lawrence is made to resemble Jesus, transformed from the prophet Moses leading his people to the suffering servant bearing a terrible burden. When the two arrive at a cluster of buildings, Farraj leaves Lawrence behind and heads further along, then returns a few moments later and urges him forward on foot. The arrival of the two at the canal, which is announced by a sounding of a boat's horn after Lawrence and Farraj emerge from one of the buildings, closes off the dangling cause of the scene before Daud's death. By having Farraj discover the canal offscreen first, then bring Lawrence to see it, the storytellers are again using retardation—delaying the audience's experience of an important moment so as to increase the sense of anticipation. The plot would have been served equally well if the two had simply ridden the camel to the canal and stopped, but such a telling of the tale would have diminished the emotional impact of the scene.

As Lawrence and Farraj look out over the canal, a British officer on a motorcycle on the far side stops and twice asks, "Who are you?" This

Figure 13. Lawrence loses his servant Daud in a quicksand in Sequence I of *Lawrence of Arabia* (1962). Compare this aftermath scene to that shown in Figure 10. *Lawrence* stretches the limits of the dramatic form because of its length, and makes lavish use of all the storytelling tools to keep the audience involved. (Frame enlargement)

question, posed as it is with the camera lingering on Lawrence, is yet another variation on the issue of Lawrence's identity.

With the journey across Sinai complete, the last four minutes of the sequence involve Lawrence's arrival in Cairo and his announcement about taking Aqaba. Lawrence and Farraj arrive at military headquarters, where they venture into the officers' club. A military policeman guarding the entrance warns him not to take Farraj inside, exposition about the rules of the bar that create tension in the scene that follows.

Lawrence proceeds to the bar and orders two glasses of lemonade, creating a stir among the men. Brighton arrives, and Lawrence tells him the news: he and the Arabs have taken Aqaba. Brighton tells him he'd better talk to General Allenby—an appointment that helps to hook the sequence into the next one. Lawrence then asks Brighton to get a room with a bed—for Farraj—closing off the dangling cause of the first scene in the sequence, and the two proceed out of the room. Brighton suggests that Lawrence get some trousers on—a payoff of Ali's line in the previous sequence, and a dialogue hook into the next sequence.

Sequence J: The First Meeting With Allenby

The tenth sequence, which runs twelve minutes, is the first one in which a character other than Lawrence serves as the protagonist. Here, the objective of a new character, General Allenby, drives the action: that of trying to persuade Lawrence to go back into the desert.

The sequence opens with Lawrence in Allenby's office, still in his Arabic clothing (which effectively closes off the "trousers" dangling cause) where he meets with General Allenby, Dryden, and Brighton. Allenby reviews his dossier, then questions Lawrence about the seizure of Aqaba. In the course of the conversation, Lawrence begins to give military advice—again picking up the dangling cause initiated by General Murray in the opening sequence of the picture. Allenby promotes Lawrence major, and tells him he wants him to go back. Lawrence resists, confessing his distress/thrill at killing Gasim, and his feeling that he is not fit for the job. At this, the end of the "first act" of the sequence is at hand: Allenby must try to persuade a reluctant Lawrence to go back into action.

Allenby's approach is not unlike that which Lawrence used on Auda—massage his ego. He first asks those present for their opinions of Lawrence's actions, which are very favorable. The four then proceed for a drink at the officers' bar; along the way Allenby continues to ask Lawrence for military advice—another form of flattery. During the course of the walk, Lawrence is visibly changed—more at ease.

The four take their place in the courtyard, and the conversation turns to the future. Lawrence tells how he will take his men and smash the railroads—a dangling cause—and even sets a deadline—thirteen weeks to bring Arabia to chaos. Allenby asks if this means Lawrence is going back, and Lawrence confirms this—resolving the tension of the sequence. The remainder of the sequence involves establishing a series of dangling causes that will help knit the first part of the movie to the second—made more emphatic by the intermission that separates this sequence from the next. Among these is the question of whether the Arabs will be allowed to control Arabia if the Turks are defeated, an issue that provides the dramatic tension of the third act of the picture.

In a brief scene afterward, Allenby reveals he won't be giving Lawrence the field artillery after all—another payoff of the issue of artillery. The sequence ends with one last dangling cause—Allenby observing that Lawrence is "riding the whirlwind," and Dryden replying, "Let's hope we're not."

Intermission

The intermission occurs after two hours and twelve minutes of film. It is thus not halfway through (it's about 62% of the way through the film) but rather occurs after the length of a typical feature film. The major event of the first part of the film—the attack on Aqaba—occurs an hour and a half in, the place where a typical "climax" of a regular length feature would occur. The journey across Sinai would amount to the third act of a regular feature, with Lawrence's meeting with Allenby an opportunity for an epilogue.

In fact, that last sequence is used to create the dangling causes that will knit the first part of the movie to the second, where the focus of the action will be along two lines outlined in that last scene: the attack on the Turkish railroads, and the freeing of the Arabs from both the Turks and their would-be new conquerors, the British.

Sequence K: Jackson Bentley's Scoop

For the second time in as many sequences, a newly introduced character, this time Jackson Bentley, serves as the protagonist. He is the first character to appear after the intermission, ascending a hill overlooking the Gulf of Aqaba. An armored car passes by him—paying off Lawrence's request for the vehicles in the previous sequence.

Bentley asks Selim, Feisal's reciter, for directions to Prince Feisal; his business card provides a visual bridge between that scene and the one following it, in which Bentley meets Feisal. The card also initiates exposition about Bentley: he is a reporter for the *Chicago Courier*. Feisal invites Bentley inside and places a watch on a table—a subtle, visual deadline for the scene—then reveals that he does not know where Lawrence—and his army—are, though he offers a guess. Bentley raises the issue of the Arabs' lack of artillery and warns Feisal about Allenby, who is untrustworthy—a dangling cause that, combined with the lack of artillery, raises again the issue of independence of the Arabs from British rule. Bentley then reveals his purpose—he wants to tell the story of Lawrence and the Arab revolt. This desire provides the primary tension of the thirteen-minute sequence.

Feisal gets up after checking his watch, signaling the deadline has been reached, then tells Bentley his army is destroying the Turkish railroad, providing exposition to the audience, in this case what has occurred during the intermission. Feisal also tells him that his army does not allow its wounded to be captured by the Turks, who will torture them. This motif is paid off later when Farraj is wounded. Bentley raises the issue of Lawrence's reputed horror at bloodshed; Feisal poses a question about how reliable Lawrence is as to mercy—a dangling cause picked up in the third act.

The scene ends with Bentley admitting he is looking for a romantic figure who will help persuade America to enter the war; Feisal replies: "Lawrence is your man." This is a dialogue hook into the following scene, which finds Lawrence blowing up a Turkish train. The end of the "first act" of the sequence is thus accomplished: its protagonist, Bentley, has been introduced; his objective has been explained, as have the obstacles.

Lawrence sets off an explosive charge that derails the train; the Arabs pour gunfire into the train till Lawrence stops them (a subtle payoff of the "mercy" issue raised by Feisal), then leads a charge. After the Arabs begin to pillage the train, Lawrence is wounded by a surviving Turkish soldier. The close brush with death only serves to embolden Lawrence, a return to the "god" motif. Lawrence makes a triumphant walk along the top of the train to the adoring cheers of his men, and the ready camera of Bentley. The manner in which he moves is a payoff of a visual motif planted in an earlier scene when he practiced flowing movements with his Arab garments just prior to meeting Auda.

With the attack on the train over, Colonel Brighton raises an issue—and a dangling cause—when he criticizes the Arabs for looting, then going home. He warns Ali it must stop. Lawrence insists they will come back; Ali warns him "not this year."

The next scene finds Bentley examining a British children's book explaining how Parliament works; he asks Ali skeptically if the Arabs will become a democracy. Ali replies that he will answer the question when he has a country—keeping alive the "Arabia is for the Arabs now" verbal motif.

Bentley carries this motif further in the next scene when he asks Lawrence what the Arabs hope to gain from the fight; Lawrence replies: "Their freedom," and says he is going to give it to them. Bentley announces he will be returning to the "fleshpots" shortly, an appointment that signals his departure.

The sequence ends with Auda telling Brighton the year is running out and that he must find something "honorable"—meaning loot—to bring home with him. This dialogue hook binds Sequence K to the next one, which opens with a shot of beautiful horses on a train, lingering on one white steed in particular.

Sequence L: The Campaign Falters

The twelfth sequence of the picture, which runs ten minutes, is unified by Lawrence's attempt to keep the campaign going despite the gradual desertion of most of his men with the onset of winter. It opens with another attack on a Turkish train. This time, Farraj is seen putting away the explosive equipment, planting a motif to be paid off later in the sequence.

The Arabs storm the train and make off with its load of horses. Auda chooses the white one for his own and rides up to Lawrence to bid him farewell, for he has his prize—closing off the dangling cause of the end of the previous sequence. Colonel Brighton asks Lawrence what he intends to do now—without an army. Lawrence telegraphs his plans: he'll go north, because that is what Allenby wants. Brighton replies that Allenby wanted the Arab army behind the town of Deraa; Lawrence retorts with a dangling cause—he will be in Deraa before Allenby reaches Jerusalem.

In the following scene, Lawrence and his men are preparing another attack on a train. Farraj injures himself while helping to set the charges, and, in a payoff of Feisal's earlier exposition about not leaving wounded behind, Lawrence is once again forced to be the executioner.

The sequence ends with a dangling cause that binds it to the next one: Ali asking Lawrence what he will do now, with only twenty men, and Lawrence replying, "I'll go north."

Sequence M: Disaster in Deraa

The final sequence of the second act begins with a recapitulation scene—Colonel Brighton and General Allenby discussing the progress—or lack thereof—of Lawrence's campaign. The question of Lawrence's identity is again raised, with Allenby asking Brighton if he thinks Lawrence has "gone native," and later wondering if Lawrence thinks he's a prophet. Allenby discloses that the Turks have put a reward of 20,000 pounds on Lawrence's head, and proffers a dangling cause—doubting that Lawrence has long to live. The scene ends with Allenby asking about next year—will Lawrence and his Arab army come back?—another dangling cause.

The scene now shifts to a desolate, wintry encampment—a stunning visual contrast to the quiet, comfortable quarters of General Allenby. Ali tries to persuade Lawrence to go easier on the men—using another dangling cause: one more failure and Lawrence will be alone. In his argument, Ali revives the "god" motif—chiding Lawrence that for him the men must walk on water. Lawrence replies in kind, asking Ali, "Do you think I'm just any man?"

Lawrence continues the motif when he enters the next chamber and asks the men, "Who will walk on water with me?" He asks who will accompany him into the town of Deraa, explaining that he promised the English generals he would be there before the English seized Jerusalem—picking up on a dangling cause of two sequences before. When the Arabs balk, Lawrence telegraphs his intent: "This afternoon I will take the Arab revolt into Deraa." Majid replies with a dangling cause: "Can you pass for an Arab in an Arab town?"

At this point, just under four minutes into the fifteen-minute sequence, its dramatic tension is established—Lawrence will lead a revolt in the town of Deraa, and will have to overcome the obstacles of too few men and the fact that he's not an Arab. Lawrence arrives in Deraa and promptly walks in a puddle ("walking on water"—the second pay-off of the line, this time in visual form) after almost being run over by the Turkish Bey, who is in the back seat of a motor car.

In a payoff of Majid's warning about not being able to pass for an Arab, Lawrence is immediately noticed by some Turkish soldiers, who seize him. He is brought to the office of the Bey, who selects him among several young men brought in. This is one of the few scenes in the picture whose emotional intensity is centered on dramatic irony—the audience's secret knowledge that the Turk has captured a man who is none other than Lawrence of Arabia, who carries a big price on his head. The intensity of the tension reaches its climax when the Bey dismisses all the other men and begins closely questioning Lawrence, describing his own misery at being assigned to Deraa, then eyeing Lawrence closely and proclaiming, "No, *that* would be too lucky," a subtle reference to the fact that Lawrence has a price on his head, and the nearest Lawrence comes to having his identity revealed.

The Bey strips Lawrence and touches him while making a subtle sexual reference, inspiring Lawrence to punch him. The Bey responds by ordering him beaten, and Lawrence endures it, in a distant echo of his comments about enduring pain in the opening sequence of the picture.

After the ordeal, Lawrence is dumped into the muddy street (the final payoff of the "walk on water" line), and Ali comes to his aid. The retreat that follows closes off the dangling cause uttered by Ali earlier about the danger of one more failure. It also marks the beginning of the "third act" of the sequence; Lawrence has failed to achieve his objective, and the consequences are explored.

Over the course of two night scenes, Lawrence remains in shock as Ali tries to nurse him back to health, telling him "You have a body, like other men"—a payoff of Lawrence's claim that he is not just any man. When Lawrence awakens in the third scene, the audience is given a glimpse of a plausible outcome of the film—the failure of the Arab revolt. He announces he is going, that he has come to the end of himself. In a reversal of his previous claim of not being just any man, he describes himself as just that: "any man." He telegraphs his intent: to go to Jerusalem by easy stages, and then to find a job that any man can do. Lawrence asks Ali if he can borrow his thick coat; Ali objects that it is "not clean"—the second payoff of Lawrence's line to Bentley about the desert being clean.

The "god" motif has come to a crashing end, as has Lawrence's ambivalent identity of Englishman versus Arab. Lawrence is disillusioned, and the movie is apparently over. This emotional "low point" marks the end of the second act. Lawrence, whose quest was to free the Arabs from Turkish and British control, has failed. He tells Ali and the remaining Arabs to trust only their own people, and to let him go back to his—a dialogue hook that knits the sequence (and act) to the next.

Sequence N: Lawrence Attempts to Resign

A British military parade, playing Western martial music, marks the transition to the third act, and reinforces the notion that Lawrence has now gone back to his own people and culture. He arrives at Allenby's headquarters, moving awkwardly again in his British uniform, and tries to chat casually with fellow officers, who secretly express the feeling that he is overdoing his attempts at camaraderie.

Character Arc

This phrase refers to the transformation a character can go through in the course of a drama, and is understood as the conflict between what a character *wants* and what the character *needs.* The character is aware of his or her *want,* but unaware of his or her *need* until the culmination of the character's story. Often, the character arc of the protagonist carries the main theme of the picture.

Although Lawrence is a complex character, in general his conscious desire is to emulate the gods and change history; his unconscious need is to realize that he is human and thus has limits. This realization occurs to him at the end of the second act, after his failure in Deraa. In *Toy Story,* (see Chapter 2), Woody's conscious desire is to maintain his place as Andy's most beloved toy; his unconscious need is to realize that he cannot will love. This revelation, too, occurs at the end of the second act.

Not all characters are capable of such transformation, and the result can be tragic. In *One Flew Over the Cuckoo's Nest* (Chapter 9), McMurphy is incapable of change—of shedding his basic sense of humanity—and is crushed. In *Being John Malkovich* (see Chapter 11), Craig is never able to overcome his obsession with Maxine and so is condemned to be "absorbed."

Subplot characters can also have arcs and culminating transformations; in this volume, notable among them are the Chief in *Cuckoo's Nest* and Buzz in *Toy Story.*

Lawrence arrives at Allenby's office just as Allenby and Dryden are finishing a meeting with Feisal, after which Lawrence discovers that a secret agreement has been signed by the French and British to rule the Arab world after the war—picking up a dangling cause from Sequence J (Lawrence's claim that "Arab is for the Arabs now").

Lawrence goes on to request reassignment for personal reasons; in fact, this request marks the end of the "first act" of the relatively short (eight and a half minute) sequence, which is unified by Lawrence's attempt to quit the Arab campaign. Allenby replies that he's making his big push on Damascus on the 16th of next month—an appointment—for which he needs Lawrence to continue his campaign with the Arabs. Lawrence presses his case and Allenby, after noting that Lawrence has blood on his back, guides him to another room to talk further.

After a brief interlude with Dryden and Bentley, the picture cuts back to Allenby, who manipulates Lawrence by stroking his ego—calling him an extraordinary man with a destiny. This approach quickly undermines Lawrence's resolve, leading to a negative resolution for the sequence—Lawrence fails in his attempt to resign. The remainder of the scene initiates a series of dangling causes—predictions by Lawrence—that he will take Damascus before Allenby's troops do, and when he has Damascus, he will keep it for the Arabs. The sequence ends with a dialogue hook: Lawrence says that the best of the Arabs won't come for money—they'll come for him.

Sequence O: The Drive to Damascus

This sequence, the second-last of the picture, is unified by Lawrence's drive to Damascus, cross-cut with the British drive to the same objective, the two parallel story lines often linked by dialogue hooks. It begins the "third-act tension" of the picture as a whole in earnest. After Lawrence's abandonment of his overall objective at the end of Act II, he returns to the game, but this time in a more narrowly focused way: on seizing Damascus before the British do and then setting up a new government free of Allied control. The issue of the Turks has now been rendered irrelevant; it is now the British Army that poses the chief obstacle.

In this vein, the opening shot of the sequence finds Lawrence in blazing-white Arab robes, riding in front of a large personal bodyguard, being greeted by a cheering throng of Arabs. He shouts "Damascus" and leads his men onward, initiating a dangling cause that hooks into the following scene. The narrative switches to a British command tent, where Allenby confers with his staff on the progress of the offensive toward Damascus. This amounts to a *recapitulation* scene (see text box, page 29), with the various officers bringing the general (and the audience) up-to-date on their situation, and one of them asking about the Arab army noted on a map in front of them.

Allenby orders Colonel Brighton to make contact with the Arab army to ascertain its whereabouts—initiating a dangling cause that is suspended through the following scene—and the scene ends with another dialogue hook: Allenby pounding on the blackboard map and telling one of his generals to "pound them" with artillery.

The movie now dissolves to a long shot of flashes of artillery on a distant battlefield concealed by hills, a spectacle being witnessed by Lawrence, Ali, and the other Arabs. Ali expresses empathy for the Turks being so pounded; Lawrence does not. This is a subtle payoff of the motif of mercy planted by Feisal in his initial conversation with Bentley, a motif that will be revisited forcefully for the remainder of the picture.

The Arab army continues onward, and a dissolve is used again to transition back to the British Army, where British troops march in the same screen direction. Allenby rides in an open-topped command car; Colonel Brighton waves him down and gets on board. Brighton wears an Arab headdress, a visual clue suggesting he has made contact with Lawrence and the Arab army, and makes his report, closing off the dangling cause of two scenes previous. He tells Allenby about Lawrence's cockiness, and predicts that the Arabs may reach Damascus before they do. He qualifies his prediction by noting the presence of a Turkish column ahead of him. Allenby ends the scene with another dialogue hook: "I wonder where they are now."

This line of dialogue leads to the transition to the village of Tafas, which the Turkish soldiers are shown abandoning after evidently destroying it and massacring its occupants. The Turks are then seen in a demoralized, bedraggled retreat across a dusty, windswept expanse.

Lawrence and the Arabs now move through the village, with a rage evidently building up inside Lawrence. The Arab army lines up along a ridge overlooking the retreating Turks, and here Lawrence is torn between the counsel of Ali, who urges him to go around the Turks and keep in mind the objective, Damascus, and the voice of one of his guards, who urges "No prisoners."

While he is in the midst of this quandary, one of the Arabs—Tallal, whose village was sacked—makes a suicide attack on the Turks. This action leads Lawrence to announce the attack with the command: "No prisoners!" What follows is the longest and most elaborate of the three battle scenes in the picture, a lopsided massacre that closes off in bright crimson the dangling cause initiated by Feisal earlier: "With Lawrence, mercy is a passion; with me, it is just good manners. You will have to see for yourself which is the more reliable." It is also a payoff of Lawrence's earlier line to Allenby describing his execution of Gasim: "I enjoyed it."

A long aftermath scene follows: a wordless, atmospheric advance by the Arabs past the carnage, punctuated by Bentley's arrival to take a photo of Lawrence after castigating Lawrence for the brutality.

The flash of Bentley's camera provides a visual transition to the last scene of the sequence, which finds Lawrence accompanying the Arabs ever forward. A man rides up to him and offers him grapes picked the previous night in Damascus— an indirect signal of their progress to their objective. The man also reports that Allenby is not yet there.

Sequence P: The Ambiguous Outcome

The final sequence, which runs almost eighteen minutes, is centered on Lawrence's attempt to create a functioning, independent government for the Arabs. It begins with a recapitulation scene that brings the audience up-to-date with events occurring since the previous scene, and launches several dangling causes that will be picked up in the rest of the sequence.

Allenby arrives in Damascus to a large crowd of jeering Arabs; Colonel Brighton informs him that Lawrence is behind it—that he and his Arab army had arrived a day and a half before and were occupying the town hall and other critical municipal ministries.

Unlike Lawrence's triumphant attack on Aqaba, his arrival in Damascus occurs offscreen, with the emotionally climactic moment coming some time before—during the massacre of the Turkish column. The storytellers have apparently chosen to emphasis the ambiguous nature of the main character and his actions, instead of investing audience emotional involvement in his military triumph.

Brighton urges Allenby to clear out Lawrence and his men by force; Dryden counsels against it, fearing a bloodbath. He informs Allenby that Feisal will arrive in two days' time—a deadline providing the time frame by which the problem must presumably be resolved. Allenby then issues his orders: troops to stay quartered in their barracks, including technical units—engineers and medics. This is a dangling cause that shapes the action and leads to Lawrence's failure.

The scene switches to the town hall, where Lawrence tries in vain to get the quarreling Arabs to cooperate with one another. The scene provides a masterful example of economy in writing—the screenwriter is able to use one scene to dramatize more than a year of wrangling between the various Arab factions that occurred historically.

In attempting to resolve the disputes, Lawrence learns that the phones do not work because the electricity does not work; Ali suggests English engineers be used to fix the electricity, and Lawrence objects, telling him that to accept the help of English engineers is to accept English government. This bit of exposition—delivered in the course of an argument—sheds light on Allenby's decision to keep Army technical units bound to the barracks. A late-arriving Arab announces that a fire has broken out; Lawrence is compelled to rush out to try to solve that crisis, and the meeting seems to dissolve into chaos.

Contrast—silence and darkness—marks the transition to the next scene, which finds Allenby practicing fly-fishing and remarking about taking it up after the war. The lights suddenly go out—the electricity has failed. Soon afterward, the Arabs are seen leaving the city, resolving Allenby's problem and signaling Lawrence's ultimate failure.

The resolution of the picture as a whole is thus at hand. The remainder is an epilogue; while there is conflict and therefore dramatic tension within the scenes, there is little in the way of tension—dramatic or ironic—that runs through the whole.

Lawrence, working in a dark, silent, and mostly empty town hall, writes a document while Auda and Ali stew nearby. Auda takes the document away from Lawrence and tries to convince him to return with him to Arabia; Lawrence refuses and utters a prayer that he will never see the desert again; Auda predicts he will return; these are two dangling causes that are never closed off. Most typically, in an epilogue, whatever dangling causes that remain are resolved, but in this case, with an ambiguous hero, the storytellers opt for a final sequence that is more open-ended.

Ali then reveals his own plans—he will stay and learn politics, an occupation he'd never dreamed of till Lawrence entered his life. He exits, and then he and Auda have one last confrontation, in which Ali confesses his deeply ambivalent feelings for Lawrence, and Auda initiates another dangling cause—that Ali will find being an "Arab" will be more difficult than he expects.

The film switches to Allenby, who receives a report from a medical officer about some situation demanding his immediate attention. Allenby sends him to Lawrence to inquire—a dialogue hook that links the scene to the next, where the same medical officer briefs Lawrence about an overcrowded Turkish military hospital. Another dialogue hook— Lawrence asking "What's it like?"—links this scene to the next, in which Lawrence visits the hospital and is overwhelmed by its squalor. Shortly after his arrival, a British medical crew arrives, resolving the lingering dangling cause about British intervention there. Lawrence is slapped by an outraged British soldier who does not recognize him.

The film now switches to Allenby's office, where Feisal attempts to salvage some authority for the Arab Council from Allenby and Dryden. Feisal predicts that many will in the future be proud to say that Lawrence was a friend of theirs—a faint echo of the opening sequence's post-funeral scene. Allenby promotes him colonel to make him more comfortable for the ride home—an appointment that, like Auda's prediction, extends beyond the end of the picture.

Lawrence exits the room; Feisal attempts to thank him one more time but it is too late; yet another relationship is left unresolved. Feisal and Allenby are left to haggle over another issue—the control over the various governmental ministries.

While these two wrangle offscreen, Lawrence passes through the officers' mess and is accosted by the same officer who'd slapped him at the military hospital. In a payoff of a line from the opening sequence (in which he reveals he'd shaken Lawrence's hand in Damascus), the man asks to shake Lawrence's hand because he "just wanted to be able to say I'd done it." Lawrence replies by asking if they'd met before, punching up the dramatic irony of the scene.

Back at Allenby's office, Feisal and Allenby continue to negotiate; Brighton, who has seemed distracted, asks to be excused. Finally, the haggling is resolved with a compromise—a British waterworks with an Arab flag on it. Afterward, Brighton is shown running for the entrance to the building, looking, apparently, for Lawrence, who is gone. The scene leaves another unresolved relationship.

In the final scene of the picture, Lawrence is being driven across a desert expanse, and the two threads that worked their way through his life—divided loyalties and an identity of the Arab world versus the British one—are played out one last time. The car passes a caravan of camels, which seizes Lawrence's attention, and a truckload of British troops. A motorcycle passes them by, hinting at the opening scene of the movie and subtly bookending it.

LAWRENCE OF ARABIA
Sequence Breakdown

Seq.	Description	Length	Running Time
	ACT I		
A	Lawrence's accidental death to start of journey to Feisal (excluding opening titles). *Unifying Aspect*: Dramatic Tension. *Protagonist*: Lawrence. *Objective*: To get to the desert.	11:30	11:30 (5%)
	Point of attack: Newspaper account of Arab attack. Also, memorial service points in direction of story.		
B	Lawrence and his Bedouin guide trek through the desert. His guide is killed at the well by Ali. *Unifying Aspect*: Dramatic Tension. *Protagonist*: Lawrence. *Objective*: To get to Prince Feisal with his guide.	17:06	28:36 (14%)
C	Lawrence arrives just as Feisal's camp is under air attack. He meets Feisal and joins in the retreat. *Unifying Aspect*: Event (meeting Feisal).	8:43	37:19 (18%)
D	Lawrence confers with Col. Brighton and Feisal in Feisal's tent. That night he comes up with his solution to the problem: seizing Aqaba, and succeeds in persuading Ali to join him. *Unifying Aspect*: Dramatic Tension. *Protagonist*: Lawrence. *Objective*: Initiate a solution to the Arab problem.	14:10	51:29 (24%)
	Predicament: Lawrence undertakes to unite the Arabs to throw off the Turks.		

ACT II
(Main tension: Will Lawrence succeed in uniting the Arabs to overthrow the Turks?)

Seq.	Description	Length	Running Time
E	The journey across the An Nafud desert, ending when they reach the far side of the Sun's Anvil. *Unifying Aspect*: Dramatic Tension. *Protagonist*: Lawrence. *Objective*: To get through the An Nafud.	16:17	1:04:58 (31%)
F	Lawrence returns to the Sun's Anvil to rescue Gasim; in the aftermath, Ali discovers Lawrence's illegitimate origins. While Lawrence is asleep, Ali burns Lawrence's clothes. *Unifying Aspect*: Dramatic Tension. *Protagonist*: Lawrence. *Objective*: To rescue Gasim.	13:27	1:18:25 (37%)
G	Lawrence tries on his new Arabic clothing, encounters Auda Abu Tayi, who threatens the other Arabs for drinking from his well. Lawrence persuades him to invite them to Wadi Rumm, where he then persuades Auda to join them in an attack on Aqaba. *Unifying Aspect*: Dramatic Tension. *Protagonist*: Lawrence. *Objective*: To get Auda to cooperate.	14:53	1:33:18 (44%)

H	The united Arab tribes set off for Aqaba; just prior to the attack, Lawrence is forced to execute Gasim. The next morning, the Arabs attack Aqaba, after which, Lawrence decides to head back to Cairo across the Sinai. *Unifying Aspect*: Dramatic Tension. *Protagonist*: Lawrence. *Objective*: To lead a successful attack on Aqaba.	15:42	1:49:00 (51%)

First Culmination: The attack on Aqaba.

I	Lawrence leads Farraj and Daud across Sinai; loses Daud in a quicksand; Lawrence and Farraj arrive in Cairo and drink at the officers' club, where Lawrence announces that they had taken Aqaba. *Unifying Aspect*: Dramatic Tension. *Protagonist*: Lawrence. *Objective*: To lead Farraj and Daud across Sinai to Cairo.	11:30	2:01:30 (57%)
J	Lawrence debriefs Gen. Allenby and tries to resign; Allenby persuades him to stay on and the two plan the next campaign. *Unifying Aspect*: Dramatic Tension. *Protagonist*: Allenby. *Objective*: To persuade Lawrence to return to Arabia.	12:04	2:12:34 (62%)

INTERMISSION

K	American reporter Jackson Bentley arrives in Aqaba and confers with Feisal, then observes Lawrence leading an attack on a Turkish train. Lawrence is wounded by a dying Turkish soldier; in the aftermath, Col. Brighton warns Lawrence that the thievery and desertion must stop. *Unifying Aspect*: Dramatic Tension. *Protagonist*: Bentley. *Objective*: A newspaper story about Lawrence.	13:20	2:25:54 (69%)
L	Lawrence leads another attack on a train, in which horses are being transported. Auda takes the horses and most of his men, leaving Lawrence's force very small. He struggles on with the campaign, losing Farraj to an accident in which he must be the executioner. *Unifying Aspect*: Dramatic Tension. *Protagonist*: Lawrence. *Objective*: To keep the campaign going.	10:02	2:35:56 (73%)
M	Col. Brighton and Gen. Allenby confer about Lawrence's chances of taking Deraa; Lawrence challenges his small group to walk on water with him; in Deraa, Lawrence's effort to raise a revolt is quickly thwarted; he is captured, tortured, and in the aftermath, tells Ali he is abandoning the cause. *Unifying Aspect*: Dramatic Tension. *Protagonist*: Lawrence. *Objective*: To foment revolt in Deraa.	15:22	2:51:18 (81%)

Second Culmination: Lawrence's failure at Deraa.

ACT III

N	The main tension—will Lawrence succeed in uniting the Arabs against the Turks—has essentially been resolved in the negative. In the third act, hope for this	8:37	2:59:55 (85%)

is revived with a new, specific focus: the campaign against Damascus, and the achievement of self-government (i.e., overthrowing the British as well as the Turks). In this sequence, Lawrence returns to British headquarters, where he discovers the secret pact the British and French have signed to rule Arabia after the war; he tries a second time to resign. Gen. Allenby again persuades him to stay on and lead the Arabs in an attack on Damascus. *Unifying Aspect*: Dramatic Tension. *Protagonist*: Lawrence. *Objective*: To resign.

O	Lawrence leads the Arabs on an attack on a fleeing Turkish column, then on into Damascus. *Unifying Aspect*: Dramatic Tension. *Protagonist*: Lawrence. *Objective*: To lead the Arabs to Damascus before the British Army gets there.	14:50	3:14:45 (92%)
P	Lawrence tries in vain to get the Arabs to unite in governing Damascus; in the end, Feisal is able to achieve partial victory and Lawrence returns to England. *Unifying Aspect*: Dramatic Tension. *Protagonist*: Lawrence. *Objective*: To establish an independent Arab government in Damascus.	17:44	3:32:29 (100%)

Resolution: **Lawrence fails to achieve his objective of freedom for the Arabs.**

The Graduate: Passive Main Character

The "passive main character" poses a vexing problem for screenwriters. As detailed in Chapter 1, the most commonly used tool in engaging audience attention is dramatic tension, which relies on a character who actively strives to achieve an objective. The implication is that a passive main character—one with little or no desire and/or little interest in achieving an objective—is a poor choice of protagonist and should be avoided.

The only problem with this argument is that some great films have been made with passive main characters, among them *Stalag 17* (1953), *Being There* (1979), and, in the present study, *The Graduate* (1967). It is thus useful to remember that a writer is confined not by rules or formulae but only by the need to keep an audience wondering what is going to happen next. In the case of *The Graduate*, the tool used to achieve this, in the central part of the film, is dramatic irony.

While it is certainly true that dramatic tension is used in the first act—seduction—and in the last act—Ben's famous pursuit of Elaine—in Act II, the story is propelled primarily by fear in the audience of what will happen when Ben's secret is revealed, and hope that he will be able to keep it concealed. While he clearly wants sex, he doesn't strive for it, and his partner is willing, so there is no obstacle to getting it— other than the care he needs to take to avoid being found out. Later, when he meets Elaine, his objective is to ditch her, and again obstacles are minimal. The excitement, again, comes from his fear of discovery.

As to sequence structure, the film is noteworthy in having only seven—two in the first act, three in the second, and two in the third.

Sequence A: Escape

The eighteen-minute opening sequence is unified by an escape attempt: Ben trying to escape from the party, once he achieves this, from the seduction attempt by Mrs. Robinson. Aside from being engaging, it is also a *tour de force* in exposition, establishing not only Ben's immediate situation, but also the web of relationships around him. Although the film is a comedy, it veers into searing pain in the second half as these relationships are ripped apart.

The picture opens with both a visual puzzle—a close-up of a young man, seen in the title sequence, who is sitting by an aquarium in such a way that it appears he's underwater—and a verbal puzzle: an offscreen voice asking the man, "What's the matter?" Very quickly, a certain amount of dramatic tension is introduced—the parents want Ben to come downstairs, and he doesn't want to.

During this conversation, the *exposition* as ammunition approach (see text box, page 22) is used. In trying to persuade Ben to come downstairs, Ben's father reveals that guests are downstairs, that they're all good friends of the family who have known him since he was born. Ben in turn expresses concern about his future. When Ben's mother enters and asks if anything's wrong, Ben's father says "no"—yielding insight into the family system: Ben's expressed needs are ignored.

After Ben is conveyed downstairs, the scene plays out as a classic escape, with Ben making three attempts to get out, the first two thwarted by suffocating guests, before he succeeds at last and closes the door in an apparent victory.

Ben's quiet moments alone—a classic aftermath scene—give the audience its first glimpse of a possible outcome to the sequence—Ben succeeds. Mrs. Robinson arrives after a brief respite, though, and the conflict resumes. It's worth noting that Ben's attempts to persuade Mrs. Robinson to leave him alone are constrained by their relationship, which has been carefully set up in the preceding four minutes: she is not only an adult, but a lifelong acquaintance and family friend. He can't just blow her off.

Soon enough, she does go away, giving Ben another apparent victory before she returns once more and asks for the ride home, an obligation from which Ben cannot escape. This brief interlude of apparent success is actually the second glimpse of a plausible outcome to the sequence: Ben succeeding in escaping.

During the next seven minutes, although Ben remains the "protagonist" of the sequence and his objective remains the same—escape—he plays an increasingly passive role, and Mrs. Robinson's attempt at seduction shapes the action. Drawing on their long-standing relationship and her parent-like authority, Mrs. Robinson cajoles him into keeping her company, plies him with a drink, puts on music, and opens up to him. Ben guesses her game—seduction—and calls her on it, giving the audience a glimpse of yet another outcome to the sequence: he confronts Mrs. Robinson and is able to go home.

Mrs. Robinson uses superb manipulative skills to salvage the situation, again drawing on her position as parent/authority figure. With Ben embarrassed by his accusation, Mrs. Robinson gets him upstairs on the pretext of looking at Elaine's portrait—a subtle introduction of one of the major characters.

Mrs. Robinson resumes and escalates her seduction attempt in the intimacy of Elaine's room, but overplays her hand and Ben again calls her on it, this time leaving the room and going downstairs. This represents the fourth glimpse at a positive outcome for Ben.

Mrs. Robinson again salvages the situation with a request that Ben bring her purse, and this leads to her final, most explicit attempt at seduction, confronting him in the bedroom, naked, and inviting him to call any time—a dangling cause picked up in the second sequence. Ben rejects her one last time as Mr. Robinson arrives.

Now Ben has successfully resisted seduction, and the "third act" of the sequence commences: escape from *Mr.* Robinson. The four-minute scene is propelled by dramatic irony: audience knowledge of what has just happened between Ben and Mrs. Robinson. The richness of the irony is explored in Mr. Robinson's advice to Ben to sow some wild oats and "have a good time with the girls," and his remark to Mrs. Robinson that Ben is the type who needs to fight women off. Mr. Robinson's remarks also reinforce the impression of the principles' close-knit relationships, reminding Ben that their fathers are partners and that he'd watched Ben grow up.

The sequence ends with the telegraphing of Elaine's arrival back home, and a dangling cause uttered ironically by Mrs. Robinson: "I'll see you soon, I hope."

Sequence B: Consummating the Affair

The second sequence, which runs just under seventeen minutes, is centered on Ben's desire to follow through on Mrs. Robinson's invitation to have an affair. While this is structured as dramatic tension—protagonist with an objective—the tension derived from it is primarily ironic—fear that the affair will be found out. This need for secrecy, and Ben's ambivalence, can be seen as the primary obstacles.

The sequence begins with a three-minute birthday-party scene, which contributes to the tension of the sequence only in the sense that it dramatizes how empty and unhappy Ben's life is with his parents. As in the opening scene of the picture, they ignore his feelings and in this case embarrass him. The scene has dramatic tension—Mr. Robinson trying to get Ben out of the house—and provides a good example of retardation: half of the scene elapses between when Ben's voice is heard from inside the house, and when his father finally throws open the door and reveals the birthday present (scuba outfit) Ben is wearing. After he gets into the pool, an aftermath scene ensues, in which Ben stands quietly isolated at the bottom.

The following scene picks up on the dangling causes left over from the first sequence—Mrs. Robinson's offer to see Ben any time, and her expressed hope that she'll see him soon. Ben is on the phone to Mrs. Robinson, inviting her to a drink at the Taft Hotel. He is smoking—a payoff of a remark made in the opening sequence by Mrs. Robinson ("The track star doesn't smoke.") Mrs. Robinson replies to his invitation by saying she'll be there in an hour, an appointment that helps to frame the following scene, which involves nothing more than Ben waiting for her.

The "first act" of the sequence is essentially set with these few words, since the bulk of the setup—Mrs. Robinson's attempted seduction and her invitation to him to call to consummate an affair—occurred in the previous sequence.

After Ben speaks to Mrs. Robinson, he wanders around the lobby of the hotel, encounters the suspicious clerk, awkwardly introduces himself at a party where he's not a guest, then finally enters a bar and waits for her. When Mrs. Robinson arrives, Ben is tasked by her with getting a room, generating a scene propelled by simple dramatic tension, the object being the room, the obstacle being the suspicious hotel clerk, and the emotion springing from fear of discovery.

Ben succeeds in getting the room, then Mrs. Robinson makes an appointment to meet him there in five minutes. This appointment sustains anticipation through Ben's long approach to the room along the corridor of the hotel, and his nervous preparations, which include a tooth brushing that pays off some dialogue planted earlier.

With Mrs. Robinson's arrival in the room, the "third act" of the sequence is at hand. The tension surrounding Ben's getting the room is resolved; now there remains only for him to consummate the affair. His awkwardness and deep ambivalence provide the obstacles to this objective. The scene culminates with Ben calling it off, in the process articulating his moral concerns and the web of relationships that will be endangered if they are discovered. These issues, implied till now but here made explicit, provide the stakes underlying the hopes and fears of the second act.

At this point in the scene, Mrs. Robinson manipulates him once more, displaying skill she'd shown in the opening sequence. She questions his manhood, and he rises to the challenge. When the room goes dark, the sequence ends, and music (which, as in *Toy Story,* serves as a curtain) signals the transition from Sequence B to Sequence C, and from first act to second.

Sequence C: The Affair

The third sequence, a short one at just over seven minutes, commences with a four-minute musical interlude portraying Ben drifting through the summer and the affair. There are several hints of conflict between him and his parents, a conflict that is developed during the scenes that follow.

During a confrontation between Ben and his father, the Robinsons arrive, creating some ironic tension, and Mr. Robinson, for a second time, tells Ben that Elaine will be coming to town soon, and asks him to give her a call—a dangling cause picked up during the next two sequences.

In the subsequent scene with his mother, the ironic tension that spikes at the tail end of the scene with the Robinsons is developed further. Here, she inquires about his late-night activities, and he struggles to keep cool to preserve the secret.

Sequence D: The Confrontation

Sequence D consists of a single scene that runs over nine minutes in length. It is something of an anomaly because it has little causal connection to the previous sequence beyond a sense that Ben is taking his father's advice and becoming more active—though not on his career or studies, but on his relationship with Mrs. Robinson.

The scene/sequence is unified by dramatic tension: Ben's desire to connect with Mrs. Robinson on more than a sexual level, and Mrs. Robinson's resistance to this. It follows a three-act structure, with Ben declaring his intent to talk to her, and succeeding in this regard, three minutes into the scene; a resulting culmination, or turning point, when their discussion turns to Elaine and escalates into a confrontation; and a resolution to the tension when the two agree to have sex after all, with Ben now the one refusing to talk.

Mrs. Robinson's warnings to Ben that he promise never to take out Elaine are dangling causes that pick up on Mr. Robinson's previous suggestions to Ben, and are realized in the subsequent sequence, which will center on the problem of Elaine.

Sequence E: Elaine

This fifteen-minute sequence is centered on Elaine's intrusion into Ben's life. As in Sequence C, the tool used to engage the audience is primarily dramatic irony. Ben clearly has a dramatic objective—alienate Elaine—but no dramatically compelling obstacle presents itself beyond perhaps creating waves in his relationship with Mr. Robinson and his parents. What generates the tension is the fear that Elaine will discover Ben's secret. The last third of the sequence echoes the last third of the movie as a whole: Ben pursues Elaine. Mrs. Robinson interferes, though, and in revealing the affair to Elaine, she resolves the ironic tension of the sequence.

The sequence begins with two simple dramatic scenes, which actually share the same line of dramatic tension: Ben's parents try to urge him to ask Elaine out. When he refuses, Ben's mother threatens to invite all the Robinsons over for dinner, forcing Ben's hand. Ben's decision to ask Elaine out, and Mrs. Robinson's enraged response, pick up on dangling causes in several previous sequences.

When Ben arrives at the Robinsons to pick up Elaine, the scene is rich with ironic tension, as Ben is fearful of Mrs. Robinson's reaction, and Mr. Robinson is completely oblivious to what is going on behind his back. Here, Ben telegraphs his agenda to Mrs. Robinson—he plans to treat Elaine to dinner and a drink and bring her right back. This effectively ends the "sequence first act," as the main character's objective is clear and he sets out to realize it.

Ben takes Elaine on a fast car ride and provides minimal verbal interaction, then leads her to a strip club, where she is humiliated. Her tears evoke a strong feeling of regret in him, and he pursues her and attempts to apologize for his rudeness. His apology extends into the next scene at a fast-food drive-in, where the two become better acquainted, and in the scene that follows this, when Ben stops his car in front of her house to let her off and it is apparent their relationship has improved considerably. Here, Ben decides not to drop her off after all—in violation of his own stated plan—and the two proceed to the Taft Hotel for a drink.

In the brief, comical scene that follows, many hotel employees recognize him and call him by the false name he'd given at the hotel initially. Ben is thus exposed to Elaine as having had an affair, though he doesn't reveal with whom. The scene is imbued with dramatic irony—fear that the truth will come out. Ben confesses his liking for her; she reveals the feeling is mutual, and the two make an appointment for a date the following day.

Figure 14. A considerable portion of *The Graduate* (1967) is driven by dramatic irony—the audience's fear that Ben's illicit affair will be found out. This scene, in Sequence E, explores the problem in a comic way—many of the Taft Hotel's workers identify Ben as "Mr. Gladstone." The fear is that Elaine will figure it out. (Frame enlargement)

The next scene features preparation by contrast—Ben is shown driving his car in the rain, a box of flowers ready, anticipating his date with Elaine. He stops the car and a woman gets inside—who is abruptly shown to be not Elaine but rather Mrs. Robinson. She warns him never to see Elaine again; he refuses to obey; she threatens to expose the affair. He rushes off to get to Elaine before Mrs. Robinson does.

Ben tries desperately to get Elaine out of the house before Mrs. Robinson arrives, but he fails, and the truth comes out at last. This shattering scene of recognition resolves at last the ironic tension created at the commencement of the affair at the end of the first act, and thus marks not only the end of the sequence but also the end of the second act. The main tension has been resolved in the negative: Ben has failed to keep the secret.

Sequence F: The Quest Begins

As in the transition between the first and second acts, a musical interlude provides the curtain that separates the second and third acts. This interlude fulfills the function of an aftermath scene, a pause that helps the audience digest the shattering power of the scene of recognition that just preceded it. Ben remains passive, either lying around in his room, or watching Elaine from a distance. There are some hints of change in him, though—his hair is left more tousled and his makeup suggests fatigue.

At the end of this interlude, Ben announces to his parents that he is marrying Elaine. This dangling cause propels the last third of the movie. In fact, the brief scene with his parents constitutes what might be considered the "first act"—or setup—of the entire third act of the film. All the exposition has been taken care of—the audience is aware of who Ben and Elaine are, all their relationships, and the history between them. In the scene with his parents, Ben reveals that he hasn't told anyone about his intention to marry Elaine, not even Elaine, and that in fact Elaine doesn't like him. The obstacles to his objective are thus laid out, so immediately upon conclusion of the scene, the third act tension—will Ben succeed in marrying Elaine?—is initiated. Dramatic tension at last takes over forcefully as the chief tool used to engage audience attention and more than two-thirds of the way into the movie, it takes on a more traditional structure.

Ben also tells his parents he is leaving for Berkeley that day, and has a suitcase in his hand, an appointment that is paid off in the next scene, when Ben is shown driving north to Berkeley. The inter-act musical interlude is picked up again during this drive and in several scenes afterward, when Ben is shown watching Elaine from a distance.

The interlude ends when Ben moves into an apartment, then pursues Elaine on a bus and makes his first contact with her. His pursuit meets her immediate resistance, intensifying the dramatic tension, and at the zoo—a destination telegraphed on their bus ride—Ben encounters his first big obstacle, Carl, Elaine's boyfriend. After Elaine and Carl depart, Ben remains quietly behind, in an aftermath scene that reinforces the strong emotions he feels for Elaine, and the dimension of the problem he faces in realizing his objective.

Ben is next shown shaving in his room, when Elaine visits him and confronts him about his appearance in Berkeley. In the course of the argument, Elaine reveals that her mother claims that Ben raped her; Ben sets her straight on this and an important obstacle to his objective is removed. In the process, though, Ben is ordered by his landlord to leave, setting up a new obstacle, and as a consequence he seems to lose his drive to his objective. He begins to pack and tells her he's not in the mood to talk. In response, Elaine unexpectedly tells him she wants him to stay, at least until he has a definite plan. This significant development is punctuated by a short aftermath scene, in which Ben watches her exit the apartment and walk down the street.

Figure 15. "I'm going to marry Elaine Robinson." With this dangling cause, Ben launches the dramatic tension that unifies the entirety of the third act of *The Graduate* (1967): will he succeed in tracking down Elaine and getting her to marry him? (Frame enlargement)

Elaine returns that night in what amounts to a continuation of the previous scene; here, the roles are reversed, as she has become the pursuer. She requests that he kiss her, and he asks her to marry him. She seems open to the idea, and tells him she'll think about it—a dangling cause picked up in the following scene.

This amounts to the end of the "second act" of the sequence, a turning point where Elaine proves to be open to the idea of marriage, and now it becomes simply a matter of Ben pursuing her so as to close the deal. For the rest of the sequence, he pursues her and badgers her about getting married, first outside a classroom, then in a gymnasium, where she announces she's seeing her boyfriend Carl that night to discuss marriage. Ben's emphatic reaction—a loud "What?"—is a dialogue hook that is picked up in the following scene at the library, where he asks Elaine how he proposed and where—suggesting a car—a payoff of the dialogue earlier in which Mrs. Robinson revealed Elaine was conceived in the back of a Ford.

The sequence reaches an apparently positive resolution outside Elaine's classroom, where Ben asks her if they'll get married the next day, and she replies, "Maybe we are, maybe we're not"—a dialogue hook that, combined with the kiss at the end of the scene, knits it to the seventh and final sequence of the picture.

Sequence G: A Chase In The Final Reel

This fifteen-minute sequence, which centers on Ben's quest to get to Elaine before she marries Carl, begins with a classic scene of preparation by contrast: Ben proceeds to buy an engagement ring, flowers, and some other presents, giving the impression of an impending wedding. This expectation ends in the surprise twist: Mr. Robinson is waiting for him in his room.

Mr. Robinson provides a grave obstacle to Ben's ambitions; he informs Ben that he's already contacted Elaine to make sure Ben can't get to her; the scene then ends with a dangling cause—a threat that if Ben ever tries to pursue Elaine he'll be arrested—which hooks the scene into the next.

Ben tries to contact Elaine by phone, then in person; he discovers she has left school, and gets a note from her apologizing and explaining her parents' anger at her. Ben next heads south to the Robinson house, where he learns from Mrs. Robinson that Elaine will soon be married.

This deadline serves to intensify the remaining dramatic tension, and disclosure to Ben (and the audience) marks the end of the "first act" of the sequence: Ben's objective and principal obstacle are made clear. Before leaving Mrs. Robinson, Ben warns her that he will find her and Mrs. Robinson expresses doubt—dialogue that hooks the scene into the next one, which finds Ben speeding back to Berkeley.

Ben stops at Carl's frat house, where he gets confirmation that Carl is indeed getting married, and finds out where: Santa Barbara. Ben resumes his speedy quest to Santa Barbara, where he stops at a gas station to try to find out where the wedding is taking place. As he hops back into his car, the gas station attendant asks him if he needs gas—a motif paid off in the following scene, when he runs out, short of the church.

Ben runs the final distance, only to discover the wedding has just ended, presenting an apparently negative resolution to the sequence and film as a whole. Upon seeing Ben, though, and surveying the angry reaction of her family, Elaine chooses him and the two make a memorable escape from the church.

They mount a bus, and sit wordlessly in one of the great aftermath scenes in cinema history.

THE GRADUATE
Sequence Breakdown

Seq.	Description	Length	Running Time
	ACT I		
A	Benjamin flees from the party, fends off Mrs. Robinson, unwinds with Mr. Robinson afterward (excluding opening titles). *Unifying Aspect*: Dramatic Tension. *Protagonist*: Ben. *Objective*: To be alone.	18:05	18:05 (18%)
	***Point of attack:* Mrs. Robinson tries to seduce Ben.**		
B	Benjamin endures humiliation with his scuba gear, then initiates the affair with Mrs. Robinson at the Taft Hotel. *Unifying Aspect*: Dramatic Tension. *Protagonist*: Ben. *Objective*: Sex.	16:56	35:01 (34%)
	***Predicament:* Benjamin is having an affair with the wife of his father's partner.**		
	ACT II **(Main tension: Will Benjamin be able to continue his affair without being found out?)**		
C	Musical montage portraying the affair; Ben's Mom becomes suspicious. *Unifying Aspect*: Dramatic Tension. *Protagonist*: Ben. *Objective*: To conceal the affair.	7:45	42:46 (42%)
D	Ben tries to engage Mrs. Robinson in talk; she warns him against asking out Elaine. *Unifying Aspect*: Dramatic Tension. *Protagonist*: Ben. *Objective*: To communicate with Mrs. Robinson.	9:13	51:59 (51%)
	***First Culmination:* Ben asks Elaine out (53:11—52%).**		
E	Ben's Dad suggests he ask Elaine out; under threat of a party he does so; he takes her on a date, falls in love, Mrs. Robinson ambushes him and the truth comes out to Elaine. *Unifying Aspect*: Dramatic Tension. *Protagonist*: Ben. *Objective*: To deal with Elaine.	15:20	1:07:19 (66%)
	***Second Culmination:* Ben has fallen in love with Elaine but his affair apparently wipes out any hope for him (1:07:19—66%).**		
	ACT III		
F	The main tension has been resolved—the affair was discovered—but a new tension has taken its place: Ben wants to marry Elaine. This sequence (and act) begins with a musical montage, proceeds with Ben's declaration that he is going to marry Elaine; he pursues her in Berkeley, at last gets her to say "Maybe." *Unifying Aspect*: Dramatic Tension. *Protagonist*: Ben. *Objective*: To get Elaine to marry him.	19:46	1:27:05 (85%)

| G | Benjamin buys a ring—then finds his plans thwarted by the arrival of Mr. Robinson. Benjamin frantically pursues Elaine—first to L.A., then back to Berkeley, and finally down to Santa Barbara for the finale. *Unifying Aspect*: Dramatic Tension. *Protagonist*: Ben. *Objective*: Elaine. | 15:20 | 1:42:25 (100%) |

Resolution: **Ben and Elaine make it to the bus.**

Epilogue: **Ben and Elaine on the bus.**

One Flew Over the Cuckoo's Nest: Midpoint Reversal

This shattering 1975 winner of five Academy Awards is powered primarily by the tool of dramatic tension—the desire of one character, R. P. McMurphy, to beat the system to avoid labor at the work farm. McMurphy runs into some substantial obstacles while in pursuit of his objective, but in the end his own "flaw"—his basic decency, humanity, and impulse to inspire joy in the life of others—brings him down. Thus, unlike some of the other pictures studied in this volume that are propelled by dramatic tension, the protagonist's struggle toward his objective is somewhat muted in *Cuckoo's Nest*. McMurphy is not constantly scheming for ways to beat the system; rather, he is constantly distracted from that objective by pursuing other kinds of activities that strike his fancy. As a consequence, the film has something of a more leisurely pace, and many of the scenes and sequences are not connected with a chain-like cause-and-effect aspect notable in other films studied herein.

The film is unified by place as well as dramatic tension: only one sequence takes place away from the state mental institution. With anticipation created by McMurphy's objective, and the sense of unity shored up by consistency of place, the filmmakers are free to explore the subject manner in an ensemble fashion, and develop several subplots exploring the theme of freedom, among these the story of the Chief and that of Billy Bibbit.

In terms of sequence structure, the film is unusual in that it has nine of them—the third act has three instead of the typical two. Consistent with the leisurely pace of the film, three of the nine are unified not by dramatic tension but by events or actions.

Sequence A: The New Arrival

The picture begins with a series of visual puzzles, accompanied by music that plants, subtly, a Native American motif. The opening image is that of an automobile approaching at either dawn or dusk, and is followed by the images of patients asleep inside an institution. The occupants of the automobile and their purpose are left a mystery, and the connection with this and the sleeping inmates is not at first clear.

Soon enough the film shows what appears to be the ward of a hospital coming to life, with the antagonist of the picture, Nurse Ratched, introduced in what appears to be the flow of a normal morning. Patients are treated to "Medication Time," accompanied by calming classical music.

When the mysterious automobile arrives at the institution and McMurphy is taken out and released into the custody of the medical personnel, the pieces of the puzzle begin to fall into place. When Nurse Ratched and her assistant Nurse Pilbow start inventorying the contents of McMurphy's bag, it is clear he will be staying at the institution for a while. McMurphy casually makes his rounds of the ward, introducing himself first to the Chief (an act that signals the Chief's coming significance in the story), then to some of the other inmates who play cards. In this scene, the motifs of card playing and of McMurphy's "dirty" set of cards are planted.

Eight and a half minutes into the opening sequence, McMurphy arrives at an intake interview with Dr. Spivey, and the remaining questions raised by the opening puzzle are answered: McMurphy has a criminal record and has been sent to the mental institution from the work farm for evaluation to see if he's mentally ill. There is also a suspicion that McMurphy is faking his mental illness in order to get off work duty. Although it's impossible to know for sure, McMurphy's mischievous nature, manifest in this scene and the previous one, suggest that he may indeed be trying to fake the mental illness.

During the course of the scene, the motif of fishing is planted (through McMurphy's observations about a photo of Dr. Spivey holding up a big fish), as is McMurphy's propensity for getting into fistfights. The scene (and sequence) end with Dr. Spivey telegraphing the future plan (McMurphy will remain there for a while for evaluation), and with McMurphy's declaration: "I think it's time we got to the bottom of R. P. McMurphy"—a dangling cause that is picked up and developed throughout the rest of the picture.

Sequence B: Getting Acquainted

The second sequence in large measure continues both the leisurely pace of the first and its general thrust: McMurphy is getting acquainted with his new home. Like Sequence A, it is unified more by an event than by dramatic tension built from the desire of a protagonist. What distinguishes the three scenes of Sequence B from Sequence A is the introduction of important information at the Dr. Spivey scene, which amounts to the point of attack of the picture. McMurphy's background and his apparent intent (to fake mental illness) infuses the subsequent scenes with a subtle ironic tension.

It could be argued that the first act of the movie as a whole ends with the interview scene in Dr. Spivey's office, because it is at this point that McMurphy's objective is substantially revealed, and the subsequent scenes find him pursuing this objective albeit at a leisurely pace. One important ingredient is still missing at that point, though: Nurse Ratched. She is introduced in the first sequence but only in a very cursory way; the central role she plays in the institution and in the story has yet to be made clear, and the initiation of her relationship with McMurphy is the subject of the second sequence (she is present in all three scenes).

The sequence opens with the first of the group therapy scenes; Nurse Ratched is the protagonist of the scene and her desire is to lead the discussion. After overcoming initial resistance, the discussion occurs—degenerating into a gruesome verbal slugfest. The scene ends with a brief aftermath beat: McMurphy and Nurse Ratched making eye contact across the room.

The film then switches to the recreational area of the institution, with no causal connection to the previous scene. McMurphy notes the barbed wire fence and a school bus loading some of the patients just outside the perimeter—planting two motifs paid off in Sequence D. The protagonist of the scene is McMurphy; his objective is to teach the Chief to play basketball. While he is trying (and, ultimately, failing at this task) Nurse Ratched is shown watching his activities from a high window.

The third and final scene of the sequence finds McMurphy and the other patients playing cards, paying off the motif established earlier. Two other important motifs are planted in the scene: gambling for cigarettes and McMurphy's interest in the World Series. McMurphy is the protagonist of the scene, and his objective is to play cards; the obstacles consist of the mental incapacity of some of the patients and the loud music. In trying to turn down the music, McMurphy has his first direct confrontation with Nurse Ratched, which ends with him pretending to swallow a pill she insists he take. Afterward, he makes a bet with the others that in one week he'll "put a bug so far up her ass she won't know whether to shit or wind a wristwatch." This dangling cause serves as a dialogue hook into the next sequence, where it is played out over the issue of a baseball game.

The end of the scene marks the end of the first act. All the principal characters have been introduced, McMurphy's objective has been made clear, and his chief obstacle—Nurse Ratched—has been introduced as well. The main tension—will McMurphy be able to beat the system?—is now in play.

Sequence C: "Want to watch the World Series?"

This seventeen-minute sequence is the first in the picture unified by dramatic tension. McMurphy is the protagonist, and his objective is to get the schedule changed so everyone can watch the World Series. It begins with a strong undercurrent of dramatic irony—the audience knows about McMurphy's bet to antagonize Nurse Ratched but she is, of course, unaware.

The opening scene is the second of the group therapy sessions, which finds McMurphy clean-shaven and wearing a white shirt in contrast to his earlier more disheveled appearance. The choice of costume suggests he is concealing his true intent from Nurse Ratched, since his clean-cut appearance belies what we know about his darker, more mischievous nature. McMurphy raises the issue of the World Series, and is rebuffed when only two other patients vote with him on the issue. His attempt to arrange the schedule so he can watch the World Series amounts to the end of the "first act" of the sequence.

Afterward in the tub room, McMurphy broods over his defeat, then makes a second attempt to see the game—by betting the others that he can lift a plumbing fixture and throw it through a window, effecting his escape to a bar downtown. He fails to lift the fixture and loses the bet—and simultaneously plants an important motif (the plumbing fixture) and demonstrates his willingness to try, and to take risks.

The next scene finds McMurphy and the patients back in group therapy, with Billy describing his attempt to propose to a girl he was in love with. This dialogue initiates Billy's subplot, providing exposition about his sensitivity, his interest in girls, his attempt at suicide, his overbearing, suffocating mother, and that mother's relationship to Nurse Ratched.

Cheswick interrupts the conversation and re-introduces the World Series. This time, inspired by McMurphy's example, all nine members of the group vote in favor of changing the schedule. Unfortunately, Nurse Ratched advises McMurphy that he needs one more vote—from one of the "chronics" who occupy the other parts of the ward. McMurphy frantically tries to persuade one to raise his hand; when at last the Chief does so, Nurse Ratched declares the session closed and offers to let him bring it up the following day.

The resolution of the tension of the sequence is negative—McMurphy fails to get his way—but in the last few minutes of it he pretends to watch the game on the television, igniting excitement on the part of the other patients, much to Nurse Ratched's disapproval.

Sequence D: A Fishing Expedition

This sixteen-minute sequence is again unified by dramatic tension. It is also the only sequence that takes place primarily outside the institution. It begins with McMurphy in Dr. Spivey's office for a follow-up interview, which serves as a recapitulation scene—we discover that McMurphy has been at the institution for four weeks, and that he's unhappy with Nurse Ratched, who plays a "rigged game." It also picks up on an issue left dangling after the first sequence—the question of whether or not McMurphy is faking mental illness. Dr. Spivey tells him he sees no evidence of such illness and opines that McMurphy has been putting them on. McMurphy objects to the doctor's conclusion, and his desire to "prove" his insanity is what drives the sequence. The scene with Dr. Spivey thus serves as the "first act" of the sequence, setting up its tension.

The film cuts to the the recreation area, where McMurphy enlists the Chief's help in climbing over the fence—paying off McMurphy's observation in the first sequence about the fence, a nearby tree and the bus waiting just beyond. The Chief's smiling reaction hints that McMurphy is having an effect on him.

McMurphy hijacks the bus with the other patients onboard, picks up his girlfriend Candy and then takes them all to a marina, where he leads them onto a boat. Candy urges McMurphy to stop, warning him he'll wind up in jail again, to which McMurphy replies that they won't throw him in jail, because he's insane. This serves to reinforce for the audience McMurphy's intention in the sequence.

The harbormaster's objections to McMurphy's seizure of the boat provide the only remaining obstacle to him, after which the actual fishing trip is played more for comic effect and lacks true tension. During the fishing expedition, Billy's subplot is developed through his interest in Candy, and McMurphy's humanity—his desire to share joy with others—is dramatized in the way he teaches the other patients to fish, and the ensuing excitement when one of the fish actually bites.

Figure 16. "Sixty-eight days!" McMurphy brags in the first culmination of *One Flew Over the Cuckoo's Nest* (1975). The moment is a high point for him, and a reasonable glimpse of a possible outcome to the story: McMurphy succeeds in fooling the institution staff that he's insane, resulting a short, easy stay there before he is freed. Shortly after this, he discovers how wrong he is, and the film proceeds to its tragic resolution, the mirror opposite of the image here. (Frame enlargement)

The sequence ends with the yacht's return to the harbor, where the police and Dr. Spivey wait.

Sequence E: Midpoint Reversal

Another scene in Dr. Spivey's office opens the fifth sequence, where a group of doctors conclude that McMurphy is in fact mentally ill. Still, Dr. Spivey believes he should be sent back to the work farm, and, ironically, it is Nurse Ratched who finally persuades him to keep McMurphy at the institution where she can try to "help" him. Nurse Ratched, McMurphy's chief antagonist, is the one who hands him a victory he'd long sought.

The joy of McMurphy's victory is reinforced in the following scene, which takes place at the basketball court, where McMurphy leads the patients in a lively game against Robinson and the other attendants. After initial setbacks, the Chief comes to life and participates, bringing a sense of exhiliaration to McMurphy and his teammates. This scene and the one that follows mark the first culmination of the picture—and the first genuine glimpse of how it might reasonably end: McMurphy escapes from the work farm and then is released after a leisurely stay at the institution.

In fact, though, the basketball scene serves as a scene of preparation by contrast, raising the audience's hope so as to enhance the sense of disaster when the reversal comes in the next scene, when attendant Washington informs a jubilant McMurphy that he is going to stay at the institution indefinitely—not for only the 68 days McMurphy had believed. This shattering revelation reverses McMurphy's objective— from trying to persuade the staff he is mentally ill to trying to persuade them of the opposite. The main tension remains the same—trying to beat the system—but his means of beating it have now been reversed.

This revelation provides the end of the "first act" of the sequence— McMurphy's objective is to come to grips with the disaster he's brought on himself. He does this during the next scene, a group therapy session in which he complains to the others about not warning him he may be locked up forever. Here, he makes another astonishing discovery—that most of the patients are voluntary and can leave at any time. This leads McMurphy to berate them for their timidity, encouraging them that they are no more insane than the average person, and giving voice to the picture's main theme: freedom. McMurphy's exhortation falls on deaf ears, however, as the other patients remain preoccupied with their own petty issues. An errant cigarette leads to pandemonium and a fight between Washington and McMurphy, in which the Chief comes to McMurphy's aid. This fight further develops two relationships heading in opposite directions: the antagonism between McMurphy and Washington, and the budding friendship between McMurphy and the Chief.

The sequence ends with McMurphy's attempts to rectify his miscalculation leading to disaster.

Sequence F: Electroshock Therapy

This ten-minute sixth sequence is centered on an event: the electroshock therapy McMurphy suffers. It begins with a scene of preparation—McMurphy, the Chief, and Cheswick are brought to a hitherto unknown floor for some unknown purpose. The place is populated by a large number of seriously disturbed patients, lending it a forbidding aspect. As soon as Cheswick's name is called, he becomes hysterical, reinforcing the sense of impending doom.

While waiting his turn, McMurphy makes the third major discovery of the picture—that the Chief is neither deaf nor mute. McMurphy suggests to the Chief that they escape and head to Canada—a dangling cause that actually signals the end of the second act. The main tension—will McMurphy beat the system?—has been resolved in the negative, and now he's decided to escape the system altogether. The escape attempt is what provides the tension for the third act.

After McMurphy's electroshock therapy, he reappears in the ward looking like a lobotomized patient—a scene of preparation by contrast that accentuates the subsequent revelation that he's faking it. McMurphy's stunt also plants the motif of the lobotomy he later undergoes.

Sequence G: A Farewell Party

This sequence, at twenty-one minutes the longest in the picture, picks up almost immediately on the dangling cause from the previous one—McMurphy's decision to escape. However, consistent with the leisurely pacing of the previous sequences in the film, Sequence G is centered not on the escape attempt but on a party. The fact that McMurphy's objective is to escape, and that when the opportunity arises he not only throws a party but arranges for Billy to lose his virginity, is a stark dramatization of his basic "flaw"—his humanitarian impulse. It is not in his character to leave without sharing the joy with others.

The sequence opens with a television program revealing the time of year—Christmas—and with Nurse Ratched bidding everyone goodnight. Shortly after she leaves, McMurphy gets to work arranging his escape by use of a phone call. He then awakens the Chief and alerts him about his plans, but the latter reveals he's incapable of joining, and provides third-act exposition about his own background and that of his father—how his father was crushed by society the way the doctors and Nurse Ratched are trying to crush McMurphy. The conversation is both a foreshadowing of what is in store for McMurphy and important information about the Chief that helps to define his character arc.

As soon as the women arrive, McMurphy begins to deal with the orderly, Turkle, who provides the only obstacle to McMurphy's escape plans. When Turkle is neutralized with bribes and booze, the way is clear for McMurphy to flee, but he lingers instead and throws a party for the ward. Like the fishing expedition, the party scene is explored for its comic aspects. Other than the underlying fear that the party may be discovered—thwarting McMurphy's escape attempt—there is little in

Figure 17. In Sequence G of *One Flew Over the Cuckoo's Nest* (1975), McMurphy has everything he needs: an open window and nothing to stop him from going through it. The film could reasonably end here, but his fatal flaw—his humanity—leads him to a very different destiny. (Frame enlargement)

the way of tension. The comedy does serve to set up by contrast the very tragic events of the following sequence.

At last, when McMurphy begins to say his good-byes, the audience is given its second glimpse of a reasonable end to the picture: McMurphy succeeds in escaping. All the elements are there: Turkle is asleep, the window is open, and he has two accomplices with a getaway car.

McMurphy's farewell to Billy is what proves his undoing and provides the reversal that plunges the film to its tragic end. After setting up Billy with Candy and predicting that the event won't take long, a lingering aftermath scene occurs in which McMurphy falls asleep—an image that ends the sequence.

Sequence H: The Morning After

The second-last sequence of the picture is unified by dramatic tension. In this case, Nurse Ratched is the protagonist, and her objective is to reassert authority over the wayward patients. It also brings Billy's subplot to a tragic resolution.

The sequence opens with a shot of the open window in bright daylight, conveying instantly the disaster that has befallen McMurphy: he's fallen asleep and the prospects for his escape are now shattered. The attendants and Nurses Ratched and Pilbow soon arrive and size up the situation. Nurse Ratched orders the window closed, apparently sealing McMurphy's fate.

The attendants soon discover Billy still in bed with Candy. Ratched berates him and threatens to tell his mother about what he's done— paying off the motif of her relationship with Billy's mother planted earlier.

When Billy is dragged away kicking and screaming, McMurphy has another opportunity to escape—by unlocking the window using keys he'd stolen from Turkle. Even though he's interrupted by Washington, he still has one last chance to climb through the window when Nurse Pilbow screams. McMurphy remains behind, and that opportunity is lost forever. He attacks Nurse Ratched upon discovering that Billy has killed himself; the sequence ends with an aftermath scene: Ratched struggling to breathe after McMurphy has been pulled off of her.

Reversals

Novice screenwriters tend to fall into one of two camps: those who center their work on character and write the screenplay based on where the character seems to want to take it, and those who center their wok on plot, and force the characters to adhere to that plot no matter what. Scripts written under the first assumption risk being vivid but shapeless, and under the latter, well-organized but empty. The most successful approach to screenwriting is a combination of the two, and the *reversal* is an example of that combination in action.

A screenplay must persuade the reader that its characters are truly alive, so it is essential for a screenwriter to allow his or her created characters total freedom to act in any manner true to the characters' nature. But while a screenwriter should not constrain a character's action, he or she does have complete control over the *circumstances* around which a character acts, and clever manipulation of circumstances is what can make a character who is truly alive adhere to the demands of plot.

An example of this action can be seen in Sequence H of *Cuckoo's Nest,* in the form of two reversals. On the night of the party, McMurphy has the window open and freedom in his grasp, and everything about his character suggests that his desire to go through that window will be irresistible—yet he hesitates. The reason is the circumstances, namely, the untimely ''good-bye'' he says to Billy, whose sexual innocence inspires him to delay his exit (thus the *reversal*). The following morning, McMurphy again has the window open and a car waiting outside, but again circumstances—this time in the form of Billy's suicide—pull him back into the plot.

Some writers believe if they give a character total freedom, he or she will leave the story and thus ruin the script. But an imaginative screenwriter can always contrive the circumstances to get the character back.

Sequence I: The Chief Flies Over the Cuckoo's Nest

The final sequence of the picture centers on the Chief's escape from the institution. It serves to resolve both the main story—McMurphy's fate—and one of the major subplots, that of the Chief.

It begins with the various patients playing cards and discussing McMurphy's fate; two competing versions are heard—one, that he's escaped, and two, that he's "upstairs" and meek as a lamb. The Chief is shown listening with concern, setting up his central role in the sequence. As to the others, their relative complacency suggests that McMurphy had no significant influence on them: no genuine change, and no freedom, lies in their future.

That night, McMurphy is returned to the ward, and the Chief tells him he's ready to escape now, and was just waiting for his return before doing so. The Chief quickly discovers that McMurphy has undergone a lobotomy and has thus been destroyed. Rather than leave him behind, the Chief kills him, then carries on the work McMurphy had begun, by using the plumbing fixture (which McMurphy had failed to lift earlier) to shatter the window and make his escape, paying off that significant motif. There follows an aftermath scene—Taber screaming for joy—before the final shot of the Chief making his way to freedom.

ONE FLEW OVER THE CUCKOO'S NEST
Sequence Breakdown

Seq.	Description	Length	Running Time
	ACT I		
A	Introduction of locale; McMurphy's arrival, initial card game and initial meeting with Dr. Spivey (includes opening titles). *Unifying Aspect*: Action (McMurphy's arrival).	14:07	14:07 (11%)
	Point of attack: Dr. Spivey suggests that McMurphy is faking insanity to get out of work duty.		
B	McMurphy has his first group therapy session, which ends in chaos, tries to teach basketball to the Chief, plays cards with the guys, confronts Nurse Ratched over the music, berates the others for being intimidated by Nurse Ratched and makes a bet that he can "put a bug up her ass." *Unifying Aspect*: Action (McMurphy getting acquainted, especially with Nurse Ratched).	17:30	31:37 (24%)
	Predicament: McMurphy is going to try to persuade the asylum staff that he's insane, and Nurse Ratched will be his chief adversary.		
	ACT II **(Main tension: Will McMurphy beat the system— will he stay at the asylum to avoid the work farm?)**		
C	McMurphy tries to persuade Nurse Ratched to change the work routine to allow them to watch the World Series. The vote fails. McMurphy tries to lift a heavy plumbing fixture and throw it through a wall so they can go see the World Series; he fails. At the next therapy session, he wins the vote only to have Ratched change the rules on him. He pretends to watch the game with the others. *Unifying Aspect*: Dramatic Tension. *Protagonist*: McMurphy. *Objective*: To win the battle of wills with Nurse Ratched over the World Series.	17:15	48:52 (37%)
D	McMurphy has a follow-up interview with Dr. Spivey and the other psychiatrists; he complains about Nurse Ratched. Spivey suggests that McMurphy is not mentally ill. Afterward, McMurphy leads the group on a fishing expedition in order to prove he's insane. *Unifying Aspect*: Dramatic Tension. *Protagonist*: McMurphy. *Objective*: To convince Dr. Spivey that he's insane.	16:47	1:05:39 (50%)
	First Culmination: Bathing scene—McMurphy thinks he's only got 68 days left (1:10:32—54%).		

| E | McMurphy has succeeded in persuading Dr. Spivey to keep him at the institution, but he soon discovers he may never leave it. He complains at the next therapy session to the others; a melee ensues. McMurphy's initial objective has now been achieved—he's succeeded in faking mental illness—but the consequence is unexpected and now he must reverse himself and try to get out, not stay in. *Unifying Aspect*: Dramatic Tension. *Protagonist*: McMurphy. *Objective*: To deal with the consequence of his success in persuading the staff he is insane. | 13:51 | 1:19:30 (60%) |
| F | McMurphy discovers that the Chief is neither deaf nor dumb. He vows they will somehow make their escape. McMurphy, Cheswick, and the Chief get shock therapy. *Unifying Aspect*: Dramatic Tension. *Protagonist*: McMurphy. *Objective*: To survive the shock therapy and prepare for his escape. | 10:14 | 1:29:44 (68%) |

Second Culmination: McMurphy sets escape plan in motion by phoning Candy.

ACT III

G	The main tension has been resolved—instead of trying to beat the system, McMurphy has decided to escape it entirely. The tension now shifts to: will this escape attempt succeed? In this sequence, McMurphy sets up his escape by means of the two women, then hangs around to throw a going-away party for the other patients. He does one more favor for Billy, then falls asleep just as escape is possible. *Unifying Aspect*: Event (the farewell party).	21:03	1:50:47 (84%)
H	Nurse Ratched and the porters return to find the place a shambles. She berates them, discovers Billy and Candy together, threatens to tell Billy's mother on him. He commits suicide; McMurphy loses his last chance to escape and instead attacks Ratched. *Unifying Aspect*: Dramatic Tension. *Protagonist*: Nurse Ratched. *Objective*: Reassert control over the patients.	11:31	2:02:18 (93%)
I	McMurphy returns to the ward lobotomized; the Chief kills him as an act of mercy, then makes his escape. *Unifying Aspect*: Dramatic Tension. *Protagonist*: The Chief. *Objective*: Escape.	9:14	2:11:32 (100%)

Resolution: McMurphy's irrepressible spirit has cost him his life, but it lives on in the Chief.

Air Force One: Eight Sequences Eight Miles Up

In this 1997 film, screenwriter Andrew Marlowe and director Wolfgang Petersen teamed to create a polished and sophisticated thriller that demonstrates effective use of the four main tools, with dramatic and ironic tension building across the range of sequences. The protagonist, President James Marshall, is also the protagonist of most of the sequences, and his objectives are an escalating series of solutions to difficulties that arise in his battle of brawn and wit with the hijackers. The sequences also carry two main subplots: the vice-president's drama with her subordinates in Washington, and the release of General Radek from prison in Russia.

Sequence A: Heading Home

The film begins with an action "teaser" that relies on pulling the audience into the story through mystery—who are these paratroopers and what do they want?—and enthralling them with rapid-fire action. This teaser lasts three minutes, and by the time it is over, the audience is ready for a solution to the mystery, which arrives in the form of a scene at a banquet hall in Moscow, where the Russian premier describes the capture of General Radek, and American President Marshall gives a speech outlining his new "get tough" approach to dictators. Although the initial action teaser has a very different subject matter and location than the rest of Sequence A, it serves as a setup for the sequence: President Marshall preparing to head back to the United States and pursue their new policy with Congress and the American people.

The sequence is unified by that action: the movement of Marshall and his entourage to Air Force One. Along the way, most of the principal characters are introduced, including the first family, the national security advisor, chief of staff, and deputy press secretary. The sequence is propelled forward through the tools of telegraphing and dangling causes: Marshall urging his national security advisor to "get behind" his new policy, and a warning from his advisors about a frosty reception in Congress. Meanwhile, the deputy press secretary lays out an itinerary for the Russian journalists, and later the president lays out his plans for watching a Notre Dame football game. These elements of the future serve the function of preparation by contrast—setting the audience up for a mundane political story that never actually transpires. The plane takes off just as Marshall joins his staff for a meeting, bringing the sequence to a close.

Sequence B: "How the hell did they get Air Force One?"

The second sequence picks up on a subtle dangling cause established in the first one: when the Russian news crew is introduced in Sequence A, its leader, a man later revealed to be Ivan Korshunov, questions a security official about why they need to have their bags inspected after they'd already done so. This is the first hint of a dark intent on the part of Korshunov, revisited and reinforced early in the second sequence when he looks at his watch and takes a furtive glance from a comrade next to him. Shortly after this, Gibbs, one of the secret service agents, murders three colleagues and sets the hijacking in motion. Gibbs's duplicity establishes a line of ironic tension that persists until the final few minutes of the film.

When the hijacking begins, the dramatic tension of the fifteen-minute sequence is established. Korshunov is the protagonist, and his objective is to hijack the plane and take the president hostage.

The chaotic hijacking scene presents the audience with its first glimpse of a reasonable outcome to the picture: that the plane lands at Ramstein Air Base and the hijacking is thwarted. Indeed, as the plane descends toward Ramstein, Korshunov reinforces what is at stake: if the plane lands, they are finished. The plane actually *does* land, but the hijackers are able to lift it back into the air, completing a significant reversal in the narrative.

As soon as the plane is airborne again and the tension thus resolved, Korshunov is told the president is no longer on board, having escaped in the pod. Carefully selected camera angles, which suggest the president has indeed escaped without actually showing him inside the pod, set up the second significant reversal in the sequence: that the president in fact never left the plane at all. When he is revealed to be still on board, both the second sequence and first act are brought to an end. All the principal characters have been introduced, Marshall has been established as the protagonist, and his objective is clear: he must defeat the hijackers and rescue the hostages. The fact that Marshall is still on board and the hijackers don't know it creates a line of dramatic irony as well, irony that parallels the main tension and is resolved along with the main tension at the end of Act II.

Sequence C: Marshall Gets His Gun

This thirteen-minute sequence is unified by dramatic tension: President Marshall's attempt to get a weapon and free the hostages. As is typical, its tension is very nearly that of the main tension of the picture as a whole. Soon after the sequence opens, Korshunov contacts Vice-President Kathryn Bennett and reveals his intention—a demand for the release of General Radek—and utters a threat—that he will execute one hostage every thirty minutes until his demand is met. This deadline creates anticipation for the duration of the sequence and into the next one.

After the conversation with Korshunov, the dramatic tension surrounding Marshall's hiding on the plane is partially resolved: the vice-president is told that the pod is empty. This leads to speculation that the president is still alive and a stowaway on Air Force One; one of the American generals tells the vice-president that they have the element of surprise on their side, and that Marshall may be their best chance—a dangling cause that hooks directly into the following scene, which finds Marshall beginning to move about secretly in the plane.

Marshall makes his way to the main deck, where he tries to make a phone call but finds the line disconnected. The film then switches back to Washington, where the vice-president and her advisors weigh the pros and cons of releasing Radek, developing further that subplot. The issue of authority is raised in the course of the conversation, initiating the subplot of political authority and succession in Washington.

The scene then switches back to Marshall, who plays a cat-and-mouse game with one of the hijackers before ambushing him and seizing his gun. At this point, the audience is given a second glimpse of a possible outcome to the picture—Marshall, now armed, has the keys to the room where the hostages are being held and seems about to release them. His attempt is thwarted by one of the hijackers, though, and in a classic reversal he winds up being hunted again after briefly enjoying the upper hand.

The sequence ends with Marshall escaping to the baggage compartment, armed but otherwise isolated and on the defensive, his existence, if not his identity, known to the hijackers.

Sequence D: Marshall Calls For Help

The fourth sequence immediately picks up on the deadline from the previous one: the execution of a hostage after thirty minutes. Korshunov goes to the room where the hostages are being kept and executes the national security advisor before ordering the First Lady and her daughter to come with him. The sequence itself is unified once again by dramatic tension: Marshall's desire to escape from his captor, in this case through the orchestrated use of an air-to-air missile fired by one of the American fighters.

After the death of the national security advisor, Korshunov torments Marshall's daughter while Marshall busies himself locating and assembling a satellite phone, which he uses to contact Washington. This victory is cut short with another reversal, as a hijacker immediately forces Marshall to disarm at gunpoint, establishing the predicament of the sequence and initiating its tension: can Marshall free himself from his captor? The president succeeds in surreptitiously ordering a missile attack from one of the escorting fighters, and after a fistfight, succeeds in freeing himself, bringing the sequence to a close.

While Marshall's victory here, shared with his subordinates in Washington by phone, is a positive development occurring at midpoint in the film, it is not quite as powerful or persuasive as the first culminations observed in other films analyzed in this volume. Still, it does provide at least a subtle glimpse of the resolution, with the president in charge of the nation again after narrowly escaping harm.

Sequence E: The Fuel Dump

This thirteen-minute sequence begins with a dangling cause: President Marshall telling the vice-president that "we've got to get this plane on the ground." Marshall quickly settles on the means by which he plans to achieve this end when he sees some milk leaking from a carton and gets the idea of draining the aircraft of fuel. His attempt to initiate a "fuel dump," and the hijackers' countermeasures, provide the dramatic tension that unifies the sequence.

Soon after Marshall starts to pursue his objective, an obstacle arises—Korshunov's attempt to smoke him out by threatening to kill the deputy press secretary. Marshall refuses to show himself, resulting in her execution; this causes him to redouble his efforts. He succeeds in cutting the appropriate wires with the help of technicians in the United States, resolving the dramatic tension of the sequence. Very quickly, though, he has to fight off a counterattack by Korshunov's men, who shoot their way into the avionics suits and stop the fuel dump. The sequence thus ends with only a partial victory by the protagonist.

Sequence F: Parachutes

The sixth sequence, which is roughly the same length as the previous three at just over twelve minutes, is unified by dramatic tension once again: Marshall's desire to get the hostages off the aircraft using the parachutes. The sequence begins with a surprise twist—Marshall is revealed to be holding a hijacker at gunpoint. Using the hijacker's keys, Marshall succeeds at last in reaching the hostages. This positive development is tempered by dramatic irony: the first person Marshall gives a weapon to is none other than Gibbs, the man the audience knows is a traitor.

The president briefs the others on the situation—he'd tried to get the plane down but the hijackers plan to refuel. One of his subordinates, Major Caldwell, immediately suggests they can use the refueling as an occasion to get the plane to a low enough altitude and speed to allow escape by way of parachutes. Although this will not solve *all* the problems—the First Lady and daughter are still held hostage—it will result in a substantial victory for Marshall. The first obstacle to the plan is Marshall's inability to contact Washington secretly in order to relay the speed and altitude instructions; this is quickly solved by a female subordinate who suggests using a fax line instead. The secrecy surrounding this plan adds a new layer of dramatic irony to the sequence on top of the dramatic tension: the hijackers must be kept in the dark about the true reasons for the lower altitude refueling.

The "second act" of the sequence thus begins, with Marshall and the subordinate making their way to the fax machine and sending it while the rest of the hostages sneak to the lower level of the plane. The fax gets through to the Situation Room in Washington, but in a clever use of retardation, it is shown arriving unnoticed, and the plot hands off to the subplot about political succession—thus delaying the answer to the question of whether or not anyone will get the word about the parachute escape plan. As the fax lies in the fax machine in the Situation Room, the vice-president is briefed by the attorney general about the potential incapacity of the president, putting her in charge. He further tells her that the president is regarded as incapacitated if a majority of the cabinet agrees to this—a dangling cause that is picked up in Sequence G. The film then switches to a news conference, further delaying the resolution of the question of whether or not the fax was read.

Back on the plane, parachutes are handed out and the tanker arrives to refuel Air Force One. Suspense about the fax instructions persist as the hostages watch the altitude and airspeed readouts. The suspense is resolved at last, to audible sighs of relief from the hostages, when the plane begins its descent. Major Caldwell tries to hand a parachute to Marshall, who refuses, insisting he'll stay until his family is freed—a dangling cause picked up in the following sequence.

Most of the hostages succeed in making their escape, but one of the hijackers manages to disrupt the escape and take the president and three subordinates—one of whom is the turncoat Gibbs—prisoner. The capture of Marshall marks the end of the sequence and second act. The main tension—will Marshall succeed in defeating the hijackers and freeing the hostages?—has been resolved ambiguously: he has succeeded in freeing most of the hostages but failed to defeat the hijackers, leaving himself in even greater danger. The tension now shifts to Marshall's own survival and that of his family.

Sequence G: "Get off my plane!"

This sixteen-minute sequence is unified by Marshall's desire to defeat Korshunov and free himself and his family. It begins with Korshunov threatening to murder the president's family if he doesn't cooperate; after he's roughed up a bit, Marshall falls to the ground, hands taped behind his back, and sees a shard of broken glass—a moment that provides the end of the "first act" of the sequence: he will try to use the glass to free himself, and, thus free, attack Korshunov.

Korshunov lays out his demands, and the president, under threat of having his daughter shot, agrees to contact the Russian president to try to get Radek freed. This act marks a shift now to the second major subplot—the release of Radek and the Russian politics this involves. As soon as Radek's release is effected, the story shifts to the other major subplot—the political succession in the United States, where the vice-president is presented with a petition to declare Marshall incapacitated and put herself in command. This actually amounts to a skillful integration of all three subplots, since the vice-president, once empowered, might rescind the request to release Radek, putting Marshall and his family back in mortal danger.

The vice-president ultimately refuses to sign, and Radek is released. His freedom is soon enough threatened, though, when Marshall manages to cut the tape that binds him and jump Korshunov. Marshall's victory in the scuffle that follows marks the culmination of the sequence—Marshall kills two of the remaining three hostages and is now in pursuit of the last one—Korshunov—who still holds his wife hostage. The General Radek subplot adds an additional layer of suspense by way of a deadline set up by Korshunov, who declares that he will not let the First Lady go until General Radek is safely away from the prison. Marshall's battle with Korshunov thus becomes more than a fight to save his wife's life, it is also a race against time to save the world from the rise of a nuclear-armed dictator and a collapse of Russia back into Communism. The use of sound makes the race more emphatic: while Marshall pursues Korshunov, inmates can be heard at Radek's prison singing the Communist anthem, the "Internationale."

Marshall manages to catch up to Korshunov, who holds a gun to the First Lady's head and forces Marshall to disarm. Korshunov then tosses away the last parachute and warns Marshall that there is no one left to fly the plane, and no parachutes, so he cannot win. This dangling cause is picked up in the final sequence, where the issue of surviving in the crippled aircraft becomes the remaining dramatic issue.

With the timely help of his wife, Marshall manages to kill Korshunov, and with his death the two major subplots are resolved: Radek is killed, and the issue of political succession in the United States is rendered moot. With Radek's death, the sequence draws to a close.

Sequence H: Air Strip Strike Team To The Rescue

The final sequence runs sixteen minutes and has as its unifying element Marshall's attempt to get himself and his fellow passengers safely on the ground. The antagonist of the picture is dead, but the storytellers have carefully preserved one hidden opponent: the traitorous secret service agent Gibbs, who remains alive and ready to sabotage this final survival effort. The difference between Korshunov and Gibbs, of course, is that Gibbs is a danger the president does not see, but the audience does.

Soon after the president takes control of the plane, the first obstacle arises—enemy fighters attempting to bring down the plane. Once this is overcome with the help of friendly fighters, the next obstacle asserts itself: damage sustained by Air Force One during the aerial combat seems to be fatal.

There follows a quick recapitulation scene in the situation room—the plane is uncontrollable, the engines are failing and it's losing fuel. At this point one of the military officers asks whether or not a plane on the map is the "Air Strip Strike Team." Upon confirmation of this, he replies, "I just had a wild idea"—a dialogue hook into the next scene, which finds a hitherto unseen plane approaching Air Force One.

A quick cutaway to a news reporter at the White House fills in some needed exposition: a daring mid-air rescue is being contemplated. This rescue attempt occupies the action for the remainder of the picture.

The remaining dramatic tension—a race to see if the president and passengers can get off the plane before it crashes—is intensified by dramatic irony spawned by the presence of Gibbs, who may betray the whole operation at any moment. With only time for one escapee left, Gibbs finally asserts himself and murders Major Caldwell and one of the rescuers before Marshall is able to subdue him and make it to the rescue plane safely. A brief epilogue involves the announcement that the rescue plane is now "Air Force One."

AIR FORCE ONE
Sequence Breakdown

Seq.	Description	Length	Running Time
	ACT I		
A	Opening titles and action teaser: Gen. Radek is captured. Then, in Moscow, President Marshall delivers a foreign policy speech, surprising his advisors and the rest of the world. He and his entourage head back to Air Force One for the return trip, and he discusses his new policy with them, and what it might portend for their careers. *Unifying Aspect*: Action (preparing to return home on Air Force One).	18:18	18:18 (15%)
B	Ivan Korshunov and his band of retrograde Communists take over plane, but fail to get President, who remains on board. *Unifying Aspect*: Dramatic Tension. *Protagonist*: Korshunov. *Objective*: To take over the plane.	15:21	33:39 (28%)

Point of attack: Secret Service guy shoots colleagues on plane.

Predicament: President Marshall is hiding on a plane that has been hijacked and must act to save his own life and that of everyone else on board.

ACT II
(Main tension: Will Marshall be able to defeat the hijackers and rescue the hostages?)

Seq.	Description	Length	Running Time
C	Marshall surveys his situation, plays hide and seek, succeeds in beating up one of the hijackers and seizing his weapon. He then makes an escape into the luggage compartment. Meanwhile Korshunov makes his demands about the release of Radek. *Unifying Aspect*: Dramatic Tension. *Protagonist*: Marshall. *Objective*: To size up the situation, get armed, and free the hostages.	13:21	47:00 (40%)
D	Korshunov executes the first hostage. Marshall tries to reach the White House by phone, then is momentarily captured, and conspires to make the plane take evasive maneuvers against a guided missile to defeat his captor. *Unifying Aspect*: Dramatic Tension. *Protagonist*: Marshall. *Objective*: To escape from his captor.	13:14	1:00:14 (51%)

First Culmination: Marshall succeeds in subduing his captor and contacting Washington.

Seq.	Description	Length	Running Time
E	Marshall succeeds in getting the plane to dump fuel, but one of Korshunov's men is able to stop it. *Unifying Aspect*: Dramatic Tension. *Protagonist*: Marshall. *Objective*: To dump fuel so as to bring the plane down.	13:07	1:13:21 (62%)

F	Marshall succeeds in getting most of the hostages off the plane with the parachutes, then gets caught. *Unifying Aspect*: Dramatic Tension. *Protagonist*: Marshall. *Objective*: To get the hostages free by using the parachutes.	12:21	1:24:42 (73%)

Second Culmination: Marshall has succeeded in getting everyone off except his family, but now he's been captured.

ACT III

G	Main tension has been resolved ambigously—Marshall has succeeded in rescuing most of the hostages but he, his family, and a few close advisors are now prisoner. A new tension arises: can he overcome his captivity by Korshunov and escape? In this sequence he agrees to Korshunov's demands, but is betrayed and fights back. After a bitter fight, Korshunov is killed in the back of the plane, and Radek is gunned down before he can make his way to freedom. *Unifying Aspect*: Dramatic Tension. *Protagonist*: Marshall. *Objective*: To defeat Korshunov and thus save his life and that of his family and subordinates.	16:09	1:41:51 (86%)
H	Marshall takes over the controls, outlasts an attack by enemy fighters, and manages to hold the plane in the air while another plane comes to effect a rescue. After a last fight with traitorous secret service agent Gibbs, he succeeds in getting off the plane and is reunited with his family in safety. *Unifying Aspect*: Dramatic Tension. *Protagonist*: Marshall. *Objective*: To get himself and his family and subordinates safely off the plane.	16:30	1:58:21 (100%)

Resolution: Marshall and the others escape to the second plane.

Being John Malkovich: The Disappearing Lead Actor

Upon initial viewing, this 1999 independent film seems a complete break from traditional storytelling, described by critics variously as "weird to the max," "different from anything that came before it," and "wonderful and inspired weirdness." A closer look reveals a remarkably imaginative use of very traditional storytelling patterns and a carefully crafted film in which the storytelling is enhanced by cinematographic and art direction choices and attention to performances. The perception of "weirdness" is a testament to the flexibility of the tools presented in this volume, and is not, in this case, an abandonment of them.

The protagonist of the film is readily identifiable as Craig, and pursuit of his desire—Maxine—is what shapes the action. The means by which Craig plans to pursue his relationship with Maxine is the portal into John Malkovich's head—a strategy set up thirty-five minutes (33%) into the film—a long setup by typical standards but not overly so. The chief obstacles he encounters in pursuit of Maxine are complications resulting from the relationship that develops between Craig's wife and Maxine. The main tension—will Craig get Maxine through use of the portal?—is resolved to the positive an hour and forty-five minutes (81%) of the way through the film, when Craig succeeds in taking over Malkovich's body and he and Maxine wind up getting married. The third act explores the implications and complications of this relationship and its eventual destruction. The resolution finds Maxine and Lotte together and Craig "absorbed" in Maxine's child—condemned to look through her eyes but have no control over what she does. The major subplots involve Craig's and Maxine's use of the Malkovich portal for business purposes, Malkovich's pursuit of the truth about Maxine, and Lester's pursuit of immortality for himself and his friends through the Malkovich "vessel body."

Along the way, the eight-sequence structure is readily apparent, the first two setting up the situation, the next four exploring the succession of complications that result from Craig's pursuit of his desire, the seventh one primarily a comical exploration of the implications of Craig's success as a puppeteer, and the last centering on Craig's decision to give up Malkovich for the sake of Maxine. In addition, extensive use is made of other tools discussed in this volume: dramatic and comic irony, dangling causes, appointments, and deadlines.

Sequence A: Craig tries to get a job

The opening of the picture is both consistent with the other films explored in this volume in its use of a puzzle to hook the audience, and unusual in its use of an apparent interior long shot (later to be revealed as more of a close-up of what turn out to be puppets). It is also unusual for a comedy in the initial tone established: the Bartok music is dark, tense, and disturbing, and the actions of the puppet (later identified as "Craig's Dance of Despair and Disillusionment") give no suggestion that the film is a comedy. The first gag—a talking parrot identified as Orrin Hatch resting on Craig's head—does not appear until more than two and a half minutes into the film. The opening does function to introduce Craig engaged in his professional work, and also plants the dance that is paid off much later.

After the opening, the tension of the first sequence is established quickly. Lotte suggests that Craig find a job until the "puppeteering thing" turns around; he protests that Derek Mantini—an apparent rival—doesn't need a day job. In the exchange, we also learn that Lotte works at a pet store, and that they have a chimp named Elijah who is apparently not feeling well. Lotte asks Craig to look after Elijah—a dangling cause that will be picked up in the second act.

In the next scene, Craig happens to be watching television when a report about a new exploit by Derek Mantini comes on—quickly paying off the plant of his name in the previous scene. Craig is sitting next to Elijah, and remarks to him how lucky he is that he has no consciousness—the misconception being a major motif in the picture, and an assumption of Craig's that proves wrong later at a critical moment in Sequence E, when Elijah overcomes his childhood trauma to untie Lotte.

In the next scene, Craig attempts to make money doing his puppetry on a street corner, and gets punched in the face for his trouble. He shows up at Lotte's pet shop with a bruised lip in the next scene, and at this point the end of the "first act" of the sequence arrives: Craig will set out to find a day job.

In the next scene he pores over the want ads and, failing to find any openings for puppeteers, locates an ad for Lester Corp. Craig circles the ad—a visual hook that links the scene to the next, which finds Craig walking down a city street and entering an office building. Craig locates the company on the $7^{1}/_{2}$ floor, and presents himself to Floris, the receptionist, who has difficulty understanding what he's saying—a verbal motif that is paid off as a running gag throughout the rest of the picture.

Soon, Craig is called in to the interview with Mr. Lester, who gives him some simple and somewhat nonsensical tests before hiring him. At the end of the scene, Craig asks why the ceilings are so low; Lester tells him that will be covered in orientation—a dialogue hook binding the scene to the next one. The tension of the opening sequence is thus resolved—Craig has secured a job—and the remaining four minutes of the sequence deal with the consequence of his hire—his orientation by means of the video presentation. Although presented as a gag, the orientation video provides important exposition about Captain Mertin, paid off late in the second act.

The orientation segment also introduces Maxine, who becomes the focus of Sequence B.

Sequence B: Craig Goes After Maxine

The twenty-minute second sequence has as its unifying element the dramatic tension surrounding Craig's pursuit of Maxine. It begins with an economical expository scene involving Craig and Lotte preparing dinner; the exposition is so subtly smuggled in it takes effort to notice it. The scene begins with a (presumably) upstairs neighbor pounding on the floor complaining about the noise of the animals, and his words are echoed by the various birds, revealing an ongoing situation. As the two prepare dinner, they are facing away from each other, a visual cue that their relationship is strained. This is reinforced verbally by Craig's apparent lack of interest in what Lotte has to say about the chimp Elijah (he is seeing a shrink in an effort to deal with some sort of childhood trauma—which is a further setup for Elijah's heroic deed in Sequence E) and his negative response to Lotte's query about having a baby (revealing her own yearning). Craig's reply, that he thinks it's best they wait to see how his "job thing pays off," is a dangling cause that hooks the scene into the next one, which takes place at Lester Corp.

Here, Craig tries to strike up a conversation with Maxine, and she immediately interprets it as an attempt to hit on her, which she rebuffs. Craig is next shown working his job; Floris makes a pass at him using indirection: maybe he could alphabetize *her*. He tells her he's in love with someone else, and she misinterprets what he says—another variation on the speech-impediment gag.

At this point, Lester arrives and in turn misinterprets Craig's interaction with Floris, warning him not to toy with her. During this brief conversation, Lester reveals his lust for Floris (after an oblique reference to it in the job interview scene) and the fact that he is 105 years old. Thus, after seventeen minutes, the two major motifs of the picture are suc-

Figure 18. Craig makes a pass at Maxine in the second sequence of *Being John Malkovich* (1999). Craig's pursuit of her love provides the unifying dramatic tension of the sequence and underlies the main tension of the film. She is introduced just after the tension of the first sequence—will Craig find employment?—is resolved. (Frame enlargement)

cinctly set forth: lust and immortality, the lust corresponding primarily to the "A" plot and the immortality informing the "C" plot of Lester's quest to leap to the "vessel body." The scene ends with the establishment of an appointment: Lester invites Craig to join him for a drink at Jerry's Juiceteria after work, to further discuss Lester's sexual fantasies.

Craig's pursuit of Maxine resumes in the following scene, in which he hoodwinks her into a date. The scene ends with another appointment: she instructs him to meet her at the Stuffed Pig at seven o'clock; if he's late, she'll walk.

The next scene finds Craig and Lester at the Juiceteria, with Lester at the tail end of an erotic story. With seven o'clock approaching, Craig excuses himself, but not before Lester makes another appointment with him: a dinner date with Craig and his wife for that Thursday. Craig quickly makes his way to the bar where he meets Maxine, who quickly rebuffs him again, this time when he reveals he's a puppeteer.

Craig now returns home, in a scene that is the first in the film to use dramatic irony: Craig conceals from Lotte his interest in Maxine. Lotte explains she spent the day feeding all the animals—a subtle reminder of her desire for a child—and then announces that the chimp will sleep with them that night—another indication of a strained marital relationship.

Craig retires to his workshop, where the puppets are used by the storytellers to make visible his inner state—his obsessive lust for Maxine. He dresses one of his puppets as Maxine, and leaves a puppet resembling Lotte hanging off to the side. After a brief shot of Lotte lying in bed alone, the film returns to Craig's workshop, where Craig acts out, using the Maxine puppet and one resembling himself, a love scene as he would like to live it. He also describes to "Maxine" that puppeteering is simply being inside someone else's skin for a while—a setup for the later discovery of the Malkovich portal.

Craig's success in seducing Maxine in the puppet play provides a contrast to the reality portrayed in the following scene, when Craig tries out the same lines on the real Maxine and is rebuffed once more.

This brings about the apparent resolution to the sequence—Craig fails to get Maxine. After a brief aftermath scene in which Craig absorbs the reality of the rejection, he discovers the Malkovich portal, experiences Malkovich finishing breakfast and taking a cab ride (in which the "jewel thief movie" verbal motif is planted), and is then dumped near the New Jersey Turnpike.

Craig returns to Maxine's office, where he explains to her the strange adventure. She is wholly unimpressed, and walks out on him. She calls him at his home, though, and suggests they go into business together to make money off the portal. Craig asks her whether it might be dangerous to toy with something so profound—a dangling cause picked up and developed throughout the rest of the picture. Maxine seduces him into accepting just as Lotte enters the apartment, adding a layer of dramatic irony that punctuates the scene.

Sequence C: The Lotte Complication

Craig's acceptance of Maxine's offer to go into business is the dangling cause that binds the second sequence with the third, and this, coupled with her statement that Craig is her "man on the inside," constitutes the end of first act. The protagonist is clear, and so is his objective—Maxine—his means to getting her—the Malkovich portal—and the obstacles—Maxine's reluctance and Craig's relationship with Lotte. These three aspects of dramatic tension inform the rest of the picture.

Sequence C, which runs just under sixteen minutes, picks up on both dangling causes—the lust and the business angle—and is unified by the tension created by Craig attempting to avoid Lotte's becoming suspicious about his budding relationship with Maxine. After this is resolved

Figure 19. The four main ingredients of *Being John Malkovich* (1999) are united in one moment at the end of Sequence B: Craig is on the phone with Maxine, discussing turning the Malkovich portal into a money-making enterprise, while Lotte is in the background, unaware. The main tension of the picture is established here. (Frame enlargement)

with a surprise twist, the remainder of the sequence involves the first customer, which is the shift to the "B" subplot.

The sequence opens with Craig and Lotte en route to dinner at Lester's place, picking up on the appointment established in the previous sequence. Dramatic irony is at play: he tells her he'll be working late nights, and justifies it by telling her about the money he'll make; naturally he conceals the other activity he plans those nights, which will doubtless be pursuing his relationship with Maxine. Lotte voices skepticism about the idea of a portal, and asks to try it out—suggesting that this would also be a way to meet Craig's partner, which plays on Craig's fears. Craig offers to take her "right now, on the way to Lester's"—a dialogue hook leading into the following scene, which finds Craig swinging open the portal door.

Lotte gathers the nerve to go into the portal, and gets inside John Malkovich while he is taking a shower. Afterward she is completely overwhelmed by the experience and wants to do it again. He protests that they'll be late for Lester—a dialogue hook into the following scene, which finds Craig and Lotte dining on an obviously Spartan meal of greens and juices at Lester's place.

During dinner, Lotte, traveling to the rest room, instead stumbles upon some sort of "shrine" for John Malkovich in one of Lester's rooms. On the ride home, she asks Craig about what he thinks might be the connection between Lester and Malkovich. He doubts there is any, and she changes the subject to sex—speculating about whether the portal is some sort of vagina. The fact that she does not bother to tell Craig about the shrine in Lester's house amounts to storytelling sleight of hand. It's not logical—why wouldn't she share this information that might yield clues to the mystery of the portal? But sharing the information would turn it into a mystery story, undermining the sexual/relationship direction in which the story actually develops. Thus the storytellers use Lotte's sexual references to distract the audience from the illogic of her actions, and the mystery aspect is safely submerged until late in the second act.

The film now switches to the offices of Lester Corp., where Craig and Maxine write an ad for their new business venture. Lotte interrupts their intimate meeting, exploiting again Craig's fear of discovery of his interest in Maxine. Lotte tells Craig she wants to do the Malkovich ride again, confessing to him that the experience has convinced her she's a transsexual. Maxine tells Craig to let her go—on the Malkovich ride. She and Lotte make lingering eye contact as Lotte exits. As soon as she's alone, Maxine calls a friend to get Malkovich's home number.

The film switches to Malkovich alone at home rehearsing a play, and soon we discover that Lotte is already inside him, enjoying the experience of his masculinity. The phone rings and Maxine is on the other end, attempting to persuade him to meet her, in the process paying off the "jewel thief movie" gag for a second time. He resists the impulse, but Lotte urges him on, and at last he writes down the appointment: Bernardo's at eight o'clock. In addition to the dramatic tension of the scene—Maxine's attempt to persuade Malkovich to go to the restaurant—dramatic irony is also at work, since Malkovich doesn't know that Lotte is "inside" him.

Afterward, Lotte tells Craig that she needs to go back to the portal at exactly eight o'clock that night, a dialogue hook leading into the following scene, which finds Malkovich waiting at a restaurant. Maxine arrives, and Lotte is indeed inside Malkovich, and both Malkovich and Lotte seem to hit it off with Maxine.

Afterward, in the car with Craig, Lotte lies about her experience, claiming Malkovich was just hanging around his apartment during her "trip," and thus introducing another layer of dramatic irony. The scene resolves the tension of the sequence: what had been a question about whether or not Lotte would discover Craig's budding romance with Maxine has been transformed into a question of whether or not Craig will discover Lotte's ersatz affair with Maxine through Malkovich. During their conversation, Craig offers her advice that touches on the theme of the picture —switching bodies will not solve her problems. It is, of course, advice he should take himself. At the end of the scene, a dangling cause is initiated by Lotte—that they should invite Maxine over for dinner. This dangles through the next scene, which focuses on the "B" subplot—the business Maxine and Craig are running—and is not picked up again until the following sequence. In the "B" plot scene, the first customer arrives and takes an exhilarating trip on the "Malkovich ride."

Sequence D: Lotte's Affair

This short sequence picks up immediately the dangling cause from two scenes prior—Maxine is over at Craig's and Lotte's for dinner. It is unified by dramatic tension—Lotte's desire to pursue her relationship with Maxine.

The dinner scene is informed primarily by dramatic irony—both Craig and Lotte are in love with Maxine, and neither knows about the other's interest. That ironic tension is resolved when both Craig and Lotte lunge for Maxine while she sits on the couch. Maxine immediately rejects Craig, and is willing to accept Lotte only when she's "in Malkovich." A wordless aftermath ensues, with Craig and Lotte sharing the couch but not looking at each other.

The film now switches to J.M. Inc., where Maxine receives a call from Lotte asking her to meet after work so they can initiate an affair—an action that picks up on the dangling cause of the scene before. Maxine agrees, creating an appointment for 4:11 that morning. Craig is shown alone in bed, a shot that echoes that of Lotte lying alone in bed in Sequence B. This scene constitutes the first culmination—Craig is alone in bed—he doesn't have Maxine or his puppeteering career, and as such is the mirror opposite of the second culmination, when he has both.

Malkovich greets Maxine at his door, and the two wait on the couch until precisely 4:11, at which time they begin to make passionate love. The scene is intensified by the dramatic irony of Lotte's secret presence inside Malkovich. Maxine's request that she call Malkovich "Lotte" almost exposes the secret, but Malkovich winds up accepting this as an eccentricity.

A brief post-coital aftermath scene follows, with Lotte lying ecstatic by the side of the New Jersey Turnpike, before she arrives home and confesses her affair with Maxine. The sequence is resolved: Lotte has successfully realized her affair with Maxine.

Sequence E: Malkovich Threatens

This seventeen-minute sequence resolves temporarily Craig's problem in the main plot, then shifts almost entirely to the subplot of the business venture, which is threatened by Malkovich's suspicions about Maxine. It begins with Craig assaulting Lotte in their apartment and forcing her to make a date with Maxine, resulting in an appointment one hour hence; after this, Craig ties her up and puts her in a cage with Elijah, the chimp.

Maxine tracks down Malkovich at a stage rehearsal, and the two soon wind up at his apartment having sex. It is quickly revealed that Craig is inside Malkovich, adding another layer of ironic tension to the scene: not only is Malkovich unaware that someone is "inside" him, but Maxine is unaware that Craig has taken Lotte's place "inside" Malkovich. To Craig's surprise, he realizes he can control Malkovich somewhat. Malkovich realizes he's losing control of his own body and becomes frightened.

Craig goes home to celebrate his newfound power, and brags to Lotte that soon Malkovich will be just another puppet in his hands—a dangling cause that is picked up and developed emphatically during the rest of the picture.

The movie now switches to Malkovich, who confers with Charlie Sheen about his unnerving experience with Maxine. The scene is sustained with dramatic tension—Malkovich ranting about his situation and Charlie trying to calm him down. In the end, Malkovich tells him he's got to get to the truth, a dangling cause that provides the central tension of the sequence.

The next scene picks up on this dangling cause: Malkovich is shown waiting furtively outside Maxine's apartment building. He follows her cab to the 7½ floor, where he discovers J.M. Inc. and confronts Craig and Maxine. Malkovich insists on going through the portal himself. This leads to a scene of preparation, in which retardation is used. A considerable amount of anticipation is created around the question posed by Craig: what happens when a man goes through his own portal? For the first time since Craig's initial journey, the lead-up to the "trip" is drawn out. Malkovich is shown slowly making his way through the tunnel till the telltale *squish* of the mud is heard. He is then thrust down the tunnel at high speed, and the payoff, thus delayed, has considerable impact: Malkovich finds himself in a world densely populated exclusively with other John Malkoviches of various sizes, ages, genders, and attire.

Malkovich flees from this world and winds up by the New Jersey Turnpike, where he confronts Craig and warns him that he will take legal action to seal the portal—a dangling cause that is closed off when Craig later succeeds in taking control of Malkovich completely.

The sequence abruptly switches back to the main plot, with Craig home to feed the animals and arguing with the still-caged Lotte. In an effective use of preparation by contrast, Craig begins, apparently, to reject his course of action, regretting that he has locked his wife up in a cage wondering if he's become a monster. Lotte tries to soothe him with words. He tells her he loves her very much, opens the cage door, and dials the phone. The film cuts away to Maxine alone at J.M. Inc., who answers the phone and speaks to Lotte, agreeing to meet her an hour hence. The impression is that Craig has come to his senses and freed his wife. The reality is just the opposite, revealed in the following shot, where Lotte is shown tied and gagged in the cage after all.

At this point, Elijah the Chimp has a flashback replaying trauma he suffered during his capture. Working through this memory enables the chimp to free Lotte from her bonds, completing his character arc, and paying off the exposition about his therapy aimed at dealing with childhood trauma.

Lotte immediately calls Maxine and tells her about Craig's actions, but in a surprise twist, Maxine finds Craig's power over Malkovich intriguing and winds up rejecting her in favor of Craig. She tells Lotte she'll be late for Malkovich and hangs up—a dangling cause that hooks the sequence to the following one. An aftermath scene ensues, with Lotte walking lonely New York streets in the rain.

Sequence F: Craig Gets His Woman

This nine-minute sequence is centered on Craig's final conquest of Malkovich and, as a result, Maxine. It immediately picks up on the appointment made previously: Maxine goes to meet Malkovich and the two make love on the dining room table—with Craig now fully in control.

The movie switches to Lotte, who remains alone in the rain, this time in a taxi. She turns up at Lester's house, and in the process initiates the second major subplot—Lester's secret scheme to achieve immortality. Because this subplot is begun so late in the picture, a considerable amount of exposition occurs just before the end of the second act—also quite unusual. Lotte confesses to Lester her obsession with Malkovich, and mentions the Malkovich "museum" she'd discovered while visiting him the last time. Lester solves the mystery of the portal, an issue that, as noted previously, was deftly avoided in Sequence C. He explains that he is none other than Captain Mertin, a character introduced in the orientation video, who discovered the portal ninety years before and used it to leap into the body of Lester, a much younger man, and thus remain alive. By leaping from one such "vessel body" to another, he can achieve immortality. He further explains that Malkovich is the next "vessel body," and he must go through the portal into Malkovich by midnight of Malkovich's 44th birthday. If he goes in too late, he'll be absorbed: diverted into the next "infant" vessel, doomed forever to look out of that person's eyes without being able to control anything. This exposition provides a deadline—Malkovich's 44th birthday—which informs the third act of the picture. Lester then introduces Lotte to a roomful of elderly friends, who Lester plans to bring with him when he makes the leap into Malkovich's body. This marks the end of the setup of the "C" plot—the exposition is complete, the protagonist of the subplot is Lester, and his objective—leaping into Malkovich by midnight of his 44th birthday—is revealed.

The film now cuts back to Maxine and Craig (as Malkovich); Craig demonstrates his "Dance of Despair and Disillusionment," paying off the dance seen in the opening of the picture. Maxine is deeply impressed, and asks that Craig stay in Malkovich forever, explaining that they'll have access to his money. Craig adds to this that he can use Malkovich's existing notoriety to launch his puppeteering career.

This conversation marks the end of the second act, for the resolution of the main tension is at hand: Craig has succeeded in getting the girl of his dreams, and faces the prospect of success as a puppeteer. The sequence ends with one more cutaway to the immortality subplot: Lester invites Lotte to join him and his friends in leaping to the Malkovich vessel body. Lotte replies by telling Lester there is something he should know about the Malkovich vessel—an oblique reference to Craig's occupation of it. The problem of getting Craig out of Malkovich becomes the central tension of Act III.

Sequence G: Craig With The World On A String

One of the aspects of *Being John Malkovich* that gives it such an unusual feel is that the actor playing the protagonist actually disappears for most of the last three sequences. The *protagonist* remains onscreen, but the actor playing him, John Cusack, does not. In fact, during the last 30% of the film—33 minutes—Cusack is onscreen for less than a minute. As the third act begins, he exists in manner only, his mannerisms and hairstyle evoked by the actor John Malkovich.

Sequence G, which runs just over nine minutes, is unified by an event—Malkovich's 44th birthday—rather than any dramatic tension. It also features a "mockumentary" about Malkovich and a performance by him at the American Ballet Theater. While these amount to brilliant comic explorations of the triumph of Craig over Malkovich's body, they lack the compelling use of any of the tools described in this volume, and as a result the sequence itself has an aimless quality. There is only a hint of conflict, during cutaways to Lester, Lotte, and their friends, and these cutaways lay the groundwork for the tension of the final sequence. But in the three major scenes of the sequence—the meeting with Malkovich's agent, the mockumentary, and the performance at the ABT, there is little conflict and therefore no compelling tension.

The sequence begins with Maxine and Craig (as Malkovich) meeting with Malkovich's agent and announcing his plans to switch careers from acting to puppeteering. A gap of eight months follows, announced by an intertitle.

Craig (as Malkovich) is then shown arriving home in time to watch a TV special on himself. The mockumentary is a comic exploration of the notion of puppetry as high art form, and also an economical means of delivering exposition—letting the audience know what has transpired since the previous scene. Among the important bits of information is the fact that Malkovich's relationship with Maxine has grown strained; this is reinforced by a cutaway to Maxine, gently caressing the lips of Craig's "Lotte" puppet.

During the mockumentary, there are two cutaways to Lester's house, where Lester, Lotte, and the elderly friends watch the same mockumentary on television. Lotte expresses disgust at the sight of Maxine with Malkovich, but Lester assures her the "travesty" will be over by morning—a dangling cause that creates at least some anticipation as the film heads to the final sequence.

When the mockumentary is over, Craig (as Malkovich) telegraphs the agenda for the evening: he is heading to the ABT for a Swan Lake benefit, and afterward hopes to celebrate his 44th birthday with Maxine. Since his 44th birthday has already been established as a deadline for Lester to enter the portal, so Craig's statement helps to create a subtle anticipation.

Craig's successful performance of Swan Lake brings the sequence to a close.

Sequence H: "Look away!"

The final sequence, which runs eleven and a half minutes, is unified by dramatic tension: Craig's decision to leave Malkovich in order to get Maxine back. It begins with Craig (as Malkovich) returning home with a birthday cake clearly marked "44," only to discover that Maxine has been kidnapped. Lester calls him and threatens to kill Maxine if Craig doesn't leave Malkovich immediately. Craig responds with what's at stake for him: if he leaves Malkovich, he'll lose his career, his money, and Maxine. Lester in turn responds by telling Craig that he and his friends are old and will die if they don't get into Malkovich by midnight—a dangling cause that provides the main line of tension during the remainder of the film.

Craig (as Malkovich) hangs up the phone and Lester concedes defeat. Lotte suggests they go into the portal and push Craig out; Lester tells her that Craig is too powerful and would just jam them into Malkovich's subconscious—an important bit of exposition that sets up the next scene, in which Lotte, angry and void of hope, tries to shoot Maxine.

Maxine runs into the portal to escape; Lotte follows her, and the two have a wild chase through Malkovich's subconscious before they are both dumped in the pouring rain on the New Jersey Turnpike. Once there, the two reconcile after Maxine reveals that she's pregnant with Lotte's baby.

The movie switches back to Craig (as Malkovich), who drinks alone in a bar, pondering his dilemma. At last he calls Lester and agrees to leave Malkovich. Craig winds up on the New Jersey Turnpike, and after a brief respite, Malkovich is taken over by Lester and his friends, just before the midnight deadline, closing off that dangling cause.

On the turnpike, Craig sees Maxine and Lotte and expresses his continuing love for Maxine. She again rejects him, and the two women take off in a car, leaving Craig to initiate one last dangling cause: he vows to go back into the portal and take over Malkovich again so Maxine will love him once more. The exposition provided earlier—that after midnight anyone entering the Malkovich portal will be "absorbed"—adds dramatic irony to Craig's stated intent.

An intertitle announces the passage of seven years, after which Charlie Sheen arrives at Malkovich's new California home. Malkovich has clearly been taken over by Lester, as evidenced by his hairstyle and red sweater, both reflecting Lester's tastes. Lester (as Malkovich) leads Charlie into the house, where they greet Lester's wife—Floris—who misinterprets Charlie's greeting, the final payoff of the speech-impedimentology gag.

Lester brings Charlie upstairs and asks him how he'd feel about living forever, then shows him a room containing a new shrine—photos of a little girl. He introduces her as Emily—a dialogue hook into the next scene, which finds a seven-year-old girl, Emily, playing at poolside with her two moms, Maxine and Lotte. After Maxine tickles her, Emily lies back and looks at her two moms admiringly, and Craig's voice is heard, calling out forlornly to Maxine, and urging Emily to "look away"—a command she ignores. The dangling cause of Craig's intent to take over Malkovich again is closed off here: he is condemned forever to occupy Emily's body but have no control over her.

BEING JOHN MALKOVICH
Sequence Breakdown

Seq.	Description	Length	Running Time
	ACT I		
A	Opening titles and puppet show; Craig tries to make money on the street as a puppeteer but gets punched; he answers an ad in the paper and lands the job at Lester Corp, then watches the orientation video. *Unifying Aspect*: Dramatic Tension. *Protagonist*: Craig. *Objective*: To get a job.	15:04	15:04 (14%)
	Point of attack: Craig sees Maxine for the first time.		
B	Craig pursues Maxine while dealing with Lester's lewdness. Craig is rejected by Maxine at the Stuffed Pig, later confesses his obsessive love for her, is rejected again, then discovers the portal. Afterward, Maxine proposes the business relationship using the portal, Craig accepts. *Unifying Aspect*: Dramatic Tension. *Protagonist*: Craig. *Objective*: Maxine.	20:06	35:10 (33%)
	Predicament: Craig will use the portal to pursue Maxine.		
	ACT II **(Main tension: Will Craig succeed in landing Maxine by using the John Malkovich portal?)**		
C	Craig pursues the business venture, but Lotte unexpectedly gets hooked on being Malkovich, and starts to fall for Maxine as well. Lotte goes on a "date" with Maxine through Malkovich. Meanwhile J.M. Inc. has its first successful customer. *Unifying Aspect*: Dramatic Tension. *Protagonist*: Craig. *Objective*: To pursue the relationship with Maxine, and the business venture, without Lotte interfering.	15:49	50:59 (48%)
D	Maxine comes over for dinner; both Lotte and Craig go after her. Maxine rejects Craig outright and will only accept Lotte when she's inside John Malkovich. Lotte arranges another date with Maxine through Malkovich; the two make love. Craig gets jealous, confronts Lotte, then confronts Maxine, who accuses him of wrongly choosing the unrequited kind of love. *Unifying Aspect*: Dramatic Tension. *Protagonist*: Lotte. *Objective*: To pursue her relationship with Maxine.	8:15	59:14 (56%)
	First Culmination: Craig alone in bed while his wife is in John Malkovich (54:25—51%).		
E	Craig kidnaps Lotte, then has a successful date with Maxine as Malkovich, in which he realizes he can control Malkovich. Malkovich responds by investigating	17:20	1:16:34 (72%)

J.M. Inc. and going on the "John Malkovich Ride"
himself. Afterward, he threatens Craig with legal action.
Craig makes another date with Maxine, pretending to
be Lotte inside Malkovich. Lotte escapes with the help
of Elijah the chimp, reveals Craig's deception to
Maxine. Maxine unexpectedly finds making love to
Craig through Malkovich intriguing, and rejects Lotte.
Unifying Aspect: Dramatic Tension. *Protagonist*:
Malkovich. *Objective*: To find out the truth about
Maxine.

F	Craig and Maxine make love; afterward he does his Dance of Despair. He and Maxine agree that he will remain inside John Malkovich forever, and pursue puppeteering, too. Meanwhile Lotte goes to Lester for help; Lester reveals his true identity (Capt. Mertin), the secret of the portal, and the human vessel. *Unifying Aspect*: Dramatic Tension. *Protagonist*: Craig. *Objective*: To get Maxine through controlling Malkovich.	9:11	1:25:45 (81%)

Second Culmination: **Craig agrees to be John
Malkovich forever, so he can stay with Maxine.**

ACT III

G	Main tension has been resolved—Craig got the girl. This sequence examines the comic implications of his married life and his new career as a puppeteer, and keeps alive the subplot of Captain Mertin and his plans. Craig watches a documentary about himself, then does a performance at the ABT. *Unifying Aspect*: Event. (Malkovich's 44th birthday).	9:04	1:34:49 (91%)
H	Craig returns home to find Maxine kidnapped. While Craig broods at his loss of Maxine, Lotte chases Maxine through Malkovich's subconscious before the two are spilled out on the road and have a final confrontation, in which Maxine reveals to Lotte that she's carrying Lotte's baby. Craig finally abandons Malkovich out of love for Maxine, only to find himself rejected again by the side of the New Jersey Turnpike. He vows to return to the portal to regain Maxine, and winds up stuck inside Emily. *Unifying Aspect*: Dramatic Tension. *Protagonist*: Craig. *Objective*: Saving Maxine's life.	11:34	1:46:23 (100%)

Resolution: **Craig loses Maxine but is condemned to
look at her through the eyes of Emily the rest of his
life.**

The Fellowship of the Ring:
The Shotgun Approach

In bringing *The Fellowship of the Ring* to the screen, the filmmakers faced two difficult problems at the outset: a large "installed base" of devoted fans who had read J. R. R. Tolkien's *The Lord of the Rings* trilogy and thus had expectations that mitigated against any major changes in the narrative for adaptation purposes; and a large and complicated narrative to adapt to the dramatic form. A critical analysis is complicated further by the fact that *The Fellowship of the Ring* is only one-third of the entire work, and must be understood to function both as a self-contained work and a piece of a larger one.

With both critical and box-office success, it is apparent that the filmmakers succeeded in overcoming these difficult obstacles. Yet upon closer scrutiny from a screenwriting viewpoint, it seems that many storytelling choices *not* made by the screenwriters might have further enhanced the impact of the work, especially in comparison with the book from which it was adapted. It thus makes a useful study because the choices the filmmakers made lay bare other choices not made, and the varying impact of these choices is readily assessed.

The fact is that most screenplays a screenwriter will encounter professionally—for example, during rewrite work for hire or from doing script consultation or story development, or even in reviewing his or her own work or that of friends—will not be masterpieces. It is by analyzing imperfect work in an informed way, and recognizing appropriate options for revision, that one can come to create a masterpiece.

This chapter will thus proceed somewhat differently from those be-fore—in examining the work, the impact of various choices will be weighed, with an eye toward what choices might have the greatest emo-tional impact on an audience. In this, it will on occasion be useful to compare the storytelling choices in the screenplay with those in the Tol-kien book.

In its broadest strokes, the script does not fit easily into the three-act structure examined in other films in this volume. This is clearly the re-sult of its overall faithfulness to the original Tolkien book, which was not a drama and thus not constrained by the needs of the dramatic form. It also seems due to the fragmentary nature of the movie—portraying about one-third of the Tolkien work, rather than that mate-rial in its entirety. The main tension certainly revolves around Frodo's involvement with the ring. Twenty-one percent of the way through the picture, Frodo is sent off on a journey by Gandalf with the ring. Since the rest of the movie involves Frodo's bearing of the ring, Frodo's initial departure for Bree functions as the end of the first act, or, at the very least, the end of the *beginning*.

It is at best an uncertain predicament. The setup is cursory; the na-ture of Frodo's journey, the sense of its duration, the nature of the ob-jective—these are not very clear. What seems to mark the initiation of the main tension is the journey away from the Shire.

The resolution of the main tension—the second culmination—is not readily apparent at all. Three-quarters of the way through the picture—the usual place where the second culmination occurs—Gandalf is killed and the Fellowship emerges in mourning from the Mines of Moria. While this marks the end of sequence, it does not change the nature of the journey in the way the end of a second act typically does. It's just another way station on that journey, made more difficult by the loss of a major character.

Upon reaching Lothlorien, 85 percent of the way through the film, the tension shifts to the question of Saruman's *Uruk-hai* soldiers defeat-ing the Fellowship. The battle with the Uruk-hai might be considered the font of third-act tension, but it's more the tension of a single se-quence, albeit a long one (twenty-one minutes). Further, it serves as just another obstacle to be overcome on the journey, rather than the intro-duction of some truly new issue. The resolution is left open-ended, with plenty of dangling causes left to hook up with the second installment of the saga.

While the main tension and therefore act breaks may not be clear, the film does rely on sequences—thirteen in all—to help convey the audience's attention forward. Both the original Tolkien work and the movie are episodic.

One aspect of *The Fellowship of the Ring* that distinguishes it from all the other films studied in this volume is the relative weakness of its protagonist. As is detailed below, in the first two sequences he is all but absent from the screen, and subsequently he seems lost in the shuffle of the many characters that accompany him. Notably, of the thirteen sequences in the film, he is the protagonist in only three.

These divergences from the typical form of feature films are not indicative of a flaw; ultimately, what matters is whether the picture successfully engages audiences and leaves them feeling satisfied. While there may have been ways to create a more thorough sense of "completeness," on the whole, the film succeeds in these tasks. The purpose of this analysis is to weigh whether or not alternative choices might have been even more effective.

Overall, probably the chief, persistent problem with how the script was executed is its failure to set up situations and characters in a way that moves the audience from observer to participant. The effect is a film that plays more like a travelogue—the audience conveyed from place to place making discoveries along the way—than a dramatically unfolding epic, with the audience engaged in the emotionally charged issues of hope and fear along the course of the journey (a comparison with *Lawrence of Arabia* is particularly useful in this regard). This is not to say that the picture does not provoke hope and fear at all; rather, that many opportunities to enhance these emotions are missed. The result is that, emotionally, the picture functions only on a very basic level: the audience hopes the characters don't come to physical harm and is afraid they might.

Furthermore, the setups that do occur tend to telegraph information in a way that undermines any chance for surprise, one of the staples of cinematic storytelling since its inception. The result is a three-hour action movie with few surprise twists. One may argue that the familiarity of Tolkien books to so many mitigates against this—no one is left to be surprised—but the surprise twist or reversal does more than delight an audience; it offers glimpses of possible outcomes and as such lends a sense of spontaneity and liveliness to the story.

Pre-Title Sequence: The 'Shotgun' Approach to Exposition

The two-hour, fifty-minute picture (exclusive of endtitles) begins with a female voice, heard over a black screen, telling the audience the world has changed. The disembodied voice, and these words, provide a powerful hook—the classic puzzle seen in the opening moments of many successful pictures—which draws the audience in at the outset.

These initial words are followed by a seven-minute narration describing the forging of twenty magical rings, nineteen of which were given to the races of elves, dwarves, and men, and one of which was created in secret by the "Dark Lord," Sauron, so that he would have power over all the others. Sauron proceeded to enslave various lands before being confronted by an army of elves and men in a great battle. Sauron appears, wearing the ring, and does considerable damage before one man, Isildur, cuts off Sauron's ring finger with a sword, causing the dark lord to implode. The narrator then traces the rest of the story of the ring—it corrupts Isildur, winds up at the bottom of a river, where it is found by a creature named Gollum, who obsesses over it for five hundred years before it gets away from him and is found by a hobbit named Bilbo. The narration ends with a dangling cause: "The time will soon come when hobbits will shape the fortunes of all."

The decision to place so much direct exposition in the opening seven minutes of the film is a problematic one for several reasons. First of all, so much information, laid out without any emotional context, is difficult for an audience to grasp without its taking notes. Here it is worth comparing this voice-over introduction with the narration Neff delivers in the opening minutes of *Double Indemnity* (Chapter 4). Neff's monologue lasts under three minutes, and even this is undergirded by a subtext: Neff is arguing with Keyes, out to prove that he was wrong. The opening voice-over in *Fellowship of the Ring* is completely neutral; the audience is simply getting information. No attempt is made to make the audience curious about the ring—a comparison with *Lawrence of Arabia* (Chapter 7) is worthwhile in this regard: the storytellers in that epic spent the first five minutes creating curiosity about the title character before the audience even gets a clear glimpse of him.

Another problem with the long opening monologue is that it displays to the audience some prodigious special effects without any preparation. Grand battle scenes, hideous orcs, a huge nuclear-type blast, and even the infamous Dark Lord appear in quick succession, without any buildup or context created for them. One of the most powerful tools of storytelling—the scene or preparation—is left unexploited. The casual introduction of Sauron is in particular a lost opportunity; one need only compare his introduction to that of the *balrog* near the middle of the film. For the latter demon, the storytellers showed skillful use of indirection and retardation: for five minutes the viewer is tantalized with hints of the monster—sounds, roars, the trembling ground, the fiery light— before actually seeing it. When it finally arrives, its visual impact is considerable, and it is easily the most spectacular character introduction in the film.

Since Sauron is a villain who manipulates so much of the action across nine hours of film, a comparison of his introduction is useful to the introduction of a magical figure in a very different kind of fantasy film—*The Wizard of Oz.* In that 1939 classic, the Wizard is mentioned in dialogue and discussed for an hour before he actually appears onscreen, and when at last he does, accompanied by fire, smoke, and considerable noise, the impact is, again, considerable.

A more mundane problem with the dramatization of Sauron's fall is that it lays bare a weakness in the backstory—the Dark Lord, empowered with the mighty One Ring, can be beaten simply by having his ring finger cut off (in the Tolkein work, Isildur cuts off the finger after Sauron has been killed).

Perhaps the biggest problem posed by the choice of starting the picture with the long history lesson is that it eliminates any chance for the exploitation of mystery in the opening sequence. By using this "shotgun" approach to giving the audience information, the viewer winds up ahead of the characters for a good portion of the first act. In this, it's worth considering *North by Northwest* (Chapter 6), in which Hitchcock and Lehman exploit mystery throughout the first forty minutes of the film. One need only imagine what the impact would have been if these storytellers had spent the first seven minutes of that film using a voiceover narration to describe in great detail the workings of Vandamm's spy operation, the role that Eve plays in it, and the CIA's use of a nonexistent agent to fool Vandamm, before introducing Roger in the middle of his busy day. Some of the most memorable scenes in cinema history would have been ruined.

Ultimately, the first seven minutes of *The Fellowship of the Ring* is emblematic of the storytelling style of the movie as a whole: the audience is an observer rather than a participant, witnessing a series of unfolding events without any sense of anticipation, hope or fear. And in adapting a work of epic size, every minute of screen time is precious, so using them up in this way means that there is less screen time available for other, critical storytelling tasks.

Sequence A: The Long-Expected Party

The first sequence, which runs from the end of the voice-over narration to the departure of Gandalf from the Shire, runs nineteen and a half minutes. There is no dramatic tension to unify the sequence, which is defined more by an event—Bilbo's party—and his subsequent departure. Central to the action is the reintroduction of the One Ring.

The sequence begins with Frodo sitting by a tree reading, then running happily to greet the wizard Gandalf, who has arrived on a one-horse wagon. Frodo asks him for news of the outside world; Gandalf engages in conversation that is for the most part inaudible to the audience. The two pass by some hobbits setting up a tent and a banner that reads "Happy Birthday Bilbo Baggins." Gandalf asks about Bilbo, remarking that he understands the party will be of "special magnificence"—the second dangling cause of the picture. Frodo tells Gandalf he suspects Bilbo is up to something—another dangling cause, and the two make an oblique reference to Bilbo's previous adventures with Gandalf. After this, Frodo bids Gandalf good-bye and jumps off the wagon. Shortly after this, Gandalf arrives at Bilbo's home.

The use of a ride through Bag End to introduce the setting of the story is a good one, but the three-minute scene suffers from two problems: one, there is no conflict and therefore no tension or anticipation created within it, and two, it is not rich enough in the information to justify its length. Essentially we discover that Hobbits are quiet folk, that Bilbo—a character who hasn't yet been introduced—is planning a party and perhaps something more, and that he had some adventure.

Bilbo welcomes Gandalf into his home and in the course of their conversation we learn that Bilbo plans to leave the Shire to finish his book, that he feels old, and that he does not plans to return. The scene runs over three minutes and suffers from the same problem as the previous one: it has no conflict in it, and thus no dramatic tension. It provides some exposition about Bilbo and telegraphs Bilbo's intentions after the party, but Bilbo is a relatively minor character in the picture, and any time spent on him is time *not* spent on introducing the audience to Frodo, who is the protagonist, and who remains something of a cipher even as the film unfolds.

The party that follows features the introduction of Sam, Merry, and Pippin, the latter two in the midst of a prank to steal and set off one of the fireworks. The flight of this "dragon" firework is a brief example of preparation by contrast—the apparently menacing device proves, after a few frightening moments, to be harmless. The dramatic highpoint of the party is Bilbo's disappearance into thin air after saying his last good-bye. He then retreats—while invisible—to his home, where he puts a golden ring back into his pocket (the device he evidently used to perform his disappearing act) and finds Gandalf already there waiting for him. There follows what amounts to the first dramatic scene in the picture—Gandalf trying to persuade a curiously resistant Bilbo to leave the magic ring behind. When at last Bilbo departs, leaving the ring, he utters a prediction: he will live happily ever after to the end of his days.

With Bilbo gone, the "third act" of the sequence begins, and this deals exclusively with the ring: Gandalf's attempt to make sense of it, and his handing it over to Frodo for safekeeping. The sequence ends with two powerful dangling causes: Gandalf's announcement that he must see to some "things," and his warning to Frodo to keep the ring secret and safe. Because of the opening narration, the scene is suffused with dramatic irony—the characters are ignorant of the history and nature of the ring, but the audience is quite aware.

Sequence B: The Truth About the Ring

The second sequence runs just under ten minutes and is centered on Gandalf's quest to determine the truth about Bilbo's ring. It begins with a cutaway to an undisclosed location that appears to be a dark, menacing castle. An anguished voice cries out, barely intelligibly, "Shire!" and "Baggins!" As soon as these words are uttered, a volcano erupts and several black-clad horsemen emerge at a gallop from some gates.

This episode runs under a minute in length and is visually striking but has no discernible storytelling function. Given given the length of the work and the need for economy, it is an example of a segment that can be cut without affecting the story. True enough, it can later be inferred, especially on second viewing, that the location is the fortress Barad Dûr in the land of Mordor, and the voice is that of Gollum, and the horsemen are the Black Riders, but none of this information is made clear during the scene and all of it gets thorough treatment later. Further, the segment's presence here eliminates an opportunity to build up audience expectation—preparation. This is, after all, the home of the Dark Lord himself, the seat of evil and the headquarters of an army of horrible orcs that threaten the whole of Middle Earth. Anticipation could have been milked considerably, even across the sequels. Inserting the image unannounced and unexplained can only diminish its impact later.

Gandalf is next seen arriving at a distant city of undisclosed name, where he researches the ring in a dusty library. Here, while he reads, some of the scenes from the opening narration are repeated, and the presence of a telltale engraving on the ring is revealed.

A cutaway follows, to a black-clad horseman terrifying a hobbit and inquiring as to Baggins; he is directed to Hobbiton. This sets up a scene of preparation by contrast, in which Frodo arrives home to a dark, empty house where the window is open and papers are blowing about, lending the place a sense of lurking danger. A hand reaches out of the shadows to touch him; it proves to be that of Gandalf, who pays off an earlier line and closes off a dangling cause from the end of the first sequence: "Is it secret? Is it safe?"

Gandalf and Frodo soon confirm it is, indeed, the One Ring. Gandalf briefly recounts for Frodo the history of the ring—the third time the audience has heard it—and then delivers exposition about the reawakening of the Dark Lord in Mordor and his desire to reclaim the ring and by its power bring on a "second darkness." He tells Frodo that Sauron must never find the ring, a dangling cause that informs the rest of the picture.

Gandalf concludes their only option is for Frodo to convey the ring out of the Shire. As Frodo packs his things, Gandalf telegraphs the plan: Frodo needs to travel across country, during the day only, and meet Gandalf in Bree, at the Inn of the Prancing Pony. He must also not reveal that his name is Baggins. Meanwhile Gandalf will go to the head of his order to try to get some answers.

Before Frodo leaves, they discover that Sam has been eavesdropping on their conversation. The sequence ends with a dialogue hook uttered in response to Sam's plea for mercy—Gandalf tells him, "I've thought of a better use for you."

Frodo is thus suddenly thrust into the heart of the story from the periphery. Unlike other films studied in this volume, in which the flow of life of the protagonist is carefully established prior to the point of attack, which interrupts that flow, in *The Fellowship of the Ring* so little time in the opening two sequences is spent with the protagonist that there is no apparent flow of life from which he is snatched. This can create the unfortunate impression that Frodo exists only because the film needs him. A stronger choice might be to make sure the opening sequences are built around him, so that his inner and outer conflicts can work together to create a more powerful effect.

Sequence C: The Journey To Bree

This thirteen-minute sequence opens with Frodo already starting out on his journey and Gandalf urging Sam to keep up. Gandalf completes the setup for the journey begun in the previous sequence by telling the two to be careful—the enemy has many spies, and the ring must be kept safe—it *wants* to be found.

Some information is missing from the setup, though—how long will it take? How many days of travel? Has Frodo ever been to Bree? Or even outside the Shire? (We learn later that Sam hasn't.) What do they think about this journey? Geography—maps—are very important in the Tolkein books, but the film is curiously lacking in a sense of geography—of distances, directions, and the spatial relationship between various lands. In contrast, the other epic analyzed in this volume—*Lawrence of Arabia*—dedicates considerable screen time in carefully setting up distances, dangers, and expectations.

After journeying for a while and then setting up camp, one of the Black Riders appears menacingly in the foreground of a twilight expanse of landscape—picking up the dangling cause of Gandalf's warnings about Sauron's spies.

Following this is a cutaway to Gandalf riding to visit Saruman, as telegraphed in the previous sequence. The two have a friendly greeting, and Saruman delivers exposition: Sauron is gathering an army great enough to launch an assault on Middle Earth. He also tells Gandalf that Sauron's forces are moving and the Black Riders have already left in search of the ring, a dangling cause that informs the remainder of the sequence. At this point Gandalf tries to run, apparently to warn Frodo, but Saruman stops him and reveals himself to be a servant of Mordor—a traitor. Gandalf refuses to join him; the two battle it out with Saruman getting the better of it.

As to this five-minute segment with Saruman, two storytelling issues can be raised. One—another chance for preparation seems to have been missed. As noted previously, the film is largely void of surprise twists. Gandalf, going in desperation to a trusted mentor, only to find out he's a traitor, is an ideal opportunity to use this storytelling technique. Instead, because of the way the segment is written and shot, it is clear very early on—and long before Gandalf seems to realize it—that Saruman is crooked.

Two—is the segment necessary at all? True enough, it allows the filmmakers to display prodigious skill with special effects, but a price is paid in the storytelling. By showing Gandalf waylaid, the audience is aware immediately that Frodo and his companions will not be seeing him at the Prancing Pony as arranged. Another chance for preparation by contrast—and a surprise twist—is thus lost (in the Tolkein work, his fate is concealed in this way, preserving the surprise twist). Another advantage of cutting the segment is that it saves five precious minutes that could be used elsewhere. In particular, the hobbits' memorable encounter with Tom Bombadil is not in the film.

The audience's foreknowledge of Gandalf's travails does have the effect of adding dramatic irony to the scenes with the hobbits: they are unaware that Gandalf will not be meeting them at Bree. Unfortunately, those scenes are not exploited for dramatic irony. No mention is made in them of Gandalf at all, nor of their hope/expectation that they will soon be with him and he'll protect them.

After Gandalf is shown indisposed with Saruman, the film switches back to the Shire, where Frodo and Sam encounter Merry and Pippin, two mischief-makers introduced during the fireworks display. The four wind up on a wooded road, where they have their first encounter with a Black Rider. A chase through the foggy, moonlit woods leads to a narrow escape at the Buckleberry Ferry, en route to Bree.

Sequence D: Bree

The fourth sequence opens with the hobbits' arrival at Bree—closing off the dangling cause initiated at the end of Sequence B—and is unified by location (the town) and to a lesser extent dramatic tension (Strider's desire to protect the hobbits from the Black Riders).

Frodo and his companions make their way to the Prancing Pony, where they discover what the audience already knows: Gandalf is not there. Very quickly, two dangling causes are picked up—Pippin reveals to some bar patrons that Frodo's name is Baggins, and Frodo trips and falls, and winds up with the ring on his finger—both violations of Gandalf's admonitions from Sequences B and C.

Before Frodo can remove the ring from his finger, the Black Riders are alerted to his presence. Strider quickly seizes Frodo as soon as he becomes visible again, and in a clever use of preparation by contrast, proves to be a great ally and protector, not the enemy he first appeared to be. Strider ends the scene with a dialogue hook: "They're coming." The Black Riders now burst through the gate and, in another effective use of preparation by contrast, are apparently set to stab the sleeping hobbits before they realize the mattresses are empty.

Strider and the hobbits are now revealed to be in a stable a short distance away. While he watches the Black Riders depart, Strider explains what they are: the *Nazgul,* undead human kings (shown in the opening narration segment) who are enslaved to Sauron. The sequence ends with a dangling cause: "They will never stop hunting you."

Sequence E: The Journey To Rivendell

The next scene finds Strider leading the hobbits across an open field. Frodo asks where they are going; Strider replies: to Rivendell, the house of Elrond. Sam notes that it means they'll be seeing the elves.

Thus begins the 16-minute fifth sequence. Again, in contrast to *Lawrence of Arabia,* the setup is cursory; no hint is given of the dimensions of the journey: how long, how far, what the dangers might be (other than Black Riders), what the expectations are, how likely they are to succeed, and what they hope to do once they get there. The audience is instead launched into another segment that resembles a travelogue— new places to see and experience—rather than drama, with its awesome power to create anticipation. Without being told what to hope for and what to be afraid of, there is no way for the audience to know.

As to why the hobbits are even following Strider, Pippin asks the others: "How do we know he's a friend of Gandalf?" and Frodo replies: "We have no choice but to trust him." Why they need to trust him is unclear. Any other possible choices the hobbits may have are not mentioned or explored, depriving the film of a crucial sense of limitless possibility. It leaves the impression that they need to trust Strider because the story requires them to.

The lack of attention given to the setup of the sequence is also in evidence in the way the dialogue is delivered—mostly offscreen or from a distance while the characters are hiking in various locales. It's easy to miss the setup entirely. Further, it seems likely the hobbits would ask such questions as why they should trust Strider, and where he plans to take them, *before* they set out on the journey (as in the book), not after they've already traveled what seems a fair distance. A fully developed dramatic scene might have delivered a more forceful setup and paid big dividends later.

After Strider tells them they're going to Rivendell and that they must not stop till nightfall, the film crosscuts to Saruman, who is busy getting in touch with Sauron through use of a palantir. Sauron instructs Saruman to build him an army "worthy of Mordor"—a dangling cause that is picked up and developed during several subsequent scenes. At this point, some deformed-looking but polite creatures (later identified as *orcs)* enter into Saruman's presence and ask him about the command from "the eye"; Saruman replies "We have work to do"—a dialogue hook into the following scene, which shows trees being torn down. We next see a beat-up-looking Gandalf awakening at the top of Saruman's tower, who looks over the edge and sees the evil work being done.

This second cutaway to the Gandalf/Saruman subplot lasts just under two minutes, and from a storytelling viewpoint it seems as unnecessary as the first such cutaway. The segment is essentially expository: Saruman is given orders to build an army. In response, he inexplicably starts tearing down trees. Meanwhile, Gandalf is still alive but apparently imprisoned. The use of these two minutes of screen time in the setup of the sequence might easily have paid much bigger dividends dramatically than their use here.

The film now switches back to the journey of Strider and the hobbits, who have come upon Weathertop, an abandoned watchtower, and will spend the night. Strider hands out some swords and tells the hobbits to keep them close, as he is going to have a look around.

Frodo is next shown awakening from sleep; he becomes instantly alarmed upon seeing that the others have started a campfire. He puts it out, but it is too late—five Nazgul are seen approaching from the base of the watchtower. It is a moment again without setup—no warning has been given *not* to start a fire, and the fact that it's a mistake is revealed to the audience at the same time that it's put out by Frodo—too late for the audience to participate in the sense of danger, except by inferring danger from Frodo's reaction.

The four hobbits are no match for the Nazgul, and in desperation Frodo puts on the ring. His disappearance only temporarily thwarts them; Frodo winds up getting stabbed. At this moment Strider shows up with a sword in one hand and a torch in the other and quickly dispatches all five. The battle scene is wonderfully shot but the storytelling again suffers: if the Nazgul are so readily defeated by the use of fire, why didn't Strider arm them with torches rather than swords? This is not an idle question, because it is one of the jobs of the storyteller to set up the rules of the world, so that, again, the audience knows what to hope for and what to be afraid of. For example, if the audience knows ahead of time that fire is effective against the Nazgul, then Frodo's act of putting out the fire could be seen as an alarming mistake. Instead, the audience is getting exposition—fire is effective—right at the end of the battle, at which time it's too late to have a dramatic impact. This problem is compounded a few scenes later, when the same Nazgul return un- harmed: apparently getting burned up only stuns them. (It is worth not- ing that in the Tolkien book, prior to the battle, Strider does indeed tell the hobbits that fire can help neutralize the Nazgul and instructs them to *build* a fire, thus providing the setup so crucial to the battle that fol- lows.)

After Strider disables the Nazgul, he goes to Frodo's side and delivers the unhappy news that the hobbit has been wounded by a Mordor blade, which is very serious and needs "elvish medicine" to heal. The group is next seen running through the woods—and here Sam an- nounces they are six days from Rivendell—the first such spatial/tempo- ral orientation in the sequence—and that Frodo will never make it—a dangling cause that propels the rest of the action until Sequence F.

Sam cries out for Gandalf in desperation, which provides a verbal link to a cutaway back to Isengard, where Gandalf remains imprisoned and the orcs are hard at work creating weapons and digging up new orcs from the muddy subterranean soil.

The film then cuts back to Strider and the hobbits, deep in the woods, with Frodo fading fast. They unexpectedly encounter Arwen, a female elf, who quickly concludes that Frodo's only hope lies in bring- ing him to Arwen's father. Strider offers to take him, but she argues that she can ride faster, and if she can reach the river, the power of her peo- ple will protect her.

The setup for the chase scene that occupies the remainder of the se- quence is now complete: the journey is six days, a deadline has been laid out (Frodo might die), the Nazgul provide a potentially deadly obstacle, and if Arwen can reach the river, she'll be safe. The result is a very effec- tive chase, in which Arwen's arrival at the river signals instantly that success has been achieved.

Arwen disposes of the Nazgul by magically manipulating the river (their weak spot—an inability to ford water—was already established at the Buckleberry Ferry), then turns to Frodo, who seems to be fading fast. Arwen's desperate reaction signals effective use of preparation by contrast: her moments of despair occur just before Frodo is successfully revived.

Sequence F: Rivendell and the Creation of the Fellowship

The fifth sequence is the longest in the film and is unified by place—the elven city of Rivendell. It has at its heart a pivotal event, the council of Elrond, at which a decision is made about the ring and the Fellowship is formed—two events that will shape the action of the rest of the picture. While the sequence has a few dramatic scenes, it suffers from lack of focus; in particular, a failure to adequately set up the momentous nature of the council of Elrond and the decision that issues from it. The establishment of the Fellowship does amount to something of a first culmination. It occurs just over the halfway point in the film, and it provides a mirror opposite of the end, when the Fellowship is dissolved.

The sequence begins with Frodo returning to consciousness and being reunited with Gandalf and the other hobbits. He also sees Bilbo, who has completed his book—closing off a dangling cause from the first sequence. While Frodo looks at Bilbo's book, he sees a map of the Shire and mentions his yearning to go back to it. He tells Bilbo that he spent his youth pretending he was elsewhere, on adventures with Bilbo, but that his own adventure did not turn out the way he expected.

The placement of this exposition here is problematic; as suggested elsewhere, this sort of information about Frodo would be useful for the audience to know in the opening sequence of the picture, since it would help put Frodo's acceptance of the task Gandalf asks of him—to carry the ring to Bree—in a very different light: the hobbit who'd long imagined himself an adventurer gets at last an opportunity to become one.

It would also cast in a very different light Frodo's desire to return to the Shire, expressed both to Bilbo and to Sam in the following scene. Instead of being mere exposition, the scenes would be rendered deeper and more resonant, because they would mark a turning point in the evolution of the main character—from a self-imagined adventurer to one who realizes such a life is not for him. His predicament would then grow more poignant when he soon realizes that he must continue on anyway—a reluctant hero. Because this information is introduced so late in the film, it has little impact.

After Sam tells Frodo they've done what Gandalf asked (bring the ring to Rivendell) and that it's time to return to the Shire, Frodo seems to have a sudden realization that Sam is right—they did what they set out to do, and it's time to go home. He looks at the ring and concludes aloud that it will be safe in Rivendell. That notion is refuted in the following scene, and in a sense it is a setup for that scene, but again the whole discussion occurs very late for both logical and storytelling reasons. Logically, it stretches credulity to believe that Frodo and Sam would have traveled so many miles without having given any thought to what they were going to do in Rivendell and what they would do after they got there. As mentioned elsewhere, these issues would more logically be addressed and settled (and revealed to the audience) prior to the departure from Bree. Such knowledge would make clear what is at stake in that journey, and set up the major reversal that occurs in Rivendell (the fact that for the hobbits, the journey is not over after all). Instead, though, the question is brought up only a few minutes before the reversal occurs, and cannot enhance the emotional impact of the journey from Bree.

After Frodo and Sam share their mutual desire to return to the Shire, the film switches to Gandalf and Elrond, where the first fully developed dramatic scene of the sequence occurs: Gandalf attempting to convince a reluctant Elrond that the ring can stay in Rivendell. It also functions as a *recapitulation* scene (see text box, page 29) and provides some exposition through its argumentative ammunition. Gandalf tells Elrond that the ring is a burden Frodo should not have had to carry, quickly picking up almost immediately the dangling cause of the previous scene— Frodo's expressed intent to return home. During their conversation, Gandalf tells Elrond that Saruman is preparing an army of orcs crossed with goblins, which will be able to move and attack during the day— exposition that explains, at last, the images seen in the earlier cutaways to Saruman. From this, Elrond concludes that the ring is not safe even in Rivendell. Gandalf suggests they must place their hope in men, who, although currently leaderless, may unite behind Strider, who is here revealed to be more than a mere ranger.

The revelation that Strider is in fact royalty would have been more effective if more thoroughly set up. Prior to Elrond's mentioning it, there is no indication in the film that the race of men is leaderless and suffering for it. The moment this is brought up, though, the answer is readily at hand, in the person of Strider. A more effective choice might have been to introduce the issue earlier and dramatize the effect of this lack of leadership on the peoples of Middle Earth. Once so dramatized, this revelation—that the outwardly humble Strider is none other than the person who can step forward and become the king for which the people are yearning—could play as a significant punctuation mark, rather than mere exposition sandwiched between other such exposition.

During the scene between Gandalf and Elrond, three unannounced and unexplained cutaways occur showing new characters—a bearded man arrives alone on horseback, a white-haired elf likewise appears with some companions, and a dwarf approaches on foot. These are later revealed to be Boromir, Legolas, and Gimli, three major characters who will soon be members of the Fellowship of the Ring after which the film and book are named. The muted introduction of these three is worth contrasting to the memorable way in which Merry and Pippin are introduced, not to mention Sherif Ali, Auda Abu Tayi, and Lawrence in *Lawrence of Arabia.*

Following Gandalf and Elrond's discussion is a scene in which Strider reads quietly and has an oblique interaction with Boromir—the man seen entering on horseback—who picks up a shattered sword, drops it, and exits. Again, with screen time very precious, it seems odd to expend it on a scene that seems to lack any dramatic or story content.

At this point, the elf Arwen enters, and a very effective dramatic scene transpires in which she guesses he is reluctant to take the mantle of leadership out of fear that he would succumb to the temptation to which Isildur succumbed. She tenderly assures him he will succeed where Isildur failed. This is a powerful dangling cause that will be revisited several times during the rest of the film. The scene ends with Arwen giving Strider a gift of jewelry, and confessing her love for him.

The film now switches to a meeting attended by Gandalf, Frodo, and Strider (henceforth Aragorn, heir to the throne of Gondor), in addition to Boromir, Legolas, Gimli, and some other unnamed serious-looking white-bearded fellows, presided over by Elrond. The latter recounts the danger they all face, and tells them there is only one choice—the ring must be destroyed, by tossing it into the fires of Mount Doom, in Mordor. Boromir raises objections—Mordor is a remarkably difficult place to journey into, containing much evil, many obstacles, poisonous air, and unfriendly orcs—important exposition delivered as ammunition. The meeting soon dissolves into a shouting match until Frodo steps forward and offers to take the ring to Mordor. The others quickly agree to accompany him. Elrond accepts the arrangement and announces the Fellowship of the Ring.

The council of Elrond is dramatically structured, with Elrond as protagonist, attempting to persuade the others of his chosen solution. Its weakness is that no other options are presented. In the Tolkein work, the council also weighs the possibility of hiding the ring with Tom Bombadil in the Barrow Downs, or transporting it overseas; the awful choice of having to return it to Mordor is only adopted when all other possibilities are eliminated. This course of action has the additional advantage of being so outrageous and foolhardy a quest that Sauron might not suspect what they were planning to do. In the film, because none of these other possibilities are mentioned, and because Elrond announces at the outset the only choice available to them, the entire council scene borders on unnecessary. The decision is pre-ordained; it is only a matter of everyone acceding to it. Further, with no other possibilities set before the audience, the sense of limitless possibility evaporates and the danger of contrivance fills its place: the reason the Fellowship must do its deed is because that's what the story requires.

Sequence G: To the Pass of Caradhras

This sequence is the second shortest in the film, running just over seven minutes. It is unified by dramatic tension—Gandalf's desire to lead the Fellowship through the Pass of Caradhras. It opens with the Fellowship setting out on its journey, seen traveling on foot through various landscapes. In this, it shares the weakness of the previous two "journey" sequences (C and E)—no exposition creating expectation. How far are they going? How long will it take? What milestones along the way might give us a sense of their progress? What obstacles will they likely face? A minute into the sequence, Gandalf provides an itinerary: they must hold forth on their course for forty days and try to get to the Gap of Rohan, and from there go east to Mordor. This is critical information, but it is delivered in voice-over only and is thus easy to miss.

After traveling a ways, the Fellowship stops for a break, and Gimli offers some counterpoint to Gandalf's itinerary, suggesting a better route might be through the Mines of Moria, where his cousin Balin will give them a royal welcome. Gandalf refuses without offering any explanation.

After this, the Fellowship is overtaken by a swarm of birds—"spies of Saruman"—and opts to hide. Gandalf concludes from this that the southern route is being watched, and they will thus be forced to take the

Pass of Caradhras, a snowy outcropping visible in the distance—thus completing the "first act" of the setup—the objective is now clear.

There follows another cutaway to Saruman, who is apparently making considerable progress building his orc/goblin army. We follow the flight of the black birds through the underground chambers to Saruman, to whom they report. Saruman wonders aloud what Gandalf will do if the mountain defeats him—will he risk a more dangerous road? This dangling cause is picked up a short time later, after Saruman uses magic to cause an avalanche, blocking the Fellowship's route through the mountain pass.

A hurried snowbound conference is held—Boromir urges them to take the road through Rohan, and Gimli repeats his suggestion that they go through the Mines of Moria. With the mention again of the mines, Saruman's voice is heard over Gandalf's image, explaining why Gandalf dreads to go there—the dwarves, apparently digging too deep, awakened some dreadful creature ("flame and shadow"). Saruman is then seen looking at an illustration of the creature, later identified as a balrog. Fortunately, this image is brief enough so as not to undermine the highly effective entrance of this character later.

With the Fellowship at an impasse, Gandalf turns to Frodo and says "Let the ring bearer decide." Frodo quickly renders his decision: the mines. This is, again, a curious way to handle exposition. As was the case in Sequence H, having a discussion about the best route to Mordor so late in the journey seems illogical; why wasn't it discussed at the outset? And why rely on Saruman's voice-over to describe Gandalf's trepidation about the Mines of Moria? Wouldn't he share his fears with the others so they could weigh their decision? (Note: in the book, he does.) And in the end, on what basis does Frodo decide? He doesn't seem to have any information. The impression is the same as that after the Council of Elrond: he makes this decision because the story needs him to. This moment is worth comparing with Lawrence's decision in *Lawrence of Arabia* to go back to rescue Gasim after the journey through the Nefud desert. The pros, cons, stakes, hopes, and fears are emphatically laid out for the audience and the characters before Lawrence decides to go. His apparently risky, foolhardy decision becomes a chance for insight into his character. In contrast, the basis of Frodo's decision, and its meaning for the quest, is a mystery.

Sequence H: The Mines of Moria

The journey of the Fellowship in the mines lasts almost twenty-eight minutes of screen time, at that unity of place and action might be appropriate for one sequence. However, the first eighteen minutes concern themselves primarily with the Fellowship battling the orcs, and the next nine are centered on the race against the balrog to the Bridge of Kazad-dûm, so the ebb and flow of dramatic tension justifies understanding it as two sequences (in the Tolkien book, the chapters have a similar division).

Gandalf's statement, "So be it," in response to Frodo's decision to go to the mines provides the dialogue hook into Sequence H. After some delay in opening the stone gates to Moria, the Fellowship enters, with Gimli promising them hospitality dwarf-style. Very quickly, though, they find the chamber filled with long-dead bodies. Legolas pulls an arrow from one and concludes it is the work of goblins. Boromir has apparently won his argument to pull out and proceed by way of the Gap of Rohan, but a tentacled creature from the water stirs and attacks them, forcing them into the cave and sealing off the entrance. Gandalf thus lights his staff and leads them on—warning them there are older and fouler things than orcs ahead of them—a dangling cause to be picked up most emphatically in Sequence I.

The discovery that the mines have been the site of a massacre seems an opportunity for some form of preparation—either direct or by contrast—but the setup here has been cursory and ambiguous, with Gandalf anticipating doom and Gimli anticipating the opposite, and neither really sharing his expectation with the other. Certainly Gimli's expectation is proven wrong quickly, but here the question is—what does he think happened? There is no discussion in which the characters exchange any ideas about what has occurred to Gimli's cousins and what this might mean for them, other than Gimli's cousins are probably all dead and whoever killed them may come after the Fellowship as well. This is the classic opportunity for a *recapitulation* scene (see text box on page 29).

The mystery of Gimli's reactions deepens later when he finds the tomb of his cousin Balin and seems somewhat surprised, leading again to the question: what was his expectation? Was he really expecting to find anyone alive after traveling so many days through ruins and dead bodies?

As the journey continues in the mines, the recurrent problem of the film—missing or minimal setup for subsequent action—recurs. Gandalf explains they have a four-day journey to the other side, and expresses a hope that their presence will go unnoticed. Rather than having this information delivered as part of a dramatic scene, which might also be an opportunity for laying out just what has likely happened to Gimli's relatives, it is delivered again in voice-over while the characters are marching. As such it is easily missed. And it is never explained just who it is they're hoping will not notice them.

After journeying a while, Gandalf stops and weighs which direction to take them. This would be another opportunity for a recapitulation scene, reviewing the issues noted above, but instead it is occupied by a pep talk that Gandalf delivers to Frodo, and a brief discussion of the creature Gollum, who is following them. Gandalf initiates here a dangling cause that will dangle beyond the end of the film—he feels that Gollum will as yet play some important role in the drama.

The journey soon resumes, and Gandalf leads them to the great underground dwarf city where Gimli finds the tomb of his cousin Balin and is devastated at the confirmation of his death. Gandalf reads from a journal describing a hopeless battle. After he's through reading, Pippin accidentally creates a disturbance, threatening to pick up the dangling cause initiated earlier by Gandalf—that they will be able to pass through unnoticed.

Preparation by contrast is used effectively after the noises fall silent—there is general relief among the nine that their whereabouts remain a secret. Too soon, though, they begin to hear noises from below, signaling danger. Sam notices that Frodo's sword is glowing blue, indicating trolls—the first payoff of this visual motif planted when Bilbo had given him the sword at Rivendell. The Fellowship proceeds to do battle with the orcs and their cave troll, managing to defeat them all, but not before Frodo is apparently run through with a lance.

Frodo emerges unharmed, though, due to the special chain mail he wears—another payoff of Bilbo's gifts to him. More orcs are heard coming, though, and Gandalf cries out: "To the Bridge of Kazad-dûm!"—a dialogue hook into the next sequence.

Sequence I: The Balrog

The nine and a half minutes of Sequence I are probably the most effective in the film, from a storytelling viewpoint. The setup is adequate—the "protagonist" in the sequence is Gandalf and his objective is to lead the other eight members of the Fellowship over the Bridge of Kazad-dûm. The obstacle is primarily the balrog, secondarily the orcs and the treacherous stone steps. The sequence also features masterful use of preparation, in this case the retardation variety: as mentioned previously, almost five minutes pass between the first hint of the balrog—through sound and light—and its arrival in all its infernal glory at the bridge. Its arrival after so much anticipation is stunning.

The sequence begins with the nine members of the Fellowship running as fast as they can through the great stone columns, with orcs springing up from below and scrambling down from above along the way. Too soon, the orcs have them surrounded and greatly outnumbered, and all appears lost. As the hopelessness of the predicament sinks in, though, there arises a loud, low growl, accompanied by a hint of flame in a distant corridor. The orcs suddenly scatter, and momentary relief turns to dread as Gandalf identifies the new intruder as a balrog, and warns them it is beyond the power of any of them.

The nine flee to a vast chamber with decaying stone stairways, and overcome these and interference from orcs to reach the bridge. Here, Gandalf turns to face the balrog after the others have made it safely across; after a brief battle, the two plunge into the chasm.

The apparent death of this major character is followed by an effective aftermath scene, rich with music, giving time for the members of the Fellowship to grieve as they reach the outside world. The sequence ends with Aragorn urging them onward, telegraphing a destination—the woods of Lothlorien—and setting a deadline—by nightfall the woods will be crawling with orcs.

Sequence J: Lothlorien

This twelve-minute sequence, like Sequence F, is unified by location, in this case Lothlorien. The elf Galadriel is the dominant character but her objective—to endure a test with Frodo and then, having survived the test, giving him advice—is specific to one scene as opposed to the whole of the sequence. The sequence also marks the transition from second to third act, or at the very least, from the "middle" to the "end" of the film. As discussed previously, the sequence does not mark a transforming, culminating moment found in many successful films, but it does offer surviving members of the Fellowship, and the audience, a chance to rest and catch their breath before resuming the journey. Further, because Gandalf, whose personality and objectives carried so much of the picture till now, is now absent, the sequence serves to focus the story more completely (and much belatedly) on the plight of Frodo.

The sequence beings with the same minimal setup as the others, with Lothlorien identified as the destination, but its distance in miles and days of travel, what the place is supposed to be like, and what the likelihood of their success in getting there are not revealed. It must be stressed again that these are not idle questions. For a viewer whose hopes and fears are tied into the prospects of success or failure of the expedition, such information is key to making an assessment as to the progress. Lothlorien has never before been mentioned. Does the decision to go there represent a new direction? Does it mean that they're making progress or losing ground? What is to be expected when they get there? Is it a refuge like Rivendell or a potential source of danger like the Mines of Moria? Is it a jumping-off point for the journey to Mordor or far from it? Knowing these things will enhance an audience's sense of hope and fear; ignorance of them reinforces the sense of travelogue—we go along for the ride, and have little sense of anticipation beyond the expectation of a change in scenery at regular intervals.

After traveling through some open fields, the Fellowship enters some woods, and here a late attempt at preparation is made: Gimli warning Frodo and Sam about some sorceress who lives in the woods. It's minimally effective both logically (wouldn't this issue have come up long before?) and from a storytelling viewpoint (it's too late to create much of a sense of anticipation). Gimli goes on to say he will not fall under her spell, and he is very observant; it is a brief use of preparation by contrast, for as soon as he offers this reassurance, the Fellowship finds itself surrounded by elves wielding bows and arrows.

Aragorn asks the leader of these elves, Haldir, for protection; Gimli insists the woods are too dangerous and that they should go back; Haldir tells them they've entered the realm of the "Lady of the Wood," who is waiting—a dialogue hook into the next scene.

Frodo and the others proceed up the stairways of some large trees and find themselves standing before Galadriel, presumably the Lady of the Wood. She recapitulates their situation—the quest stands on the edge of a knife, and may fail, to the ruin of all. She makes withering eye contact with a very nervous Boromir, then urges them to rest—a dialogue hook into the next scene, which finds the Fellowship lounging about at the foot of the trees.

Two recapitulation scenes follow that set up dangling causes for the subsequent sequence. In the first, Boromir confides in Aragorn his doubts about restoring Gondor to its former glory now that his father is ailing. In the second, Frodo is silently summoned into the presence of Galadriel, who recounts what is at stake in the Fellowship's quest and warns him that one member of the Fellowship will try to get the ring; this is a powerful dangling cause that sets up a major question in the following sequence: will Boromir seize the ring? Frodo then offers the ring to Galadriel, who confesses but rejects it. Frodo confesses his fear about carrying on; she tells him that even the smallest person can change the course of the future—another dangling cause, which ends the sequence.

Sequence J: Assault of the Uruk-hai

The second-to-last sequence of the film is also the second longest, at twenty-one minutes, and is centered on the question of whether or not the Fellowship can overcome the attack of Saruman's orc/goblin soldiers (*Uruk-hai*). This dramatic question is what carries the bulk of the third act of the picture.

The sequence begins with a cutaway to Saruman, who gives his troops a pep talk—"Cut them down; do not stop till they are found; do not know pain, do not know fear, you will taste man-flesh!" These dangling causes, and the orders he gives to Lurtz, the lead Uruk-hai— "One of the halflings carries something of value—bring them alive and unspoiled; kill the others"—essentially complete the setup, or "first act," of the sequence. The surviving members of the Fellowship need to continue their journey; the chief obstacle will be Saruman's Uruk-hai, operating under cruel orders.

The film crosscuts between the Fellowship setting out on canoes and the quick march of the Uruk-hai. The destination of Frodo and his companions is even more vague for this sequence than for any of the others; they are simply moving onward, presumably toward Mordor. No milestones are offered and therefore there is no way to gauge their progress. There is also no way to know how close or far the Uruk-hai are from the Fellowship, information that would certainly help to enhance the audience's sense of hope or fear.

Frodo and his companions eventually beach their boats, and at a campsite, Aragorn gives the first sense of a plan: they will move across the lake at nightfall and approach Mordor from the north on foot. Gimli objects to the route, recounting some forbidding terrain on the way; Aragorn insists it is the plan. At this point Legolas shares with Aragorn a sense of impending danger and urges them to continue on immediately. Shortly afterward, Frodo and Boromir are discovered missing.

The two are deeper into the woods, where Boromir tries to take the ring from Frodo—picking up the dangling cause of Galadriel's warning. Frodo manages to escape from Boromir, and finds himself in the presence of Aragorn. Frodo tells him to look after the others, telegraphing the notion that Frodo will go on alone.

At this point Aragorn notices that Frodo's sword is glowing blue— signaling the presence of orcs. It is the second payoff of this prop; unfortunately in both payoffs (here and in the Mines of Moria) the characters notice the glow before the audience has a chance to see it. If the order had been reversed, the ironic tension created—the audience realizing orcs are near before the characters do—would have been very intense.

Frodo flees and Aragorn is left to take on the army of Uruk-hai alone until the other members of the Fellowship arrive to help. Boromir is killed in the battle, closing off the dangling cause of his vow to restore glory to Gondor, though Aragorn promises to carry on in that regard, initiating another cause that dangles beyond the end of the film. Aragorn, Gimli, and Legolas manage to prevail, but not before Merry and Pippin are hauled off to Isengard.

Sequence K: Frodo and Sam Go On Alone

The final sequence finds Frodo at water's edge. He recalls Gandalf's words about doing the best he can with what is given to him, and, thus fortified, gets into one of the boats. Sam arrives soon after and swims out to join him. After a few moments of suspense in which it seems Sam might drown, Frodo pulls him. Sam tells him he never means to leave Frodo, another cause that will dangle beyond the end of the picture. The two embrace and journey on together.

The movie switches to Aragorn, Legolas, and Gimli, who decide to rescue Merry and Pippin. Aragorn leads them back into the woods with the words "Let's hunt some orc," and yet another dangling cause is initiated, to be picked up in the sequel.

At the end of the picture, Frodo and Sam look out at their ultimate destination—Mordor—and they both initiate the final dangling causes of the picture: Frodo hoping the others find a safer route, and doubting they'll ever see them again, and Sam suggesting they may yet.

FELLOWSHIP OF THE RING
Sequence Breakdown

Seq.	Description	Length	Running Time
	ACT I		
	Opening Narration	7:14	7:14 (4%)
A	The long-expected party; Bilbo disappears; Gandalf confronts him about the ring; he goes away; Gandalf tells Frodo to keep the ring secret and safe. *Unifying Aspect*: Dramatic Tension. *Protagonist*: Bilbo. *Objective*: To make a memorable exit.	19:26	26:40 (15%)
B	Gandalf researches at library and returns; Black Riders set out; Gandalf sends Frodo and Sam on a journey to Bree. *Unifying Aspect*: Dramatic Tension. *Protagonist*: Gandalf. *Objective*: To learn about the ring.	9:45	36:25 (21%)
	ACT II **(Main tension: Will Frodo convey the ring to safety?)**		
C	Gandalf is betrayed by Saruman; Frodo and Sam are joined by Merry and Pippin. The company narrowly escapes the Black Riders and makes it to Bree. *Unifying Aspect*: Dramatic Tension. *Protagonist*: Frodo. *Objective*: To get to Bree.	12:46	49:11 (29%)
D	Frodo and friends are befriended by Strider at the Prancing Pony. The Black Riders narrowly miss them. *Unifying Aspect*: Dramatic Tension. *Protagonist*: Strider. *Objective*: To help the hobbits.	7:53	57:04 (33%)
E	Strider leads the hobbits on the journey to Rivendell; Saruman puts the hurt on Gandalf. Frodo is wounded by one of the Black Riders. After Strider fights them all off, the elf Arwen conveys him safely to Rivendell. *Unifying Aspect*: Dramatic Tension. *Protagonist*: Strider. *Objective*: To guide the hobbits to Rivendell.	16:19	1:13:23 (43%)
F	Frodo recovers in Rivendell; Gandalf and Elrond debate what to do about the ring; Boromir, Legolas and Gimli are introduced; the Fellowship of the Ring is established at the Council of Elrond. *Unifying Aspect*: Location (Rivendell) and Action (the creation of the Fellowship).	21:55	1:35:18 (56%)
	First Culmination: The forming of the fellowship (56%).		
G	Gandalf leads the Fellowship on the first leg of its journey, which takes them to the Pass of Caradhras, which Saruman's magic renders impassable. *Unifying Aspect*: Dramatic Tension. *Protagonist*: Gandalf.	7:40	1:42:58 (60%)

Objective: To lead the Fellowship through the Pass of
Caradhras.

H	The Fellowship enters the Mines of Moria and after battling a tentacled monster. They discover that the dwarves within have been massacred. They battle orcs and a cave troll, and Frodo is run through by a lance, only to be saved by a magical chain mail. *Unifying Aspect*: Dramatic Tension. *Protagonist*: Gandalf. *Objective*: To lead the Fellowship through the Mines of Moria.	18:43	2:01:41 (71%)
I	The Fellowship flees from the Balrog, escapes across the Bridge of Kazad-dûm. Gandalf confronts the Balrog there and tumbles into the chasm with him. *Unifying Aspect*: Dramatic Tension. *Protagonist*: Gandalf. *Objective*: To lead the Fellowship to and across the Bridge of Kazad-dûm.	9:19	2:11:00 (76%)
J	The Fellowship travels to Lothlorien. Once there, they rest while the elf Galadriel warns Frodo about the danger that Boromir poses to the Fellowship. *Unifying Aspect*: Location (Lothlorien).	12:11	2:23:11 (84%)

Second Culmination: **The arrival at Lothlorien.**

ACT III

K	The Fellowship sets off by boat but is overtaken by Saruman's Uruk-hai. Boromir tries to get ring but Frodo overcomes him. The battle with orcs ensues, in which Boromir dies. Frodo escapes while Merry and Pippin are taken prisoner. *Unifying Aspect*: Dramatic Tension. *Protagonist*: Frodo. *Objective*: To carry on the quest despite trouble with Boromir and the Uruk-hai.	21:01	2:44:12 (96%)
L	Frodo and Sam set out alone to Mordor, while Aragorn, Legolas, and Gimli decide to go off and rescue Merry and Pippin. *Unifying Aspect*: Dramatic Tension. *Protagonist*: Frodo. *Objective*: To set off for Mordor.	6:18	2:50:30 (100%)

Sources

Archer, William. *Play-Making: A Manual of Craftsmanship*. Boston: Small, Maynard & Co., 1912.

Aristotle, *Poetics*.

Bordwell, David, Janet Staiger, and Kristin Thompson. *The Classical Hollywood Cinema: Film Style and Mode of Production to 1960*. New York: Columbia University Press, 1985.

Bordwell, David. *Narration In The Fiction Film*. Madison: University of Wisconsin Press, 1985.

Clark, Barrett H. *European Theories of the Drama*. New York, NY: Crown Publishers, 1970.

Elsaesser, Thomas, and Warren Buckland. *Studying Contemporary American Film*. New York: Oxford University Press Inc., 2002.

Field, Syd. *Screenplay: The Foundations of Screenwriting*. New York: Dell, 1994.

Forster, E. M. *Aspects of the Novel*. New York, NY: Harcourt Brace, 1927.

Howard, David, and Edward Mabley. *The Tools of Screenwriting*. New York, NY: St. Martin's Press, 1996.

Rimmon-Kenan, Shlomith. *Narrative Fiction: Contemporary Poetics*. London: Routledge, 1983.

Thompson, Kristin. *Storytelling In The New Hollywood: Understanding Classical Narrative Technique*. Cambridge: Harvard University Press, 1999.

Index

Aeschylus, 5
aftermath scenes
  defined, 54 (box)
  examples, 54, 55, 68, 69 (caption),
    83, 85, 87, 94, 121, 125, 127, 129,
    139, 146, 148, 152, 153, 155, 160,
    167, 169, 186, 190, 192, 219
Air Force One (1995), 18, 172–81
American Beauty (1999), 8
Animal Crackers (1930), 24
Apartment, The (1960), 17
appointments, *see under* telegraphing
Archer, William, 6
Aristophanes, 5
Aristotle, 4–5, 11

Being John Malkovich (1999), 13, 18,
    136 (box), 145, 182–198
Being There (1979), 10
"Big Four" storytelling tools, 7–12,
    20, 44
"black moment," 37
Bordwell, David, 5, 12
Bullets Over Broadway (1994), 17

Cannes (Film Festival), 81
Chandler, Raymond, 64
Chapman University, 2, 19
character arc
  defined, 33 (box)
  discussed, 52 (box), 136 (box)
  examples of, 32, 192

Chinatown (1974), 14, 15, 18
coda
  defined, 18
Columbia University, 2
comic relief, 32
Curiosity
  used to hook an audience, 14
  used in exposition, 21
  examples of, 21, 65, 66, 82, 115–16
    (puzzle), 121, 146 (puzzle), 159,
    202 puzzle)
Cusack, John, 193

dangling cause
  defined, 8
  referenced, 17, 18
  examples of, 22, 28, 30, 35, 38, 46,
    48, 51, 53, 54, 58, 59, 60, 66, 68,
    69, 70, 71, 72, 73, 74–75, 76, 80,
    84, 85, 86, 87, 89, 90, 91, 91 (cap-
    tion), 99, 100, 101, 103, 106, 107,
    108, 110, 111, 115, 116, 117, 118,
    119, 120, 121, 122, 123, 124, 126,
    127, 128, 129, 130, 131, 132, 133,
    134, 135, 137, 138, 139, 140, 141,
    147, 148, 149, 150, 152, 153 (cap-
    tion), 154, 160, 161, 165, 173,
    174, 176, 177, 178, 183, 185, 187,
    189, 190, 191, 192, 195, 196, 200,
    202, 204, 205, 206, 207, 208, 209,
    210, 211, 212, 213, 214, 216, 217,
    218, 220, 221, 222

Daniel, Frank, *xiii, xiv,* 10
deadlines, *see* telegraphing
De Laurentiis, Dino, 81
dialogue hook, *see also* dangling cause
  defined, 26
  examples of, 26, 31, 66, 89, 100,
    102, 104, 116, 119, 122, 126, 130,
    132, 133, 136, 137, 138, 141, 154,
    161, 179, 184, 188, 189, 195, 206,
    209, 210, 217, 218, 220
Double Indemnity (1944), 11, 18, 64–
  77, 202
dramatic irony
  defined, 9–10
  examples of, 36, 41, 45, 50, 51, 56,
    58, 59, 60, 65, 68, 69, 70, 71, 72
    (caption), 73, 74, 85, 92 (cap-
    tion), 98, 104, 106, 108, 110, 111,
    122, 125, 135, 141, 145, 150, 151,
    151 (caption), 161, 174, 176, 177,
    179, 183 (discussed), 186, 187,
    188, 189, 190, 195, 205, 208
  comic irony, 59, 60, 183
  ironic tension, 23, 28, 49, 51, 53, 55,
    60, 61, 70, 73, 74, 75, 80, 82, 92,
    93, 101, 102, 103, 104, 109, 140,
    148, 149, 150, 151, 152, 172, 173,
    190, 222
dramatic question,
  defined, 10–11
  examples of, 15, 16, 22, 23, 26, 27,
    57, 75
dramatic relief, 32, 57
dramatic tension
  defined, 10
  examples of, 1, 22, 27, 39, 40, 41,
    44, 47, 48, 49, 51, 57, 58, 62, 63,
    64, 65, 67, 68, 70, 78, 79, 80, 82,
    83, 85, 92, 93, 95, 96, 99, 100,
    101, 103, 104, 107, 108 (caption),
    109, 110 (caption), 111, 112, 113,
    119, 120, 124, 131, 134, 140, 142,
    143, 144, 145, 146, 148, 150, 153,
    155, 156, 157, 158, 161, 162, 167,

    170, 171, 172, 173, 174, 175, 176,
    177, 180, 181, 184, 185 (caption),
    187, 189, 191, 194, 197, 198, 204,
    208, 215, 217, 223, 224

epilogue
  defined, 18
  examples of, 37, 40, 60, 63, 67, 76,
    79, 111, 113, 125, 140, 157, 179
Euripides, 5
exposition
  defined, 22 (box)
  examples of, 21, 43, 45, 47, 48, 60,
    65, 67, 69, 83, 102, 108, 116, 122,
    132, 140, 146, 166, 179, 184, 192,
    193, 194, 195, 202, 207, 210, 211,
    212, 213, 214, 216

Fellini, Federico, 80, 81
Fellowship of the Ring, The (2001), 18,
  199–224
Field, Syd, 4
first culmination
  defined, 16
  examples of, 30, 39, 56, 62, 72
    (box), 73, 78, 112, 114, 127, 143,
    156, 163, 164, 170, 175, 180, 190,
    197, 212, 223
Forster, E.M., 6
fractals, 11

Graduate, The (1967), 10, 17, 145–157

Harvey (1950), 10
Hitchcock, Alfred, 97

inciting incident, 14
in medias res, 14, 98
indirection
  defined, 31 (box)
  discussed, 42
  examples of, 30, 46, 51, 52, 53, 54,
    56, 58, 59, 60, 66, 68, 115, 126,
    185, 203

In the Good Old Summertime (1949), 41

ironic tension, *see under* dramatic irony

irony, *see* dramatic irony

Lawrence of Arabia (1962), 8, 17, 18, 114–45, 202, 207, 216

Lehman, Ernest, 97

Lord of the Rings Trilogy, 199

"low point," 17, 57

main character (see also *protagonist*), 14, 193

main tension
  defined, 10–11
  examples of, 15, 16, 17, 23, 26, 27, 47, 49, 55, 62, 68, 75, 78, 79, 80, 90, 95, 101, 102, 107, 112, 142, 143, 152, 156, 161, 170, 171, 174, 177, 180, 182, 185 (caption), 187 (caption), 193, 197, 200, 201, 223

Malkovich, John, (actor), 193

Marlow, Andrew W., *xiii, xiv*, 2

Midnight Run (1988), 15, 17

midpoint culmination, *see* first culmination

Moliere, 4–5

motifs
  defined 45
  discussed, 42
  examples of, 25, 26, 27, 32, 43, 44, 46, 47, 48, 49, 51, 53, 54, 58, 59, 60, 61, 66, 71, 75, 76, 84, 88, 91, 117, 118, 119, 121, 122, 123, 124, 125, 126, 127, 128, 132, 133, 134, 135, 138, 155, 159, 160, 161, 162, 167, 169, 184, 185, 186, 218

mystery (used in hooking an audience), 172, 188, 203

narration, 97

narrative, 97

Nights of Cabiria (1957), 12, 80–96

North by Northwest (1959), 9, 11–12, 14, 97–113, 203

omniscient narration, 9

One Flew Over The Cuckoo's Nest (1975), 8, 136 (box), 158–171

"passive main character," 145

point of attack
  defined, 14
  discussed, 50
  examples of, 26, 39, 62, 66, 78, 95, 112, 142, 160, 170, 180, 197, 223

predicament
  defined, 15
  examples of, 26, 39, 50, 62, 78, 95, 112, 142, 156, 170, 175, 180, 197, 200, 223

Preparation
  by contrast, 30, 35, 53, 70, 71, 72 (box), 73, 76, 82, 84, 86, 87, 88, 89, 92, 94, 118, 119, 120, 124, 127, 152, 154, 164, 165, 173, 191, 205, 206, 208, 209, 212, 218, 220
  defined, 24 (box)
  discussed, 202
  examples of, 24, 56, 70, 92, 108, 165, 191, 203, 206, 207, 217, 218, 220,

protagonist, 14, 22, 39, 40, 49, 52 (box), 52, 55, 56, 62, 63, 64, 65, 66, 74, 78, 79, 85, 95, 98, 102, 112, 113, 121, 130, 131, 132, 142, 143, 144, 145, 147, 156, 157, 160, 161, 167, 170, 171, 172, 173, 174, 176, 180, 181, 182, 193, 197, 198, 201, 205, 206, 215, 218, 223, 224

recapitulation scenes
  defined, 29 (box)
  examples of, 30, 70, 102, 107, 108 (caption), 134, 138, 139, 162, 179, 213, 217, 218, 220

recognition (scenes of), 9, 37, 53, 55, 60, 103, 106, 107, 152

resolution
  defined, 18
  discussed, 52 (box)
  examples of, 40, 57 (caption), 63,
    75, 76, 80, 84, 90, 91, 96, 99, 109,
    113, 122, 124, 127, 137, 140, 144,
    150, 155, 157, 162, 163 (caption),
    171, 175, 181, 182, 186, 200
retardation
  defined, 24 (box)
  examples of, 24, 55, 103, 105, 119,
    129, 148, 177, 191, 203, 218
revelation (scene of), 9, 104, 110, 125
reversal
  defined, 168 (box)
  examples of, 34, 37, 67, 68, 69, 70,
    71, 73, 89, 167, 175, 201, 213

Saving Private Ryan (1998), 11–12
second culmination
  defined, 17
  examples of, 34, 39, 63, 75, 79, 90,
    91 (caption), 95, 107, 113, 127–8,
    143, 156, 171, 181, 190, 198, 200
Sequence A defined, 13–14
Sequence B defined, 15
Sequence C defined, 15
Sequence D defined, 15–16
Sequence E defined, 16
Sequence F defined, 16–17
Sequence G defined, 17
Sequence H defined, 18
Sheen, Charlie, 191, 195
Shop Around the Corner, The (1940),
    9–10, 18, 29, 41–63
Sophocles, 5
Stalag 17 (1953), 145
subplots, 16, 18, 42, 51, 52 (box), 53,
    56, 69, 158, 162, 163, 167, 168,
    172, 174, 175, 177, 178, 183, 186
    (as "A" and "B" plots), 188, 189,
    190, 192, 193, 210

subtext
  defined, 22
  examples of, 46, 65
Sunset Boulevard (1950), 14, 16, 17

telegraphing
  defined, 7–8
  discussed, 80
  examples of, 21, 22, 28, 29, 49, 98,
    99, 102, 106, 107, 115, 118, 123,
    133, 134, 135, 147, 151, 159, 173,
    194, 201, 206, 207, 219, 222
  appointments, 7, 46, 47, 49, 54, 66,
    67, 73, 84, 86, 89, 90, 98, 100,
    104, 107, 108, 109, 116, 128, 130,
    133, 137, 141, 148, 149, 151, 153,
    183 (discussed), 186, 188, 189,
    190
  deadlines (ticking clock), 7, 21, 34,
    35, 36, 73, 109, 117, 124, 128,
    131, 132, 139, 155, 174, 178, 183
    (discussed), 193, 195, 211, 219
theme, 20, 23, 33, 34, 52, 56, 136
    (box), 164, 189
third act tension, 152, 165, 200
Thompson, Kristin, 5–6, 12
"three act structure," 1, 10–12, 52
    (box), 80, 114, 115, 150, 200
ticking clock, see telegraphing
Tolkien, J.R.R., 199, 200, 201, 207,
    215, 217
Tootsie (1982), 16, 18
Top Hat (1935), 10
Toy Story (1995), 17, 19, 20–40, 41,
    42, 45 (box), 149
Toy Story 2 (1999), 20

University of Southern California,
    xiii, 2, 19

Wilder, Billy, 64
Wizard of Oz, The (1939), 203

You've Got Mail, (1998), 9, 29, 41, 42